Beyond Methods:

Macrostrategies for
Language Teaching

B. KUMARAVADIVELU

Yale University Press   *New Haven and London*

Published with assistance from the Louis Stern Memorial Fund.

Publisher: Mary Jane Peluso
Manuscript Editor: Jeffrey Schier
Production Controller: Aldo R. Cupo
Designer: James J. Johnson
Editorial Assistant: Emily Saglimbeni
Marketing Manager: Timothy Shea

Set in New Aster type by Integrated Publishing Solutions.
Printed in the United States of America.

Library of Congress Cataloging-in-Publication Data

Kumaravadivelu, B., 1948–
Beyond methods : macrostrategies for language teaching / B.
Kumaravadivelu.
    p. cm.—(Yale Language Series)
Includes bibliographical references and index.
ISBN 0-300-09573-2 (paperback : alk. paper)

1. Language and languages—Study and teaching. I. Title.
P51 .K88 2003
418'. 0071—dc21

2002014040

A catalogue record for this book is available from the British Library.

The paper in this book meets the guidelines for permanence and durability of the Committee
on Production Guidelines for Book Longevity of the Council on Library Resources.

10 9 8 7 6 5 4 3 2

Yale Language Series

Dedicated with gratitude to the memory of my father

தந்தை மகற்கு ஆற்றும் நன்றி அவையத்து
முந்தி யிருக்கச் செயல்

A father earns the gratitude of his children
by nurturing them to be preeminent
in the Assembly of the Learned.

(*Thirukural*, verse 67, circa 100 A.D.)

Contents

Acknowledgments

I wish to record my sense of gratitude to the entire Yale team, particularly to Mary Jane Peluso, publisher, whose sustained encouragement enabled the whole project to reach fruition; to Jeffrey Schier, manuscript editor, whose meticulous care made the manuscript more readable; and to Emily Saglimbeni for her efficient support work. It has been a pleasure to work with them all.

My debt to those who have contributed to the thinking underlying this book is immeasurable. I cannot mention them all here, but they include professors R. N. Ghosh, N. Krishnaswamy, N. S. Prabhu, and M. L. Tickoo at the Central Institute of English and Foreign Languages in India, where I was initiated into English language teaching; professors Dick Allwright, Mike Breen, and Chris Candlin at the University of Lancaster in England, where I continued my academic interest; and professors Alton Becker, Susan Gass, and Larry Selinker at the University of Michigan, where I completed my formal education. My personal and professional association with these colleagues have immensely shaped and reshaped my own pedagogic orientation. I also owe a debt to my past and present graduate students—too many to name here—who argued with me, challenged me, and forced me to clarify my thoughts, thereby making me a better teacher and a better thinker.

Always supportive of my academic ambitions, my family members—Arunagiri, Velliangiri, Janaki, and Gowri—have encouraged me to go where they have never gone before. My wife, Revathi, herself an academic, has always been there for me, offering me professional critique and personal care. Our two little children, Chandrika and Anand, have not only happily adjusted to the demands of their professorial parents but have also created for us a joyous space outside our demanding professional pursuits. To all of them, I say: Thank you.

Beyond Methods

Introduction

"It is not instruction," said Ralph Waldo Emerson, "but provocation that I can most accept from another soul." What I have attempted to offer in this book is not instruction but provocation, though provocation of the positive kind. I have tried to

- stimulate the critical thought processes of those involved in second and foreign language (L2) learning, teaching, and teacher education;
- spur them to self-reflective action that is firmly grounded in a situational understanding of their own learning and teaching environment, and
- urge them to go beyond the limited, and limiting, concept of method and consider the challenges and opportunities of an emerging postmethod era in language teaching.

What This Book Is About

This book is about language teaching in a postmethod era. It reflects the heightened awareness that the L2 profession witnessed during the waning years of the twentieth century:

- an awareness that there is no best method out there ready and waiting to be discovered;
- an awareness that the artificially created dichotomy between theory and practice has been more harmful than helpful for teachers;
- an awareness that teacher education models that merely transmit a body of interested knowledge do not produce effective teaching professionals; and

- an awareness that teacher beliefs, teacher reasoning, and teacher cognition play a crucial role in shaping and reshaping the content and character of the practice of everyday teaching.

To shape the practice of everyday teaching, teachers need to have a holistic understanding of what happens in their classroom. They need to systematically observe their teaching, interpret their classroom events, evaluate their outcomes, identify problems, find solutions, and try them out to see once again what works and what doesn't. In other words, they have to become strategic thinkers as well as strategic practitioners. As strategic thinkers, they need to reflect on the specific needs, wants, situations, and processes of learning and teaching. As strategic practitioners, they need to develop knowledge and skills necessary to self-observe, self-analyze, and self-evaluate their own teaching acts.

To help teachers become strategic thinkers and strategic practitioners, I present in this book a macrostrategic framework consisting of ten macrostrategies derived from theoretical, empirical, and experiential knowledge of L2 learning, teaching, and teacher education. The framework represents a synthesis of useful and usable insights derived from various disciplines including psycholinguistics, sociolinguistics, cognitive psychology, second language acquisition, and critical pedagogy. It has the potential to transcend the limitations of the concept of method and empower teachers with the knowledge, skill, attitude, and autonomy necessary to devise for themselves a systematic, coherent, and relevant theory of practice.

How the Book Is Organized

The book consists of thirteen chapters. The first deals with the concept of teaching in general and the second with the concept of post-method pedagogy in particular. Thus, these two chapters lay the philosophical and conceptual foundation needed to make sense of what follows. The last chapter pulls together ideas from different chapters, and offers a classroom observational scheme that can be used by teachers to monitor how well they theorize what they practice, and to practice what they theorize.

Each of the ten intervening chapters focuses on individual macrostrategies. They all follow the same format with three broad sections: macrostrategy, microstrategies, and exploratory projects:

- the macrostrategy section provides theoretical, empirical, and experiential rationale underpinning a particular macrostrategy;
- the microstrategies section provides sample microstrategies that illustrate how to realize the goals of the particular macrostrategy in a classroom situation; and
- the exploratory projects section provides detailed guidelines for teachers to conduct their own situated teacher research aimed at generating new ideas for realizing the goals of a particular macrostrategy in their specific learning and teaching context.

All the chapters have built-in reflective tasks that encourage readers to pause at crucial points along the text and think critically about the issues in light of their own personal as well as professional experience. In addition to these reflective tasks, several chapters contain authentic classroom interactional data that illustrate the issues raised and the suggestions made.

How to Use the Book

The chapters in the book need not be read and used sequentially. Each is written as a self-contained unit and, therefore, can be used separately. It would, however, be beneficial to start with the first two chapters to understand the rationale behind the macrostrategic framework. The next ten chapters on specific macrostrategies can be read in any order although, as will become clear, certain macrostrategies closely relate to each other to form a meaningful cluster. The last chapter shows how the framework can be used for monitoring classroom aims and activities. Similarly, the reflective tasks and the exploratory projects can be carried out selectively depending on teachers' experience and their perceived needs.

Regardless of the sequence in which the book is read and used, it is worthwhile to keep its primary purpose in mind: to facilitate the growth and development of teachers' own theory of practice. This is not a recipe book with ready-made solutions for recurring problems. Rather, it is designed to give teachers broad guiding principles to assist them in the construction of their own context-specific postmethod pedagogy. Readers will quickly recognize that neither the suggested microstrategies nor the proposed projects can be used without suitably modifying them to meet the linguistic, conceptual, and communicative capacities of a given group of learners.

Because this is not a recipe book, it does not specify any one particular way of "doing" the teaching. To do so, I believe, is to diminish the complexity of teaching as well as the capacity of teachers. Using their own language learning and teaching experience as a personal knowledge base, the theoretical insights on macrostrategies as a professional knowledge base, the suggested microstrategies as illustrative examples, and the exploratory projects as investigative tools, teachers should be able to develop their own distinct way of teaching. In their attempt to become self-directed individuals, teachers may follow the same operating principles discussed in this book, but the style and substance of the theory of practice they eventually derive will be quite different.

CHAPTER 1

Conceptualizing Teaching Acts

To teach is to be full of hope.
—LARRY CUBAN, 1989, p. 249

We often hear educators say that teaching is both an art and a science. I take this to mean that teaching is basically a subjective activity carried out in an organized way. In fact, there are educators who believe that teaching lacks a unified or a commonly shared set of rules, and as such cannot even be considered a discipline. As Donald Freeman points out,

> when we speak of people "teaching a discipline" such as math or biology, we are separating the knowledge or content from the activity or the teaching. These traces of activity that teachers accumulate through the doing of teaching are not seen as knowledge; they are referred to as experience. Experience is the only real reference point teachers share: experiences as students that influence their views of teaching, experiences in professional preparation, experience as members of society. This motley and diverse base of experience unites people who teach, but it does not constitute a disciplinary community.
>
> (Freeman, 1998, p.10)

It is this motley and diverse base of experience that makes teaching challenging as well as engaging, fulfilling as well as frustrating.

It is no wonder that diverse experiences lead to diverse perceptions about teaching. In his inspiring book *The Call to Teach* David Hansen characterizes teaching as a vocation. Recalling its Latin root *vocare*, meaning "to call," he explains vocation as a summons or bidding to be of service. According to him, teaching as a vocation "comprises a form of public service to others that at the same time provides the individual a sense of identity and personal fulfillment" (Hansen, 1995, p. 2). He compares the language of vocation with the language that goes with other terms that are used to characterize teaching: job, work, career, occupation, and profession. For Hansen,

- a *job* is an activity that provides sustenance or survival. It comprises highly repetitive tasks that are not defined and developed by those performing them.

- *vocation* goes well beyond sustenance and survival; it guarantees personal autonomy and personal significance.

- *work* may ensure personal autonomy and can therefore yield genuine personal meaning but, unlike vocation, it need not imply being of service to others.

- a *career* describes a long-term involvement in a particular activity but differs from vocation in similar ways that job and work do, that is, it need not provide personal fulfillment, a sense of identity, nor a public service.

- an *occupation* is an endeavor harbored within a society's economic, social, and political system, but persons can have occupations that do not entail a sense of calling in the same way vocations do.

- a *profession* broadens the idea of an occupation by emphasizing the expertise and the social contribution that persons in an occupation render to society. However, profession differs from vocation in two important ways. First, persons can conduct themselves professionally but not regard the work as a calling, and can derive their sense of identity and personal fulfillment elsewhere. Second, perks such as public recognition and rewards normally associated with professions run counter to personal and moral dimensions of vocations.

Hansen believes that it is the language of vocation that "brings us closer to what many teachers do, and why they do it, than does the language of job, work, occupation or profession" (ibid., p. 8).

As these terms clearly show, "the doing of teaching" defies classification. The goal of teaching, however, seems to be rather obvious. Teaching is aimed at creating optimal conditions for desired learning to take place in as short a time as possible. Even such a seemingly simple statement hides a troublesome correlation: a cause-effect relationship between teaching and learning. That is, the statement is based on the assumption that teaching actually causes learning to occur. Does it, really? We know by experiential knowledge that teaching does not have to automatically lead to learning; conversely, learning can very well take place in the absence of teaching. The entire edifice of education, however, is constructed on the foundation that teaching can contribute to accelerated and accomplished learning.

The overall process of education certainly involves several players—educational administrators, policy makers, curriculum planners, teacher educators, textbook writers, and others—each constituting an important link in the educational chain. However, the players who have a direct bearing on shaping and reshaping the desired learning outcome are the classroom teachers. This is not very different from saying that the success or failure of a theatrical production depends largely on the histrionic talent of the actors who actually appear on the stage. It is true that several individuals have worked hard behind the scenes to make that production possible: the director, the scriptwriter, and the production manager, to name a few. But if the actors do not perform well on the stage, and if they are not able to connect with the audience, then all the behind-the-scenes activities will come to naught.

In fact, the educational role played by teachers in the classroom is much more demanding and daunting than the theatrical role played by actors on the stage for the simple reason that the failure of an educational enterprise has more far-reaching consequences for an individual or for a nation than the failure of a theatrical production. Such is the significance of the teacher. Nevertheless, there is very little consensus about the precise role the teacher is expected to play.

The Role of the Teacher

The role of the teacher has been a perennial topic of discussion in the field of general education as well as in language education. Unable to precisely pin down the role and function of the teacher, the teaching profession has grappled with a multitude of metaphors. The teacher has been variously referred to as an artist and an architect; a scientist and a psychologist; a manager and a mentor; a controller and a counselor; a sage on the stage; a guide on the side; and more. There is merit in each of these metaphors. Each of them captures the teacher's role partially but none of them fully.

Instead of delving deep into the familiar metaphors, I believe it is much more beneficial to view the historical role and function of classroom teachers to understand how the concept of teacher role has developed over the years, and how that development has shaped the nature and scope of institutionalized education. From a historical perspective, one can glean from the current literature on general education and language teaching at least three strands of thought: (a) teachers as passive technicians, (b) teachers as reflective practitioners, and (c) teachers as transformative intellectuals.

Teachers as Passive Technicians

The basic tenets of the concept of teachers as technicians can be partly traced to the behavioral school of psychology that emphasized the importance of empirical verification. In the behavioral tradition, the primary focus of teaching and teacher education is content knowledge that consisted mostly of a verified and verifiable set of facts and clearly articulated rules. Content knowledge is broken into easily manageable discrete items and presented to the teacher in what might be called *teacher-proof* packages. Teachers and their teaching methods are not considered very important because their effectiveness cannot be empirically proved beyond doubt. Therefore, teacher education programs concentrate more on the *education* part than on the *teacher* part. Such a view came to be known as the *technicist* view of teaching and teacher education.

The primacy of empirical verification and content knowledge associated with the technicist view of teaching overwhelmingly privileges one group of participants in the educational chain—professional experts! They are the ones who create and contribute to the professional knowledge base that constitutes the cornerstone of teacher education programs. Classroom teachers are assigned the role of passive technicians who learn a battery of content knowledge generally agreed upon in the field and pass it on to successive generations of students. They are viewed largely as apprentices whose success is measured in terms of how closely they adhere to the professional knowledge base, and how effectively they transmit that knowledge base to students.

In this technicist or transmission approach, the teacher's primary role in the classroom is to function like a conduit, channeling the flow of information from one end of the educational spectrum (i.e., the expert) to the other (i.e., the learner) without significantly altering the content of information. The primary goal of such an activity, of course, is to promote student comprehension of content knowledge. In attempting to achieve that goal, teachers are constrained to operate from handed-down fixed, pedagogic assumptions and to seldom seriously question their validity or relevance to specific learning and teaching contexts. If any context-specific learning and teaching problem arises, they are supposed to turn once again to the established professional knowledge base and search for a formula to fix it by themselves.

Viewing teachers as passive technicians is traditional and is still in vogue in many parts of the world. It might even be said, with some justification, that the technicist view provides a safe and secure environment for those teachers who may not have the ability, the resources, or the willingness to explore self-initiated, innovative teaching strategies. The technicist approach to teaching and teacher education is clearly characterized by a rigid role relationship between theorists and teachers: theorists conceive and construct knowledge, teachers understand and implement knowledge. Creation of new knowledge or a new theory is not the domain of teachers; their task is to execute what is prescribed for them.

Such an outlook inevitably leads to the disempowerment of teachers whose classroom behavior is mostly confined to received knowledge rather than lived experience. That is why the technicist approach is considered "so passive, so unchallenging, so boring that teachers often lose their sense of wonder and excitement about learning to teach" (Kincheloe, 1993, p. 204). The concept of reflective teaching evolved partly as a reaction to the fixed assumptions and frozen beliefs of the technicist view of teaching.

Reflective task 1.1

What are the advantages and disadvantages of the role and function of teachers as passive technicians? Think about some of your own teachers whom you might call technicists. What aspect of their teaching did you like most? Least? Is there any aspect of technicist orientation that you think is relevant in your specific learning and teaching context?

Teachers as Reflective Practitioners

While there has recently been a renewed interest in the theory and practice of reflective teaching, the idea of teachers as reflective practitioners is nothing new. It was originally proposed by educational philosopher John Dewey in the early twentieth century. He has articulated his seminal thoughts on reflective teaching in several of his books, particularly in *How We Think* (1933). In a nutshell, Dewey makes a distinction between action that is routine and action that is reflective. Routine action is guided primarily by an uncritical belief in tradition, and an unfailing obedience to authority, whereas reflective action is prompted by a conscious and cautious "consideration of any belief or practice in light of the grounds that support it and the further consequences to which it leads" (Dewey, 1933, p. 4).

In the Deweyan view, teaching is seen not just as a series of predetermined and presequenced procedures but as a context-sensitive action grounded in intellectual thought. Teachers are seen not as passive transmitters of received knowledge but as problem-solvers possessing "the ability to look back critically and imaginatively, to do cause-effect thinking, to derive explanatory principles, to do task analysis, also to look forward, and to do anticipatory planning" (ibid., p. 13). Reflective teaching, then, is a holistic approach that emphasizes creativity, artistry, and context sensitivity.

Exactly half a century after the publication of Dewey's book came further thoughts on reflective teaching. In 1983, Don Schon published a book titled *The Reflective Practitioner* in which he expands Dewey's concept of reflection. He shows how teachers, through their informed involvement in the principles, practices, and processes of classroom instruction, can bring about fresh and fruitful perspectives to the complexities of teaching that cannot be matched by experts who are far removed from classroom realities. He distinguishes between two interlocking frames of reflection: reflection-on-action and reflection-in-action.

Reflection-on-action can occur before and after a lesson, as teachers plan for a lesson and then evaluate the effectiveness of their teaching acts afterward. Reflection-in-action, on the other hand, occurs during the teaching act when teachers monitor their ongoing performance, attempting to locate unexpected problems on the spot and then adjusting their teaching instantaneously. Schon rightly argues that it is the teachers' own reflection-in/on-action, and not an undue reliance on professional experts, that will help them identify and meet the challenges they face in their everyday practice of teaching.

Because the term *reflective teaching* has been used so widely, its meaning has become rather diffused. Concerned that the essence of the concept might get diluted even further, Kenneth Zeichner and Daniel Liston thought it fit to talk about what it is that will *not* make a teacher a reflective practitioner. In their 1996 book *Reflective Teaching: An Introduction,* they caution that "not all thinking about teaching constitutes reflective teaching. If a teacher never questions the goals and the values that guide his or her work, the context in which he or she teaches, or never examines his or her assumptions, then it is our belief that this individual is not engaged in reflective teaching" (Zeichner and Liston, 1996, p. 1).

They then go on to summarize what they consider to be the role of a reflective practitioner. According to them, a reflective practitioner

- "examines, frames, and attempts to solve the dilemmas of classroom practice;
- is aware of and questions the assumptions and values he or she brings to teaching;
- is attentive to the institutional and cultural contexts in which he or she teaches;
- takes part in curriculum development and is involved in school change efforts; and
- takes responsibility for his or her own professional development" (ibid., p. 6).

By delineating these five roles, Zeichner and Liston make it clear that learning to teach does not end with obtaining a diploma or a degree in teacher education but is an ongoing process throughout one's teaching career. Reflective teachers constantly attempt to maximize their learning potential and that of their learners through classroom-oriented action research and problem-solving activities.

While the concept of teachers as reflective practitioners has been around for quite some time in the field of general education, it has only recently started percolating in the domain of language teaching. In *Training Foreign Language Teachers: A Reflective Approach* (1991), Michael Wallace offers ways in which a reflective approach can be applied to many areas of teacher development, including classroom observation, microteaching, and teacher education. In a book titled *Reflective Teaching in Second Language Classrooms* (1994), Jack Richards and Charles Lockhart introduce second language teachers to ways of exploring and reflecting upon their classroom experiences, using a carefully structured approach to self-observation and self-evaluation.

These initial efforts to spread the values of reflective teaching among second and foreign language teachers have been further strengthened by Donald Freeman and Karen Johnson. In his book *Doing Teacher Research: From Inquiry to Understanding* (1998), Freeman demonstrates how practicing teachers can transform their classroom work by doing what he calls teacher research. He provides a teacher-research cycle mapping out the steps and skills associated with each part of the research process. In a similar vein, Johnson, in her book *Understanding Language Teaching: Reasoning in Action* (1999), examines how "reasoning teaching represents the complex ways in which teachers conceptualize, construct explanations for, and respond to the social interactions and shared meanings that exist within and among teachers, students, parents, and administrators, both inside and outside the classroom" (p. 1).

Reflective task 1.2

Consider the true meaning of being a reflective practitioner in a specific learning and teaching context. What are the obstacles you may face in carrying out the responsibilities of a reflective teacher? And how might you overcome them?

The concept of teachers as reflective practitioners is clearly a vast improvement over the limited and limiting concept of teachers as passive technicians. However, the reflective movement has at least three serious shortcomings:

- First, by focusing on the role of the teacher and the teacher alone, the reflective movement tends to treat reflection as an introspective process involving a teacher and his or her reflective capacity, and not as an interactive process involving the teacher and a host of others: learners, colleagues, planners, and administrators.
- Second, the movement has focused on what the teachers do in the classroom and has not paid adequate attention to the sociopolitical factors that shape and reshape a teacher's reflective practice.

- Third, in spite of its expressed dislike for the teachers' excessive reliance on established professional wisdom, the movement contributed very little to change it.

Out of these and other concerns has emerged the concept of teachers as transformative intellectuals.

Teachers as Transformative Intellectuals

The idea of teachers as transformative intellectuals is derived mainly from the works of a particular group of educationists called critical pedagogists. They include general educationists such as Henry Giroux (1988), Peter McLaren (1995), and Roger Simon (1987), and language teaching professionals such as Elsa Auerbach (1995), Sarah Benesch (2001), and Alastair Pennycook (2001). All of them are heavily influenced by the educational philosophy of the Brazilian thinker Paulo Freire. Through a quarter century of writings ranging from *Pedagogy of the Oppressed* (1972) to *Pedagogy of the Heart*, published posthumously in 1998, Freire tirelessly espoused the cause of sociopolitical emancipation and individual empowerment through the democratic process of education.

Following Freire's philosophy, critical pedagogists believe that pedagogy, any pedagogy, is embedded in relations of power and dominance, and is employed to create and sustain social inequalities. For them, schools and colleges are not simply instructional sites; they are, in fact, "cultural arenas where heterogeneous ideological, discursive, and social forms collide in an unremitting struggle for dominance" (McLaren, 1995, p. 30). Classroom reality is socially constructed and historically determined. What is therefore required to challenge the social and historical forces is a pedagogy that empowers teachers and learners. Such a pedagogy would take seriously the lived experiences that teachers and learners bring to the educational setting.

Critical pedagogists view teachers as "professionals who are able and willing to reflect upon the ideological principles that inform their practice, who connect pedagogical theory and practice to wider social issues, and who work together to share ideas, exercise power over the conditions of their labor, and embody in their teaching a vision of a better and more humane life" (Giroux and McLaren, 1989, p. xxiii). In order to reflect such a radical role assigned to teachers, Giroux characterized them as "transformative intellectuals." In his 1988 book *Teachers as Intellectuals: Toward a Critical Pedagogy of Learning,* Giroux points to "the role that teachers and administrators might play as transformative intellectuals who develop counterhegemonic pedagogies that not only empower students by giving them the knowledge and social skills they will need to be able to function in the larger society as critical agents, but also educate them for transformative action" (Giroux, 1988, p. xxxiii).

By requiring teachers to be sociopolitically conscious and to be assertive in acting upon their sociopolitical consciousness, the concept of teachers as transformative intellectuals stretches their role beyond the borders of the classroom. As transformative intellectuals, teachers are engaged in a dual task: they strive not only for educational advancement but also for personal transformation.

To achieve educational advancement, they try to organize themselves as a community of educators dedicated to the creation and implementation of forms of knowledge that are relevant to their specific contexts and to construct curricula and syllabi around their own and their students' needs, wants, and situations. Such a task makes it imperative for them to maximize sociopolitical awareness among their learners using consciousness-raising, problem-posing activities.

To achieve personal transformation, they try to educate themselves and their students about various forms of inequality and injustice in the wider society and to address and redress them in purposeful and peaceful ways. The dual role, thus, requires teachers to view pedagogy not merely as a mechanism for maximizing learning opportunities in the classroom but also as a means for transforming life in and outside the classroom.

What exactly do transformative teachers do? Using a related term, postformal teachers, to refer to teachers as transformative intellectuals, Joe Kincheloe (1993, pp. 201–3) summarizes their teaching as:

- *inquiry oriented:* teachers cultivate and extend research skills that help them and their students to explore problems they themselves have posed about life in and outside the classroom;
- *socially contextualized:* aware of the sociohistorical context and the power dimensions that have helped shape it, teachers always monitor and respond to its effect on themselves, their students, and the social fabric;

- *grounded on a commitment to world making:* teachers realize that appropriate knowledge is something that is produced by inter-action of teacher and student in a given context, and act on that realization;
- *dedicated to an art of improvisation:* teachers recognize that they operate in classroom conditions of uncertainty and uniqueness and therefore are able and willing to improvise their lesson plans and instructional procedures;
- *dedicated to the cultivation of situated participations:* teachers pro-mote student discussion in class by situating the class in the words, concerns, and experience of the students;
- *extended by a concern with critical self- and social-reflection:* teach-ers conceptualize classroom techniques that encourage intro-spection and self-reflection;
- *shaped by a commitment to democratic self-directed education:* teachers consider ways of helping themselves and their students gain a sense of ownership of their own education;
- *steeped in a sensitivity by pluralism:* familiarize themselves with the linguistic and cultural diversity of their student population and conceptualize multiple perspectives on issues that matter to them and to their students;
- *committed to action:* teachers come to see thinking as a first step to action and continually design plans of action to carry out their critical thoughts; and
- *concerned with the affective dimension of human beings*: teachers think in terms of developing both the emotional and logical sides of their students and themselves.

Reflective task 1.3

What are the implications of becoming/being a transformative intellectual? For what reasons would you support or oppose the expanded role that teachers as transformative intellectuals are expected to play? To what ex-tent do teacher education programs with which you are familiar prepare student teachers to become transformative intellectuals—in terms of im-parting necessary knowledge, skill, and attitude?

The three perspectives on the role and function of teachers—as passive technicians, as reflective practitioners, and as transformative intellectuals—have evolved over time and have overlapping characteristics. Table 1.1 provides a summary of salient features that clearly illustrate the overlap.

Table 1.1 The Roles of the Teacher: a summary

	Teachers as passive technicians	Teachers as reflective practitioners	Teachers as transformative intellectuals
Primary role of teacher	conduit	facilitator	change agent
Primary source of knowledge	professional knowledge + empirical research by experts	professional knowledge + teacher's personal knowledge + guided action research by teachers	professional knowledge + teacher's personal knowledge + self-exploratory research by teachers
Primary goal of teaching	maximizing content knowledge through prescribed activities	all above + maximizing learning potential through problem-solving activities	all above + maximizing sociopolitical awareness through problem-posing activities
Primary orientation to teaching	discrete approach, anchored in the discipline	integrated approach, anchored in the classroom	holistic approach, anchored in the society
Primary players in the teaching process (in rank order)	experts + teachers	teachers + experts + learners	teachers + learners + experts + community activists

The overlapping and expanding characteristics of teacher roles can be related in terms of a hierarchy as well, as shown in Fig. 1.1. This hierarchy is interpreted to mean that teachers' role as transformative intellectuals includes some of the characteristics of teachers'

Teachers as transformative intellectuals	>	Teachers as reflective practitioners	>	Teachers as passive technicians

Figure 1.1 A hierarchy of teacher roles

role as reflective practitioners, which in turn include some of the characteristics of teachers' role as passive technicians.

It is useful to treat the three perspectives not as absolute opposites but as relative tendencies, with teachers leaning toward one or the other at different moments. What is crucial to remember, however, is that passive technicians can hardly become transformative intellectuals without a continual process of self-reflection and self-renewal. One major aspect of that process relates to the teachers' ability and willingness to go beyond the professional theories transmitted to them through formal teacher education programs and try to conceive and construct their own personal theory of teaching. In other words, the process of transformative teaching demands that teachers take a critical look at the dichotomy between theory and practice, between theorists and practitioners.

Theory and Practice

It is generally agreed that teachers' classroom practice is directly or indirectly based on some theory whether or not it is explicitly articulated. Teachers may have gained this crucial theoretical knowledge either through professional education, personal experience, robust commonsense, or a combination. In fact, it has been suggested that there is no substantial difference between common sense and theory, particularly in the field of education. Cameron et al. (1992, pp. 18–19), for instance, assert that common sense is different from theory "only by the degree of formality and self-consciousness with which it is invoked. When someone purports to criticize or 'go beyond' commonsense, they are not putting theory where previously there was none, but replacing one theory with another."

That most successful teaching techniques are in one way or another informed by principled theories does not seem to be in dispute. What have become controversial are questions such as what constitutes a theory, who constructs a theory, and whose theory counts as theory. Traditionally, there has been a clearly articulated separation between theory and practice. For instance, in the context of L2 education, theory is generally seen to constitute a set of insights and concepts derived from academic disciplines such as general education, linguistic sciences, second language acquisition, cognitive psychology, and information sciences. These and other allied disciplines provide the theoretical bases necessary for the study of language, language learning, language teaching, and language teacher education.

Practice is seen to constitute a set of teaching and learning strategies indicated by the theorist or the syllabus designer or the materials producer, and adopted or adapted by the teacher and the learner in order to jointly accomplish the stated and unstated goals of language learning and teaching in the classroom. Consequently, there is, as mentioned earlier, a corresponding division of labor between the theorist and the teacher: the theorist conceives and constructs knowledge and the teacher understands and applies that knowledge. Thus, the relationship between the theorist and the teacher is not unlike that of the producer and the consumer of a commercial commodity. Such a division of labor is said to have resulted in the creation of a privileged class of theorists and an underprivileged class of practitioners.

Professional Theory and Personal Theory

Well aware of the harmful effects of the artificial division between theory and practice, general educationists correctly affirm that theory and practice should inform each other, and should therefore constitute a unified whole. Their stand on the theory/practice divide is reflected in a distinction they made between a "professional theory" and a "personal theory" of education. Charles O'Hanlon summarizes the distinction in this way:

> A professional theory is a theory which is created and perpetuated within the professional culture. It is a theory which is widely known and understood like the developmental stages of Piaget. Professional theories are generally transmitted via teacher/professional training in colleges, polytechnics and universities. Professional theories form the basis of a shared knowledge and understanding

about the "culture" of teaching and provide the opportunity to develop discourse on the implicit and explicit educational issues
raised by these theoretical perspectives . . .

A personal theory, on the other hand, is an individual theory
unique to each person, which is individually developed through the
experience of putting professional theories to the test in the practical situation. How each person interprets and adapts their previous
learning particularly their reading, understanding and identification of professional theories while they are on the job is potentially
their own personal theory (O'Hanlon, 1993, pp. 245–6).

Implied in this distinction is the traditional assumption that
professional theory belongs to the domain of the theorist and personal theory belongs to the domain of the teacher. Although this approach does not place theory and practice in positions of antitheti-
cal polarity, it nevertheless perpetuates the artificial divide between
theory and practice and between the theorist's professional theory
and the teacher's personal theory. Another drawback is that this approach offers only limited possibilities for practicing teachers because they are not empowered to design their personal theories
based on their own experiential knowledge; instead, they are encouraged to develop them by understanding, interpreting, and testing the
professional theories and ideas constructed by outside experts (Kumaravadivelu, 1999a).

Critical pedagogists have come out strongly against such an approach. They argue that it merely forces teachers to take orders
from established theorists and faithfully execute them, thereby leaving very little room for self-conceptualization and self-construction
of truly personal theories. They go on to say that supporters of this
teacher-as-implementer approach "exhibit ideological naiveté. They
are unable to recognize that the act of selecting problems for teachers to research is an ideological act, an act that trivialized the role
of the teacher" (Kincheloe, 1993, pp. 185–6). A huge obstacle to the
realization of the kind of flexibility and freedom that critical pedagogists advocate is that the artificial dichotomy between the theorist and the teacher has been institutionalized in the teaching community and that most teachers have been trained to accept the
dichotomy as something that naturally goes with the territory.

Reflective task 1.4

What might be a productive connection between a theorist's professional theory and a teacher's personal theory? Which one, according to you, would be relevant and reliable for your specific learning and teaching context? Is there (or, should there be) a right mix, and if so, what?

Teacher's Theory of Practice

Any serious attempt to help teachers construct their own theory of practice requires a re-examination of the idea of theory and theory-making. A distinction that Alexander (1984, 1986) makes between theory as product and theory as process may be useful in this context. Theory as product refers to the content knowledge of one's discipline; whereas, theory as process refers to the intellectual activity (i.e., the thought process) needed to theorize. Appropriately, Alexander uses the term *theorizing* to refer to theory as intellectual activity. Theorizing as an intellectual activity, then, is not confined to theorists alone; it is something teachers should be enabled to do as well.

According to Alexander, a teacher's theory of practice should be based on different types of knowledge: (a) speculative theory (by which he refers to the theory conceptualized by thinkers in the field), (b) the findings of empirical research, and (c) the experiential knowledge of practicing teachers. None of these, however, should be presented as the privileged source of knowledge. He advises teachers to approach their own practice with "principles drawn from the consideration of these different types of knowledge" (Alexander 1986, p. 146), and urges teacher educators "to concentrate less on what teachers should know, and more on how they might think" (ibid., p. 145). In other words, the primary concern of teachers and teacher educators should be the depth of critical thinking rather than the breadth of content knowledge.

Extending Alexander's notion of teacher theorizing, and drawing from research conducted by others, Donald McIntyre (1993) differentiates three levels of theorizing.

- At the first, *technical* level, teacher theorizing is concerned with the effective achievement of short-term, classroom-centered instructional goals. In order to achieve that, teachers are content with using ideas generated by outside experts and exercises designed by textbook writers.

- At the second, *practical* level, teacher theorizing is concerned with the assumptions, values, and consequences with which classroom activities are linked. At this level of practical reflectivity, teachers not only articulate their criteria for developing and evaluating their own practice but also engage in extensive theorizing about the nature of their subjects, their students, and learning/teaching processes.

- At the third, *critical* or *emancipatory* level, teacher theorizing is concerned with wider ethical, social, historical, and political issues, including the institutional and societal forces which may constrain the teacher's freedom of action to design an effective theory of practice.

Incidentally, the three levels correspond roughly to the three types of teacher roles—teachers as passive technicians, reflective practitioners, and transformative intellectuals—discussed earlier.

Reflective task 1.5

What are the benefits, and who stands to benefit, if teachers become effective producers of their own personal theories? What, in your specific learning and teaching context, are the possibilities and limitations you face if you wish to theorize from your practice?

In Closing

This chapter has been concerned mainly with the general nature of teaching as a professional activity. Whether teachers characterize their activity as a job or as work, career, occupation, or vocation, they play an unmistakable and unparalleled role in the success of any educational enterprise. Whether they see themselves as passive technicians, reflective practitioners, transformative intellectuals, or as a combination, they are all the time involved in a critical mind engagement. Their success and the satisfaction they derive from it depends to a large extent on the quality of their mind engagement. One way of enhancing the quality of their mind engagement is to recognize the symbiotic relationship between theory, research, and practice, and between professional, personal, and experiential knowledge.

In the next chapter, I shall attempt to relate the general nature of teaching as a professional activity to the emerging concept of post-method pedagogy in the specific field of second and foreign language education.

CHAPTER 2

Understanding Postmethod Pedagogy

> As fashions in language teaching come and go, the
> teacher in the classroom needs reassurance that there is
> some bedrock beneath the shifting sands. Once solidly
> founded on the bedrock, like the sea anemone, the
> teacher can sway to the rhythms of any tides or currents,
> without the trauma of being swept away purposelessly.
>
> —WILGA RIVERS, 1992, p. 373

William Mackey, a distinguished professor of language teaching at the University of London and the author of an authoritative book on method, *Language Teaching Analysis*, lamented that the word *method* "means so little and so much" (1965, p. 139). The reason for this, he said, "is not hard to find. It lies in the state and organization of our knowledge of language and language learning. It lies in wilful ignorance of what has been done and said and thought in the past. It lies in the vested interests which methods become. And it lies in the meaning of method" (p. 139). What Mackey said nearly four decades ago is true of today as well.

Most of us in the language teaching profession hear and use the term *method* so much and so often that we hardly pause to think about its meaning. In this chapter, I discuss the meaning of method. The discussion is in five parts. In the first part, I attempt to tease out the conceptual as well as terminological confusion surrounding the concept of method. In the second, I describe the limited and limiting nature of method and the widespread dissatisfaction it has created among teachers and teacher educators. In the third, I discuss how a state of heightened awareness about the futility of searching for the best method has resulted in a postmethod condition. Then, I highlight the basic parameters of a postmethod pedagogy that seeks to transcend the limitations of method. Finally, I present the outlines of a macrostrategic framework that is consistent with the characteristics of a postmethod pedagogy—a framework on which I will elaborate throughout the rest of this book.

The Concept of Method

A core course in *Theory and Practice of Methods*, with the same or a different title, is an integral part of language teacher education programs all over the world. A survey of 120 teacher education programs in Teachers of English to Speakers of Other Languages (TESOL) in the United States, for instance, shows that the Methods course functions as the primary vehicle for the development of basic knowledge and skill in the prospective teacher (Grosse, 1991). The survey also shows that specific classroom techniques receive "the greatest amount of attention and time in the methods courses" (p. 32) and that the three books that top the list of textbooks that are widely prescribed for methods classes "deal almost exclusively with specific language teaching methods" (p. 38).

The term *methods*, as currently used in the literature on second and foreign language (L2) teaching, does not refer to what teachers actually do in the classroom; rather, it refers to established methods conceptualized and constructed by experts in the field. The exact number of methods that are commonly used is unclear. A book published in the mid sixties, for instance, provides a list of fifteen "most common" types of methods "still in use in one form or another in various parts of the world" (Mackey, 1965, p. 151). Two books published in the mid eighties (Larsen-Freeman, 1986; and Richards and Rodgers, 1986)—which have long-occupied the top two ranks among the books prescribed for methods classes in the United States—provide, between them, a list of eleven methods that are currently used. They are (in alphabetical order): Audiolingual Method, Communicative Methods, Community Language Learning, Direct Method, Grammar-Translation Method, Natural Approach, Oral Approach, Silent Way, Situational Language Teaching, Suggestopedia, and Total Physical Response.

It would be wrong to assume that these eleven methods provide eleven different paths to language teaching. In fact, there is considerable overlap in their theoretical as well as practical approaches to L2 learning and teaching. Sometimes, as Wilga Rivers (1991, p. 283) rightly points out, what appears to be a radically new method is more often than not a variant of existing methods presented with "the fresh paint of a new terminology that camouflages their fundamental similarity." It is therefore useful, for the purpose of analysis and understanding, to cluster these methods in terms of certain identifiable common features. One way of doing that is to classify them as (a) language-centered methods, (b) learner-centered methods, and (c) learning-centered methods (Kumaravadivelu, 1993a).

Reflective task 2.1

Individually or with a peer partner, reflect on the meaning of method. Then, try to guess how the meaning of method might be treated in (a) language-centered, (b) learner-centered, and (c) learning-centered methods.

Language-Centered Methods

Language-centered methods are those that are principally concerned with linguistic forms, also called grammatical structures. These methods (e.g., audiolingual method) seek to provide opportunities for learners to practice preselected, presequenced linguistic structures through form-focused exercises in class. The assumption is that a preoccupation with form will ultimately lead to a mastery of the target language and that learners can draw from this formal repertoire whenever they wish to communicate in the target language outside the class. According to this belief, language development is largely intentional rather than incidental, that is, it takes place through conscious effort as in the case of adult L2 learning and not through unconscious processes as in the case of child L1 acquisition.

Language-centered methods treat language learning as a linear, additive process. That is, they believe language develops primarily in terms of what William Rutherford (1987) calls "accumulated entities." In practice, a set of grammatical structures and vocabulary items are carefully selected for their potential use and graded from simple to complex. The teacher's task is to introduce them one at a time and help the learner practice them until the learner internalizes them. Secondly, language-centered methods generally advocate explicit introduction, analysis, and explanation of linguistic systems.

That is, they believe that the linguistic systems are simple enough and that our explanatory power sophisticated enough to provide explicit rules of thumb, and explain them in such a way that the learner can understand and assimilate them.

Learner-Centered Methods

Learner-centered methods are those that are principally concerned with language use and learner needs. These methods (e.g., some versions of communicative methods) seek to provide opportunities for learners to practice preselected, presequenced grammatical structures as well as communicative functions (i.e., speech acts such as apologizing, requesting, etc.) through meaning-focused activities. The assumption is that a preoccupation with both form and function will ultimately lead to target language mastery and that the learners can make use of both formal and functional repertoire to fulfill their communicative needs outside the class. In this approach, as in the case of language-centered methods, language development is considered largely intentional rather than incidental.

Learner-centered methods aim at making language learners grammatically accurate and communicatively fluent. They take into account the learner's real-life language use for social interaction or for academic study, and present necessary linguistic structures in communicative contexts. Proponents of learner-centered methods, like those of language-centered methods, believe in accumulated entities. The one major difference is that in the case of the latter, the accumulated entities represent linguistic structures, and in the case of the former they represent structures plus notions and functions. Furthermore, just as language-centered methods advocate that the linguistic structures of a language could be sequentially presented and explained, learner-centered methods also advocate that each functional category could be matched with one or more linguistic forms and sequentially presented and systematically explained to the learner.

Learning-Centered Methods

Learning-centered methods are those that are principally concerned with learning processes. These methods (e.g., the Natural Approach) seek to provide opportunities for learners to participate in open-ended meaningful interaction through communicative activities or problem-solving tasks in class. The assumption is that a preoccupation with meaning-making will ultimately lead to grammatical as well as communicative mastery of the language and that learners can learn through the process of communication. In this approach, unlike the other two, language development is considered more incidental than intentional.

According to learning-centered methods, language development is a nonlinear process, and therefore, does not require preselected, presequenced systematic language input but requires the creation of conditions in which learners can engage in meaningful activities in class. Proponents of learning-centered methods believe that language is best learned when the learner's attention is focused on understanding, saying and doing something with language, and not when their attention is focused explicitly on linguistic features. They also hold the view that linguistic systems are too complex to be neatly analyzed, explicitly explained, and sequentially presented to the learner.

In seeking to redress what they consider to be a fundamental flaw that characterizes previous methods, proponents of learning-centered methods attempt to draw insights from the findings of research in second language acquisition. They claim that these insights can inform the theory and practice of language teaching methods. As a result, the changes they advocate relate to all aspects of learning and teaching operations: syllabus design, materials production, classroom teaching, outcomes assessment, and teacher education.

Reflective task 2.2

Recall the method of teaching followed by your teacher when you learned an L2 in a formal, classroom context. Was it language-centered, learner-centered, learning-centered, or a combination? Alternatively, if you have been recently teaching an L2, think about how your classroom practices do or do not fit in with these categories of methods.

It is worthwhile to remember that language-, learner-, and learning-centered methods, in their prototypical version, consist of a *specified* set of theoretical principles and a *specified* set of classroom procedures. Theoretical principles are insights derived from linguistics, second language acquisition, cognitive psychology, information sciences, and other allied disciplines that provide theoretical bases for the study of language, language learning, and language teaching. Classroom procedures are teaching and learning techniques indicated by the syllabus designer and/or the materials producer, and adopted/adapted by the teacher and the learner in order to jointly accomplish the goals of language learning and teaching in the classroom.

Classroom teachers have always found it difficult to use any of the established methods as designed and delivered to them. In fact, even the authors of the two textbooks on methods widely used in the United States were uneasy about the efficacy of the methods they selected to include in their books, and wisely refrained from recommending any of them for adoption. "Our goal," Richards and Rodgers (1986, p. viii) told their readers, "is to enable teachers to become better informed about the nature, strengths, and weaknesses of methods and approaches so they can better arrive at their own judgments and decisions." Larsen-Freeman (1986, p. 1) went a step further and explicitly warned her readers that "the inclusion of a method in this book should not be construed as an endorsement of that method. What *is* being recommended is that, in the interest of becoming informed about existing choices, you investigate each method" (emphasis as in original).

Limitations of the Concept of Method

The disjunction between method as conceptualized by theorists and method as conducted by teachers is the direct consequence of the inherent limitations of the concept of method itself. First and foremost, methods are based on idealized concepts geared toward idealized contexts. Since language learning and teaching needs, wants, and situations are unpredictably numerous, no idealized method can visualize all the variables in advance in order to provide situation-specific suggestions that practicing teachers sorely need to tackle the challenges they confront every day of their professional lives. As a predominantly top-down exercise, the conception and construction of methods have been largely guided by a one-size-fits-all, cookie-cutter approach that assumes a common clientele with common goals.

Not anchored in any specific learning and teaching context, and caught up in the whirlwind of fashion, methods tend to wildly drift from one theoretical extreme to the other. At one time, grammatical drills were considered the right way to teach; at another, they were given up in favor of communicative tasks. At one time, explicit error correction was considered necessary; at another, it was frowned upon. These extreme swings create conditions in which certain aspects of learning and teaching get overly emphasized while certain others are utterly ignored, depending on which way the pendulum swings.

Yet another crucial shortcoming of the concept of method is that it is too inadequate and too limited to satisfactorily explain the complexity of language teaching operations around the world. Concerned primarily and narrowly with classroom instructional strategies, it ignores the fact that the success or failure of classroom instruction depends to a large extent on the unstated and unstable interaction of multiple factors such as teacher cognition, learner perception, societal needs, cultural contexts, political exigencies, economic imperatives, and institutional constraints, all of which are inextricably interwoven.

The limitations of the concept of method gradually led to the realization that "the term method is a label without substance" (Clarke, 1983, p. 109), that it has "diminished rather than enhanced our understanding of language teaching" (Pennycook, 1989, p. 597), and that "language teaching might be better understood and better executed if the concept of method were not to exist at all" (Jarvis, 1991, p. 295). This realization has resulted in a widespread dissatisfaction with the concept of method.

Dissatisfaction with Method

Based on theoretical, experimental, and experiential knowledge, teachers and teacher educators have expressed their dissatisfaction with method in different ways. Studies by Janet Swaffer, Katherine Arens, and Martha Morgan (1982), David Nunan (1987), Michael Legutke and Howard Thomas (1991), Kumaravadivelu (1993b), and others clearly demonstrate that, even as the methodological band played on, practicing teachers have been marching to a different drum. These studies show, collectively and clearly, that

- teachers who are trained in and even swear by a particular method do not conform to its theoretical principles and classroom procedures,
- teachers who claim to follow the same method often use different classroom procedures that are not consistent with the adopted method,

- teachers who claim to follow different methods often use same classroom procedures, and
- over time, teachers develop and follow a carefully delineated task-hierarchy, a weighted sequence of activities not necessarily associated with any established method.

In short, confronted with "the complexity of language, learning, and language learners every day of their working lives in a more direct fashion than any theorist does," teachers have developed the conviction that "no single perspective on language, no single explanation for learning, and no unitary view of the contributions of language learners will account for what they must grapple with on a daily basis" (Larsen-Freeman, 1990, p. 269).

Justifiable dissatisfaction with established methods inevitably and increasingly led practicing teachers to rely on their intuitive ability and experiential knowledge. As Henry Widdowson (1990, p. 50) observes: "It is quite common to hear teachers say that they do not subscribe to any particular approach or method in their teaching but are 'eclectic'. They thereby avoid commitment to any current fad that comes up on the whirligig of fashion." He further asserts that "if by eclecticism is meant the random and expedient use of whatever technique comes most readily to hand, then it has no merit whatever" (p. 50).

While there have been frequent calls for teachers to develop informed or enlightened eclecticism based on their own understanding of the strengths and weaknesses of established methods, teacher education programs seldom make any sustained and systematic effort to develop in prospective teachers the knowledge and skill necessary to be responsibly eclectic. Nor do any of the widely prescribed textbooks for methods courses, to my knowledge, have a chapter titled "Eclectic Method."

Reflective task 2.3

Continuing your thoughts on the previous reflective task, consider whether your teachers (when you learned your L2) or you (if you have recently taught an L2) have followed what might be called an eclectic method. If yes, what actually made the method "eclectic"? And, what are the difficulties in developing an eclectic method?

The difficulties faced by teachers in developing an enlightened eclectic method are apparent. Stern (1992, p. 11) pointed out some of them: "The weakness of the eclectic position is that it offers no criteria according to which we can determine which is the best theory, nor does it provide any principles by which to include or exclude features which form part of existing theories or practices. The choice is left to the individual's intuitive judgment and is, therefore, too broad and too vague to be satisfactory as a theory in its own right." The net result is that practicing teachers have neither the comfort of a context-sensitive professional theory that they can rely on nor the confidence of a fully developed personal theory that they can build on. Consequently, they find themselves straddling two methodological worlds: one that is imposed on them, and another that is improvised by them.

Teachers' efforts to cope with the limitations of method are matched by teacher educators' attempts to develop images, options, scenarios, tasks, or activities based on a fast-developing knowledge of the processes of second language acquisition and on a growing understanding of the dynamics of classroom learning and teaching. Scholars such as Earl Stevick, Alice Omaggio, and Robert Di Pietro, to name just a few, provided the initial impetus to cope with the limitations of method in a sustained and systematic way, but they all tried to do it within the conceptual confines of methods. Drawing from "a wider range of methods—some old, some new, some widely used, some relatively unknown" (1982, p. 2), Earl Stevick attempted to aid teachers in identifying and evaluating many of the alternatives that are available for their day-to-day work in the classroom.

Alice Omaggio (1986) advocated a proficiency-oriented instruction that focuses on "a hierarchy of priorities set by the instructor or the program planners rather than a 'prepackaged' set of procedures to which everyone is expected to slavishly subscribe" (p. 44). Robert Di Pietro (1987) proposed strategic interaction with scenarios that motivate students "to converse purposefully with each other by casting them in roles in episodes based on or taken from real life" (p. 2).

Several others extended the lead given by the three scholars mentioned above and attempted to nudge the profession away from the concept of method. David Nunan (1989) sought to assign "the search for the one right method to the dustbin" by helping teachers "develop, select, or adapt tasks which are appropriate in terms of

goals, input, activities, roles and settings, and difficulty" (p.2). Dick
Allwright investigated and introduced the concept of exploratory
teaching that teachers can pursue in their own classroom settings
(see, for instance, Allwright and Bailey, 1991). Chiding the profession
for its obsession with method, Stern (1992) proposed "teaching
strategies" based on intralingual-crosslingual, analytic-experiential,
and explicit-implicit dimensions. His comprehensive and coherent
approach to language teaching is derived from "flexible sets of concepts which embody any useful lessons we can draw from the history of language teaching but which do not perpetuate the rigidities
and dogmatic narrowness of the earlier methods concept" (p. 278).

While scholars such as Allwright, Nunan, and Stern pointed out
the pedagogic limitations of the concept of method, others focused
on its larger, rather insidious, sociocultural and political agenda.
Alastair Pennycook (1989) explained how the concept of method
introduces and legitimizes "interested knowledge" that plays an
important role in preserving and promoting inequities between
the participants in the learning, teaching, and teacher education
processes. Educationist Donaldo Macedo (1994, p. 8) called for an
"anti-methods pedagogy," declaring that such a pedagogy "should
be informed by critical understanding of the sociocultural context
that guides our practices so as to free us from the beaten path of
methodological certainties and specialisms."

Emerging gradually over the years, and accelerating during the
last decade, are critical thoughts that question the nature and scope
of method, and creative ideas that redefine our understanding of
method. Having witnessed how methods go through endless cycles
of life, death, and rebirth, the language teaching profession seems
to have reached a state of heightened awareness—an awareness
that, as long as we remain in the web of method, we will continue
to get entangled in an unending search for an unavailable solution;
that such a search drives us to continually recycle and repackage
the same old ideas; and that nothing short of breaking the cycle can
salvage the situation. Out of this awareness has emerged what I
have called a "postmethod condition" (Kumaravadivelu, 1994a).

Postmethod Condition

The postmethod condition signifies three interrelated attributes.
First and foremost, it signifies a search for an alternative to method

rather than an alternative method. While alternative methods are primarily products of top-down processes, alternatives to method are mainly products of bottom-up processes. In practical terms, this means that, as discussed in Chapter 1, we need to refigure the relationship between the theorizer and the practitioner of language teaching. If the conventional concept of method entitles theorizers to construct professional theories of pedagogy, the postmethod condition empowers practitioners to construct personal theories of practice. If the concept of method authorizes theorizers to centralize pedagogic decision-making, the postmethod condition enables practitioners to generate location-specific, classroom-oriented innovative strategies.

Secondly, the postmethod condition signifies teacher autonomy. The conventional concept of method "overlooks the fund of experience and tacit knowledge about teaching which the teachers already have by virtue of their lives as students" (Freeman, 1991, p. 35). The postmethod condition, however, recognizes the teachers' potential to know not only how to teach but also how to act autonomously within the academic and administrative constraints imposed by institutions, curricula, and textbooks. It also promotes the ability of teachers to know how to develop a critical approach in order to self-observe, self-analyze, and self-evaluate their own teaching practice with a view to effecting desired changes.

The third attribute of the postmethod condition is principled pragmatism. Unlike eclecticism which is constrained by the conventional concept of method, in the sense that one is supposed to put together practices from different established methods, principled pragmatism is based on the pragmatics of pedagogy where "the relationship between theory and practice, ideas and their actualization, can only be realized within the domain of application, that is, through the immediate activity of teaching" (Widdowson, 1990, p. 30). Principled pragmatism thus focuses on how classroom learning can be shaped and reshaped by teachers as a result of self-observation, self-analysis, and self-evaluation.

One way in which teachers can follow principled pragmatism is by developing what Prabhu (1990) calls "a sense of plausibility." Teachers' sense of plausibility is their "subjective understanding of the teaching they do" (Prabhu, 1990, p. 172). This subjective understanding may arise from their own experience as learners and teachers, and through professional education and peer consultation. Since teachers' sense of plausibility is not linked to the concept of method, an important concern is "not whether it implies a good or bad method, but more basically, whether it is active, alive, or operational enough to create a sense of involvement for both the teacher and the student" (Ibid., p. 173).

The three major attributes of the postmethod condition outlined above provide a solid foundation on which the fundamental parameters of a postmethod pedagogy can be conceived and constructed.

Reflective task 2.4

Pause for a minute and consider what possible criteria a postmethod pedagogy has to meet in order to overcome the limitations of a method-based pedagogy.

Postmethod Pedagogy

Postmethod pedagogy allows us to go beyond, and overcome the limitations of, method-based pedagogy. Incidentally, I use the term *pedagogy* in a broad sense to include not only issues pertaining to classroom strategies, instructional materials, curricular objectives, and evaluation measures but also a wide range of historiopolitical and sociocultural experiences that directly or indirectly influence L2 education. Within such a broad-based definition, I visualize postmethod pedagogy as a three-dimensional system consisting of pedagogic parameters of particularity, practicality, and possibility. I briefly outline below the salient features of each of these parameters indicating how they interweave and interact with each other (for more details, see Kumaravadivelu, 2001).

The Parameter of Particularity

The parameter of particularity requires that any language pedagogy, to be relevant, must be sensitive to a particular group of teachers teaching a particular group of learners pursuing a particular set of goals within a particular institutional context embedded in a particular sociocultural milieu. The parameter of particularity then is opposed to the notion that there can be an established method with a generic set of theoretical principles and a generic set of classroom practices.

From a pedagogic point of view, then, particularity is at once a goal and a process. That is to say, one works *for* and *through* particularity at the same time. It is a progressive advancement of means and ends. It is the ability to be sensitive to the local educational, institutional and social contexts in which L2 learning and teaching take place (see Chapter 11 on ensuring social relevance). It starts with practicing teachers, either individually or collectively, observing their teaching acts, evaluating their outcomes, identifying problems, finding solutions, and trying them out to see once again what works and what doesn't (see Chapter 13 on monitoring teaching acts). Such a continual cycle of observation, reflection, and action is a prerequisite for the development of context-sensitive pedagogic theory and practice. Since the particular is so deeply embedded in the practical, and cannot be achieved or understood without it, the parameter of particularity is intertwined with the parameter of practicality as well.

The Parameter of Practicality

The parameter of practicality relates to a much larger issue that directly impacts on the practice of classroom teaching, namely, the relationship between theory and practice that was discussed in Chapter 1. The parameter of practicality entails a teacher-generated theory of practice. It recognizes that no theory of practice can be fully useful and usable unless it is generated through practice. A logical corollary is that it is the practicing teacher who, given adequate tools for exploration, is best suited to produce such a practical theory. The intellectual exercise of attempting to derive a theory of practice enables teachers to understand and identify problems, analyze and assess information, consider and evaluate alternatives, and then choose the best available alternative that is then subjected to further critical appraisal. In this sense, a theory of practice involves continual reflection and action.

If teachers' reflection and action are seen as constituting one side of the practicality coin, their insights and intuition can be seen as constituting the other. Sedimented and solidified through prior and ongoing encounters with learning and teaching is the teacher's un-explained and sometimes unexplainable awareness of what consti-tutes good teaching. Teachers' sense-making (van Manen, 1977) of good teaching matures over time as they learn to cope with compet-ing pulls and pressures representing the content and character of professional preparation, personal beliefs, institutional constraints, learner expectations, assessment instruments, and other factors.

The seemingly instinctive and idiosyncratic nature of the teacher's sense-making disguises the fact that it is formed and re-formed by the pedagogic factors governing the microcosm of the classroom as well as by the sociopolitical forces emanating from outside. Consequently, sense-making requires that teachers view pedagogy not merely as a mechanism for maximizing learning op-portunities in the classroom but also as a means for understanding and transforming possibilities in and outside the classroom. In this sense, the parameter of practicality metamorphoses into the pa-rameter of possibility.

The Parameter of Possibility

The parameter of possibility is derived mainly from the works of critical pedagogists of Freirean persuasion. As discussed in Chapter 1, critical pedagogists take the position that any pedagogy is impli-cated in relations of power and dominance, and is implemented to create and sustain social inequalities. They call for recognition of learners' and teachers' subject-positions, that is, their class, race, gender, and ethnicity, and for sensitivity toward their impact on ed-ucation.

In the process of sensitizing itself to the prevailing sociopolitical reality, the parameter of possibility is also concerned with individ-ual identity. More than any other educational enterprise, language education provides its participants with challenges and opportu-nities for a continual quest for subjectivity and self-identity for, as Weeden (1987, p. 21) points out, "Language is the place where ac-tual and possible forms of social organization and their likely so-cial and political consequences are defined and contested. Yet it is also the place where our sense of ourselves, our subjectivity, is constructed." This is even more applicable to L2 education, which brings languages and cultures in contact (see chapters 11 and 12 for more details).

To sum up this section, I have suggested that one way of conceptualizing a postmethod pedagogy is to look at it three-dimensionally as a pedagogy of particularity, practicality, and possibility. The parameter of particularity seeks to facilitate the advancement of a context-sensitive, location-specific pedagogy that is based on a true understanding of local linguistic, sociocultural, and political particularities. The parameter of practicality seeks to rupture the reified role relationship by enabling and encouraging teachers to theorize from their practice and to practice what they theorize. The parameter of possibility seeks to tap the sociopolitical consciousness that participants bring with them to the classroom so that it can also function as a catalyst for a continual quest for identity formation and social transformation.

Inevitably, the boundaries of the particular, the practical, and the possible are blurred. As Figure 2.1 shows, the characteristics of these parameters overlap. Each one shapes and is shaped by the other. They interweave and interact with each other in a synergic relationship where the whole is greater than the sum of its parts. The result of such a relationship will vary from context to context depending on what the participants bring to bear on it.

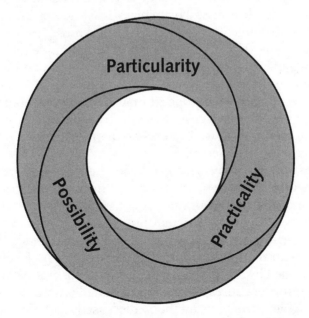

Figure 2.1. Parameters of a postmethod pedagogy

Reflective task 2.5

Do the parameters of particularity, practicality, and possibility seem appropriate to you? If they do, in what way can they guide you in your practice of everyday teaching?

If we assume that the three pedagogic parameters of particularity, practicality, and possibility have the potential to form the foundation for a postmethod pedagogy, and propel the language teaching profession beyond the limited and limiting concept of method, then we need a coherent framework that can guide us to carry out the salient features of the pedagogy in a classroom context. I present below one such framework—a macrostrategic framework (Kumaravadivelu, 1994a).

Macrostrategic Framework

The macrostrategic framework for language teaching consists of macrostrategies and microstrategies. Macrostrategies are defined as guiding principles derived from historical, theoretical, empirical, and experiential insights related to L2 learning and teaching. A macrostrategy is thus a general plan, a broad guideline based on which teachers will be able to generate their own situation-specific, need-based microstrategies or classroom techniques. In other words, macrostrategies are made operational in the classroom through microstrategies. The suggested macrostrategies and the situated microstrategies can assist L2 teachers as they begin to construct their own theory of practice.

Macrostrategies may be considered theory-neutral as well as method-neutral. Theory-neutral does not mean atheoretical; rather it means that the framework is not constrained by the underlying assumptions of any one particular professional theory of language, language learning, or language teaching. Likewise, method-neutral does not mean methodless; rather it means that the framework is not conditioned by any of the particular set of theoretical principles or classroom procedures normally associated with any of the particular language teaching methods discussed in the early part of this chapter.

I list below ten macrostrategies with brief descriptions. Each one will be discussed in detail in subsequent chapters. These macrostrategies are couched in imperative terms only to connote their operational character. The choice of action verbs over static nouns to frame these macrostrategies should not therefore be misconstrued as an attempt to convey any prescriptive quality or frozen finality. The macrostrategies are:

- *Maximize learning opportunities*: This macrostrategy envisages teaching as a process of creating and utilizing learning opportunities, a process in which teachers strike a balance between their role as managers of teaching acts and their role as mediators of learning acts;
- *Minimize perceptual mismatches*: This macrostrategy emphasizes the recognition of potential perceptual mismatches between intentions and interpretations of the learner, the teacher, and the teacher educator;
- *Facilitate negotiated interaction*: This macrostrategy refers to meaningful learner-learner, learner-teacher classroom interaction in which learners are entitled and encouraged to initiate topic and talk, not just react and respond;
- *Promote learner autonomy*: This macrostrategy involves helping learners learn how to learn, equipping them with the means necessary to self-direct and self-monitor their own learning;
- *Foster language awareness*: This macrostrategy refers to any attempt to draw learners' attention to the formal and functional properties of their L2 in order to increase the degree of explicitness required to promote L2 learning;
- *Activate intuitive heuristics*: This macrostrategy highlights the importance of providing rich textual data so that learners can infer and internalize underlying rules governing grammatical usage and communicative use;
- *Contextualize linguistic input:* This macrostrategy highlights how language usage and use are shaped by linguistic, extralinguistic, situational, and extrasituational contexts;
- *Integrate language skills:* This macrostrategy refers to the need to holistically integrate language skills traditionally separated and sequenced as listening, speaking, reading, and writing;
- *Ensure social relevance*: This macrostrategy refers to the need for teachers to be sensitive to the societal, political, economic, and educational environment in which L2 learning and teaching take place; and

- *Raise cultural consciousness*: This macrostrategy emphasizes the need to treat learners as cultural informants so that they are encouraged to engage in a process of classroom participation that puts a premium on their power/knowledge.

Reflective task 2.6

Individually or with a peer partner, go over the list of macrostrategies again. Which ones already inform your day-to-day teaching? Which ones are not relevant to your learning/teaching context? Based on your professional and experiential knowledge, can you add to this list of macrostrategies?

The basic insights for the macrostrategic framework are drawn mostly from theoretical, empirical, and experiential knowledge grounded in classroom-oriented research. The classroom research perspective adopted here is governed by the belief that a pedagogic framework must emerge from classroom experience and experimentation. It is also motivated by the fact that a solid body of classroom research findings is available for careful consideration and judicious application. It should, however, be recognized that the classroom research path is by no means the only path that has the potential to lead to the construction of a pedagogic framework. There may very well be other, equally valid paths one can take.

Whatever orientation one pursues, what should be remembered is that practicing and prospective teachers need a framework that can enable them to develop the knowledge, skill, attitude, and autonomy necessary to devise for themselves a systematic, coherent, and relevant personal theory of practice that is informed by the parameters of particularity, practicality, and possibility. While the purpose of such a framework is to help teachers become autonomous decision-makers, it should, without denying the value of individual autonomy, provide adequate conceptual underpinnings based on current theoretical, empirical, and experiential insights so that their teaching act may come about in a principled fashion.

The parameters of particularity, practicality, and possibility along with the suggested macrostrategies constitute the operating principles that can guide practicing teachers in their effort to construct their own situation-specific pedagogic knowledge in the emerging postmethod era. How these operating principles are interconnected and mutually reinforcing can be pictorially represented in the form of a wheel.

As Figure 2.2 shows, the parameters of particularity, practicality, and possibility function as the axle that connects and holds the center of the pedagogic wheel. The macrostrategies function as spokes that join the pedagogic wheel to its center thereby giving the wheel its stability and strength. The outer rim stands for language learning and language teaching. There are, of course, hidden or unknown wheels within wheels—individual, institutional, social, and cultural factors—that influence language learning, language teaching, and language use in a given communicative situation.

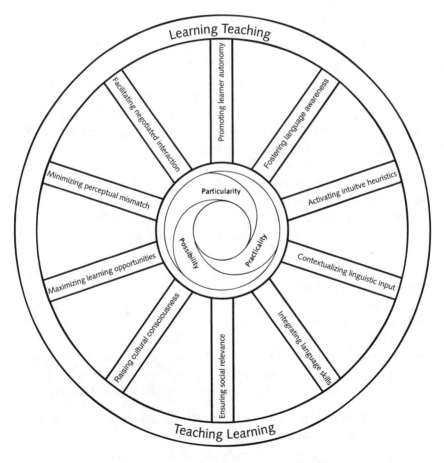

Figure 2.2. The Pedagogic Wheel

What the pedagogic wheel also indicates is that the ten macrostrategies are typically in a systemic relationship, supporting one another. That is to say, a particular macrostrategy is connected with and is related to a cluster of other macrostrategies. For instance, as will become clear in the following pages, there may be a single exercise or a task that can facilitate negotiated interaction, activate intuitive heuristics, foster language awareness, and raise cultural consciousness all at once. Clustering of macrostrategies may be useful depending on specific teaching objectives for a given day of instruction. When teachers have an opportunity to process and practice their teaching through a variety of macrostrategies, they will discover how they all hang together.

In Closing

There are at least three broad, overlapping strands of thought that emerge from what we have discussed so far. First, the traditional concept of method with its generic set of theoretical principles and classroom techniques offers only a limited and limiting perspective on language learning and teaching. Second, learning and teaching needs, wants, and situations are unpredictably numerous. Therefore, current models of teacher education programs can hardly prepare teachers to tackle all these unpredictable needs, wants, and situations. Third, the primary task of in-service and pre-service teacher education programs is to create conditions for present and prospective teachers to acquire the necessary knowledge, skill, authority, and autonomy to construct their own personal pedagogic knowledge. Thus, there is an imperative need to move away from a method-based pedagogy to a postmethod pedagogy.

One possible way of conceptualizing and constructing a postmethod pedagogy is to be sensitive to the parameters of particularity, practicality, and possibility, which can be incorporated in the macrostrategic framework. The framework, then, seeks to transform classroom practitioners into strategic thinkers, strategic teachers, and strategic explorers who channel their time and effort in order to

- reflect on the specific needs, wants, situations, and processes of learning and teaching;
- stretch their knowledge, skill, and attitude to stay informed and involved;

- design and use appropriate microstrategies to maximize learning potential in the classroom; and
- monitor and evaluate their ability to react to myriad situations in meaningful ways.

In short, the framework seeks to provide a possible mechanism for classroom teachers to begin to theorize from their practice and practice what they theorize.

In the next ten chapters, I discuss the macrostrategic framework in greater detail, providing theoretical, empirical, and experiential support for each of the ten macrostrategies. I also provide illustrative microstrategies and exploratory projects to show how a particular macrostrategy can be implemented in a classroom situation. In the final chapter, I demonstrate how the macrostrategic framework can be used by teachers to self-observe, self-analyze, and self-evaluate their own teaching acts.

CHAPTER 3

Maximizing Learning Opportunities

> We cannot really teach a language; we can only create
> conditions under which it will develop in the mind
> in its own way.
>
> —VON HUMBOLDT, 1836, as paraphrased in
> Noam Chomsky, 1965, p. 51

Our first and foremost duty as teachers is to maximize learning opportunities for our learners. To say that is to state the obvious. It is difficult to disagree with such a commonplace statement. We may, however, disagree on the details. That is, we may have different responses to questions such as: What constitutes learning opportunities? How do we know learning opportunities have or have not been created? Do learners utilize learning opportunities created by teachers? Is it the responsibility of the teacher alone to create learning opportunities? Can learners also create learning opportunities? Do teachers recognize learning opportunities created by learners? Do learners see learning opportunities as learning opportunities? These are some of the questions that I will be addressing in this chapter.

Teaching, however purposeful, cannot automatically lead to learning for the simple reason that learning is primarily a personal construct controlled by the individual learner. Every teaching act will be seen through the prism of what the individual learner brings to it as well as takes from it. If learning is indeed controlled by the learner, then teachers can only try to create the conditions necessary for learning to take place. The success of their attempt is, of course, dependent on their learners' willing cooperation to make use of the conditions that have been created. It is because of this collaborative nature of learning and teaching that Dick Allwright (1986, p. 6) defined classroom instruction as "the interactive process whereby learning opportunities are created." An interesting aspect of this definition is that it avoids what he calls a "provider;" that is to say, both teachers and learners are considered to be most valuable players in managing the creation and utilization of learning opportunities in the classroom.

Traditional Players

If classroom management should be directed toward the creation and utilization of learning opportunities, and if that managerial role is jointly vested with teachers and learners, then we need to reconsider the role of some of the factors that we have traditionally believed to be crucial for classroom management. Specifically, we may have to get away from the long-cherished notion that pedagogic success is determined by a combination of a well-planned teachers' agenda supported by a well-designed textbook based on a well-conceived syllabus. We need to recognize the possibility that creation and utilization of learning opportunities are

- not bound by teachers' agenda,
- not bound by teaching materials, and
- not bound by syllabus specifications.

These three factors are all predetermined even before the classroom interaction with learners begins. Traditional classroom management with its emphasis on these predetermined factors has certain inherent limitations.

Limitations of Teachers' Agenda

Teachers generally have a prepared teaching agenda in the form of lesson plans, written or otherwise. No doubt lesson plans offer a sense of direction to classroom activity. However, teachers know that they cannot become prisoners of their own agenda. They need to constantly monitor how the lesson is unfolding and make suitable changes as necessary. While the prepared lesson plan may offer a general road map to teachers, the specific route they follow, the speed limits they impose, and the unexpected detours they take will all depend on the "road conditions" they encounter in the classroom.

Most often, teachers' prepared agenda focus almost exclusively on what is taught whereas, in reality, what is taught is different from what is available to learn. In making this important distinction, Allwright (1981, p. 7) points out that what is available to learn is "a result of the interactive nature of classroom events." That is, beyond the teachers' planned agenda, the unfolding classroom interaction provides opportunities for teachers to explain something in the target language, and for learners to ask questions. All the things said in the target language by all the participants are available for all the learners to learn, if they pay attention to them. In other words, learners join their teachers in generating language input that is potentially available for everybody to learn. In doing so, they change the course of their teacher's agenda.

Limitations of Teaching Materials

By their very nature, teaching materials represent the product of careful and creative planning on the part of textbook writers; they are not the result of any interactive process of classroom events. They are frequently looked upon as carriers of grammatical structures or vocabulary items that have to be introduced to the learners. Commercially produced for mass consumption, they can hardly address the specific interactive needs and wants of a given group of learners.

Because of these limitations, it is better to treat a text as a pretext (or, even as a pretext, an excuse). That is, it should be treated as no more than a springboard to launch the interactive process in the classroom. In that sense, textbooks should function as source-books rather than course-books (Prabhu, 1987, p. 94). The language that is needed for the interactive process has to be negotiated by the learner with the help of the teacher, whose job it is to maximize learning opportunities in class.

Limitations of Syllabus Specifications

Just as a prescribed textbook, a syllabus is also a preplanned and presequenced inventory of linguistic specifications handed down, in most cases, to teachers and learners. The practicing teacher is expected to chart a course of action in the classroom to achieve the goals of syllabus specifications. The teacher tries to do that either by using textbooks that closely follow those syllabus specifications or by designing supplementary activities that are appropriate to the needs of a particular group of learners. In doing so, teachers recognize that "syllabus as a source of teacher reference can only effect learning through methodological mediation" (Widdowson, 1990, p. 130). In other words, without effective methodological mediation, a syllabus remains a lifeless list of linguistic labels.

The preplanned syllabus, just like the prescribed textbook, can be treated only as a pre-syllabus that has to be negotiated through classroom interactive process. Pit Corder (1967) has talked about the notion of a "built-in syllabus" that the learners themselves construct by selecting what can be learned from the choices available in the predetermined syllabus presented to them. What the participants actually do during the interactive process will inevitably convert the *teaching syllabus* that the teachers bring to class into a *learning syllabus* with which both teachers and learners feel comfortable. In fact, in the very process of that conversion, both teachers and learners will find themselves creating and utilizing a wide range of learning opportunities.

I am not suggesting that predetermined lesson plans, textbooks, and syllabuses are unnecessary or that they have no role to play in generating learning opportunities in class, only that they are insufficient to achieve their stated purposes. The reason is simple: creation and utilization of learning opportunities in the classroom are ultimately in the hands of teachers and learners who are engaged in a joint exploration of learning and teaching. Such an interactive process effectively minimizes the role of teachers' prepared agenda, the textbook, and the syllabus and, conversely, maximizes the role of the teacher and the learner in the classroom.

Reflective task 3.1

Focus on any language teacher education program (pre-service or in-service) that you are recently associated with, either as a student or as a teacher. What has been the main thrust of that program: (a) learning how to use teaching techniques, write lesson plans, use textbooks, and follow syllabuses, or (b) learning how to manage classroom interaction in order to generate learning opportunities in class? What specific changes do we have to make in a teacher education program to shift its main thrust from (a) to (b)?

Learning Opportunities

The inadequacy of the teaching agenda, the textbook, and the syllabus—mainly because of their predetermined nature—presents a challenge for the classroom participants who are actually responsible for creating and utilizing learning opportunities. I shall now discuss how teachers and learners can generate learning opportunities inside and outside the classroom.

Learning Opportunities Inside the Classroom

Two aspects of classroom management that will have a huge impact on the generation of learning opportunities inside the classroom are learner involvement and teacher questioning. I will briefly touch on these two aspects of classroom management and then use examples of authentic classroom interactional data to exemplify some of my points.

LEARNER INVOLVEMENT

Clearly, the best way we can maximize learning opportunities in our classes is through meaningful learner involvement. Considering that the learners are actually in control of their learning, and that they all come to the class with varied notions about what constitutes teaching and what constitutes learning, we have no sensible option but to involve them in the process of maximizing learning opportunities. Learner involvement will help both the learners and the teachers in making informed choices: the learners will be able to find their own path to learning, and the teachers will be able to create the optimal environment necessary for learning to take place. Any other prepackaged shortcut we may bring to the classroom is bound to be inadequate.

An important facet of learner involvement is what Bonny Norton has called learner investment. The notion of learner investment "presupposes that when language learners speak, they are not only exchanging information with target language speakers, but they are constantly organizing and reorganizing a sense of who they are and how they relate to the social world. Thus an investment in the target language is also an investment in a learner's own identity, an identity which is constantly changing across time and space" (Norton, 2000, pp. 10–11). Therefore, one way of maximizing learning opportunities in the classroom is to seriously "listen" when language learners speak, and build on what they say. In other words, the learners' voice in the classroom should not be treated merely as language practice, but "must be regarded as constituting the very fabric of students' lives and as determining their investment in learning the target language" (McKay and Wong, 1996, p. 603).

Recognizing the learners' voice also means recognizing their attempt to create learning opportunities for themselves and for other participants in class. When learners ask a question or say something, even if it appears to be far removed from the topic at hand, they might possibly be creating learning opportunities. They may also be indicating that they are capable of not only contributing to the classroom discourse but also navigating it in a direction not anticipated by the teacher. Therefore, by utilizing learning opportunities created by learners, teachers can send an important message to them: their voice counts and they, too, are partners in the joint production of classroom discourse.

TEACHER QUESTIONING

Yet another possibility for creating learning opportunities is for the teacher to ask the right type of questions that will trigger meaningful interaction. In the field of general education, Hugh Mehan (1979) has identified four types of questions that normally occur in a classroom setting:

- *choice* questions that call upon the learners to agree or disagree with the teacher's statement and/or choose a yes or no response from a list provided by the teacher;
- *product* questions that ask the learners to provide a factual response such as a name, a place, etc.;
- *process* questions that ask for the learners' opinions or interpretations; and
- *metaprocess* questions that ask the learners to formulate the grounds for their reasoning, or to produce the rule or procedure by which they arrived at or remembered answers.

Although choice and product questions do have a place in L2 classroom teaching, process and metaprocess questions, by nature, are likely to facilitate negotiated interaction (see Chapter 5 for more details), and, therefore, create more learning opportunities.

Studies on L2 development have generally focused on two types of questions:

- *display* questions that permit predetermined answers already known to the teacher; and
- *referential* questions that permit open-ended answers containing new information.

Researchers in L2 development have found that nearly 79 percent of the questions asked in the classroom are display questions, which clearly contrasts with the use of referential questions in conversations outside the class (Long and Sato, 1983). They have also found that learners' responses to referential questions were propositionally longer and grammatically more complex than their responses to display questions (Brock, 1986).

As can be expected, process/metaprocess or referential questions have the potential to generate learning opportunities. They have the capacity to elicit new pieces of information from learners. They also have the capacity to prompt them to actively engage their reasoning skills, and not just passively draw from memory, as choice and product questions are prone to do. Scott Thornbury goes even further and argues that "the effort involved in asking referential questions prompts a greater effort and depth of processing on the part of the teacher." With that understanding, he good-humoredly challenges the classroom teacher: "Try conducting a lesson in which every question is referential!" (Thornbury, 1996, p. 281).

Reflective task 3.2

Try to recall, as specifically as possible, instances of learner involvement and teacher questioning in the most recent class you taught or attended. Do you think learning opportunities were generated in that class? If yes, how were they achieved? If not, what might be the reasons?

ILLUSTRATIONS OF LEARNER INVOLVEMENT
AND TEACHER QUESTIONING

The pedagogical significance of the issues raised above will become even more apparent as we look at the following classroom interactional data. Before we proceed, a note about the way the transcription of classroom data is presented in this book: First, the meaning of a conversational *turn*. I use the term *turn* throughout to refer to a single, unitary contribution to classroom talk by a teacher or a student or a group of students raising their voice in chorus, irrespective of the length of the linguistic unit (a conversational filler, a word, a clause, a sentence, etc.) and irrespective of the discoursal functions (question, statement, evaluation, etc.). For instance, Episode 1 given below has thirty turns (serially numbered).

Second, for the purpose of simplicity, I use the following broad transcription convention, which does not show features like intonation, pause time, etc.:

T	Teacher
S	Student (unidentified)
S1, S2 . . .	Student (identified, by number)
SS	Unidentified subgroup of class
SSS	Whole class
x	Incomprehensible, probably one word
xx	Incomprehensible, probably one phrase
xxx	Incomprehensible, more than a phrase
Uh, mmm	Conversation fillers
. . .	Pause

Now to the interactional data. I mentioned earlier that teaching activity that has the potential to lead to the creation and utilization of learning opportunities depends largely on learner involvement and teacher questioning. Consider the following episode from an intermediate level ESL *Speaking* class. The teacher was trying to gather from students controversial topics, some of which she wanted to take up for further discussion. After collecting a couple of topics from students, she introduced one of her own: euthanasia, or mercy killing. Notice that when a student asked for the meaning of the word (turn 10), the teacher did not immediately give a definition. Instead, she asked other students to volunteer.

Episode 3.1

1   T: What are some other controversial topics, S4, can you try?

2   S4: Divorce.

3   T: Divorce? (writes on the board)

4   S: AIDS.

5   T: Good. That's very controversial. How about . . . have you heard the term . . . euthanasia?

6   S: Yah.

7   S1: How do you pronounce this?

8   T: Eu-tha-na-sia.

9   S1: Euthanasia.

10 S2: What does it mean?

11 T: Explain. Somebody explain what euthanasia is?

12 S3: If you . . . if you kill somebody with . . . for example . . . if you feel sorry for somebody because this person is . . . very ill and has no choice . . .

13 T: Hmmm . . .

14 S3: (turning to S2 who asked the question) Do you understand?

15 S2: I understand.

16 S3: Hmmm.

17 T: (to class) Do you understand what euthanasia is . . . no?

18 S4: People . . . that taken . . . xxx.

19 S5: Mercy killing.

20 S4: taken . . .

21 S5: It can be very mercy killing.

22 T: Right, mercy killing.

23 S5: There are two kinds of . . .

24 T: Positive and negative . . . right . . . mercy killing is another word for it (writes on board). Have you heard of that?

25 S: Ah . . . hmmm.

26 T: Have you heard of that before?

27 S: No.

28 T: OK, let's say . . . you have . . .

29 S: xx.

30 T: No . . . let's say you have a grandmother who is very sick and can't get out of bed, can't take care of herself and all she wants to do is die . . . and she asks you to let her die . . . that's what euthanasia is . . . if the doctor lets the patient die . . . OK?

(Data source: Kumaravadivelu, 1992)

Even after a fairly satisfactory answer was given by a student (turn 12), the teacher turned to other students (turn 17) to make sure that everybody had understood the concept of euthanasia. It is only after a lengthy dialogue that she gave her own explanation (turn 30). The episode presents a situation where the teacher created not only an opportunity for students to learn a new concept but also conditions for learners to interact with her and with other students.

Contrast that with what the teacher of an advanced level *Communication Skills* class did in the following brief exchange. The class was discussing an essay on rural development in developing countries. The students were asked to read the essay at home and come prepared for a discussion on rural development projects in their countries. Most of the students from the Middle East and Southeast Asia reported problems in rural development in their countries. The teacher then turned to a student from Turkey:

Episode 3.2

1 T: S5, what about Turkey? Do people in rural areas have electricity and running water?

2 S5:   Yah . . . most of them . . . uh . . . this problem has been solved five . . . we did . . . past five or seven years.

3 T: OK.

(Data source: Kumaravadivelu, 1992)

Here was a student who said that the problems of rural electrification and water supply were solved five or seven years ago. A logical step here for the teacher would be to create more learning opportunities for other students by asking the Turkish student to give more information on what the government and the people of Turkey did to solve rural developmental problems. That would have given the other students in class not only some valuable information and additional linguistic input but also an opportunity to participate in meaningful interaction. It would have also involved the Turkish student himself in an interactive situation. Instead, the teacher merely said "OK" and moved on.

My interview with the teacher after the class revealed that he did not have any particular reason in mind for closing the learner discourse; it just did not occur to him to pursue the matter any further. He realized later that he had lost an opportunity to engage the minds of the learners, and also to relate the Turkish case as an example for some of the issues raised in the prescribed essay. The loss is all the more noticeable because this was a class about developing communication skills, and the teacher was expected to create as many opportunities as possible for the learners to communicate in the target language.

Reflective task 3.3

On any given day in any given class, so many learning opportunities go unrecognized and unrealized by teachers as well as learners. How do factors such as poor classroom management, or rigid relationships between teachers and learners, or lack of training or lack of motivation, or X (insert a factor that occurs to you) contribute to this situation?

While the first two episodes illustrate the success or failure on the part of the teacher to create learning opportunities, the next two highlight the importance of the teacher's attempt (or failure) to utilize the learning opportunities created by the learners. It should be remembered that the classroom teacher is only one of the participants—one with greater competence and authority, of course—but only a participant nonetheless, and as such s/he cannot afford to ignore any contributory discourse from other partners engaged in a joint venture to "accomplish lessons" (Mehan, 1979).

One crucial way to ensure the accomplishment of lessons is for the teacher to show a willingness to utilize learning opportunities created by the learner, even if the learner talk, from the teacher's point of view, is not highly relevant to the task at hand. More often than not, a learner talk has much wider implications for classroom learning than most teachers seem to realize. Consider the following episode from a low proficiency level *Reading* class. The lesson in the prescribed textbook was titled *Dangerous Growth of Deserts,* and the teacher, as a prereading strategy, was helping the learners analyze the key words in the title:

Episode 3.3

1	T:	Who can tell me what this word . . . is (writes *Deserts* on the board) . . . Yes?
2	S1:	xx.
3	T:	Hmm?
4	S:	It's a fruit . . . or—
5	T:	No . . . that's . . .
6	S2:	That's a . . .
7	T:	That's . . . (writes *Desserts* next to *Deserts* on the board).
8	S3:	Deserts . . . ah . . . without . . . water . . .
9	T:	Without what?
10	SS:	Water.
11	T:	OK. Good.
12	SS:	Sand . . .
13	T:	What is it? Dry without water . . . sand . . . what do we call it? Dry what? xx.
15	T:	Is it a dry fruit . . . dry what?
16	S4:	Dry place.
17	T:	OK. Good. Dry land or dry place . . . is a desert. What does the other one mean? Desserts? . . . S1?
18	S1:	uh . . . I don't . . .
19	S:	Sweet . . . ice cream . . .
20	T:	OK. It can mean fruit or ice cream or cake. When do we eat it?
21	S:	After . . . dinner.
22	T:	OK. After we've eaten dinner. We'll have dessert. So the difference between deserts and desserts is quite a bit, isn't it?

(Data source: Kumaravadivelu, 1992)

A learner (turn 4) mistook *deserts* for *desserts* and answered incorrectly, thereby creating a learning opportunity for himself and, probably, for some others as well. The teacher, instead of ignoring the learner's incorrect response or simply calling it wrong, wrote the two words on the board but went ahead with her original question related to *deserts*. Once that discussion was accomplished, she utilized the learning opportunity created by the learner and returned (turn 17) to the student's initial response to make sure that all the learners understood the difference between *deserts* and *desserts*.

A point that needs to be stressed here is that, in a class of learners with similar language proficiency, if one learner indicates, directly or indirectly, any difficulty in understanding a particular linguistic item or a propositional content, we can assume that there may be several others who experience a similar difficulty. Therefore, a particular learner's problem of comprehension should be brought to the attention of the whole class and dealt with suitably. Failing to do so would indicate failure on the part of the teacher to utilize effectively the learning opportunity created by the learner. Often teachers do not dwell on the learner discourse and unintentionally ignore learning opportunities created by learners, as the following episode testifies.

The teacher in this intermediate level *Speaking* class planned to discuss wedding customs in different cultures. She used six pictorial cues to stimulate a discussion on wedding customs in the United States and hoped that the learners, who were from different cultural backgrounds, would talk about their own. Focus on how she handled the learners' questions about two problematic words: *reception* and *miscellaneous*.

Episode 3.4

1   T: Now, you are going to ask questions, OK. I have six pictures here. First one is the bride; second is the groom; third we have bridesmaids; four we have groomsmen; five we have reception and six has . . . just let's say miscellaneous. OK? I'm going to give each one of you a picture. On the back of the picture, I've written two questions. I'll give you some time. I want you to think of some more questions that you can ask the other students . . . OK . . . and then you are going to lead a discussion . . .

2   S: Uh . . . xx.

3   T: I'll give you the groomsmen . . . OK? Would you like . . . you
         have the reception. Do you want a picture . . . here is the mis-
         cellaneous. Take a few minutes . . . think of some more ques-
         tions . . . and then you can ask other students . . . OK?

4   S1: (to another) Know this?

5   T: You have a question?

6   S1: This means bridesmaid?

7   S2: What does this mean?

8   T: (answering an inaudible question raised by the S sitting next
         to her) Reception is a party . . .

9   S1: Groomsmen . . . you know . . .

10 S2: (gestures; directed to T)

11 T: (T again busy with the S sitting next to her) Miscellaneous?
         ah . . . I'll use a simple word . . . don't worry (goes to the
         board and erases *Miscellaneous* and writes *other items related
         to wedding*)

12 S1: Like this . . . I can't identify who is the groom in this pic-
         ture . . .

13 T: That's what you'll ask other students a little later . . .

(Data source: Kumaravadivelu, 1992)

A video replay of this episode indicates that the teacher was responding to a question (not picked up by the microphone) asked by
a learner sitting next to her (the class was arranged in a semicircu-
lar fashion to facilitate group discussion). She answered: "Reception is a party" (turn 8) clearly in response to the learner's query
on the meaning of the word *reception*. This turned out to be a private exchange between the teacher and one particular learner. The
teacher did not seem to realize that other learners might have
the same problem.

A much more revealing exchange occurred moments later. Another learner sitting close to the teacher had apparently asked her
(not picked up by the microphone) the meaning of the word *miscellaneous*—a difficult vocabulary item for low intermediate level
learners. The teacher repeated the word *miscellaneous* (turn 11)
with a rising intonation and quietly walked over to the board, say-

ing, "I'll use a simple word . . . don't worry." She erased "miscellaneous" and wrote: "other items related to wedding."

A video replay of this episode shows that the other students in
class were unaware of what was happening. The teacher ignored a
learning opportunity she herself created when she introduced the
word *miscellaneous*. She also failed to bring to the attention of the
other students the question raised by a learner, thereby failing to
utilize an excellent learning opportunity created by that individual.

Reflective task 3.4

It was stated earlier that what is taught is different from what is available to
learn. The teachers in these episodes focused on helping the learners understand euthanasia, desert/dessert, etc. Read the four episodes again. Apart
from what the teachers explicitly taught, what else was actually "available"
for the learners to learn if they were paying full attention to the input and interaction in class?

The discussion so far has highlighted the importance of learner involvement and teacher questioning in maximizing learning opportunities in class. The analysis of classroom interactional data, in
particular, has revealed the collaborative nature of the creation and
utilization of learning opportunities. Such a collaborative work can
form the basis for a more systematic participatory research aimed
at generating learning opportunities outside the classroom.

Learning Opportunities Outside the Classroom

When we think about participatory research, we seldom think about
involving our learners. If, however, we consider teachers and learners as co-participants in the generation of learning opportunities,
then it makes sense to involve them in this process. The fundamental belief governing participatory research is that human beings have
a natural tendency to observe, analyze, and reflect on life experience.
In our specific context, the term *participatory research* may be used
narrowly to refer to sustained and systematic activities in which

learners and teachers together explore all the available avenues to generate learning opportunities in and outside the classroom.

One such avenue is to try to connect the classroom with the local community and with the global community, and thereby enhance the creation and utilization of learning opportunities.

CONNECTING WITH THE LOCAL COMMUNITY

Among those suggesting several variations of participatory research aimed at creating opportunities for teachers and learners to connect with the community outside the classroom are Shirley Brice Heath (1983, 1993), Sudia McCaleb (1994), Bonny Norton Pierce (1995), Kumaravadivelu, (1999b), and Geneva Smitherman (2000). They all emphasize the necessity to create opportunities for the learners to develop their oral and written communication skills as well as their critical thinking skills by analyzing and understanding how language rules and language use operate in various communicative settings.

The following five recommendations about the aims and activities of participatory research that are useful for teachers and learners can be derived from a close reading of the authors cited above:

(1) *Form communities of learners.* The goal here is to bring together teachers, students, family members, and community activists to form what may be called *learning communities:* socially cohesive and mutually supportive groups seeking self-awareness and self-improvement. In order to realize that goal, participants may be encouraged to assume the role of mini-ethnographers so that they can, at a personal level, investigate their own difficulties in adjusting to a new culture, or a new educational system, or a new language, and, at a social level, explore family and community concerns and aspirations, and their impact on their education.

(2) *Interact with competent speakers of the target language.* This can be done by encouraging the learners to use their still developing target language and engage in conversations with competent speakers of the language during social and cultural events whether at school, in the neighborhood, or in the community at large. To make that engagement meaningful and critical, the learners may be asked, at lower levels of proficiency, to give a brief oral or written report about their social interaction. At higher levels of proficiency, they may be asked to reflect on and write about how language use is socially structured in terms of power and prestige.

(3) *Develop a habit of keeping diaries or journals.* It is beneficial for participants to keep diaries or write journal entries about issues that directly concern them. They may be encouraged to reflect and write about a wide range of topics including their developing sense of who they are and how they relate to the outside world, and how they and other members of the learning community react and respond to various sociocultural issues. They may also use the diaries and journals to write about how they handled communication breakdowns arising from their language difficulties, and to keep track of their own progress in learning their L2.

(4) *Exchange information with teachers and peers.* Participants can share their diary and journal entries on certain common topics, comparing and contrasting their experiences and perspectives with interested members of the learning community. Teachers may select a few interesting exchanges of information and use them, with permission from the participants concerned, to structure their classroom activities. In this way, teachers can forge a direct link between the classroom and larger social processes as seen by the learners.

(5) *Adapt and create new teaching materials.* In addition to using their diary and journal entries, participants can bring to class any news stories or write-ups that can be adapted and used as teaching materials. This opens up the participants' creative involvement in identifying and selecting interesting reading materials that can be used in the classroom. This activity, by itself, may give them a greater sense of purpose and a greater degree of commitment to shaping their own learning agenda.

Reflective task 3.5

To what extent do these recommendations make sense to you in your specific learning and teaching context? In other words, what challenges will you face if you wish to follow some of them? How can you overcome the challenges?

The practice of participatory research briefly outlined above will necessarily change from class to class, from context to context. As McCaleb rightly points out, there are no right or wrong ways of doing this kind of research. The thoughts and knowledge that each one of the members of the learning community brings to the process is valuable. They all contribute to this research by listening to each other, asking questions, doing interviews, writing, and constantly thinking about how to improve what they are already doing (McCaleb, 1994, p. 143). In fact, such an endeavor can be enriched by moving from the local community to the global community.

CONNECTING WITH THE GLOBAL COMMUNITY

In these days of global communication, one exciting option available for teachers and learners is to bring the global community into the local classroom. They can easily do this by using the Internet as a tool for participatory research. The Internet offers unlimited possibilities for teachers and learners to connect the word and the world. Using the Internet, teachers and learners can easily gain rich and varied knowledge on global matters, and develop their own critical perspectives about them. They can also, if they wish, access useful materials with explicit pedagogical focus on grammar and vocabulary or on reading and writing. For illustrative examples of using the Internet as a tool, see the microstrategies described below. For an easy-to-use guide to language and culture on the Internet, see, for example, Carl Blyth (1998).

In several North American and European countries, individual learners and teachers have ready access to Internet facilities, either at home or at school. In other settings, educational institutions provide common facilities for learners and teachers in computer labs. In countries such as China, Egypt, India, and Nigeria, almost every major city has "Internet Cafés," where users have Internet access at a nominal cost. Even in places where Internet facilities are either expensive or simply unavailable, there are always the traditional sources of information in the form of magazines, newspapers, radio, and TV, all of which now devote a considerable amount of time and space to issues related to economic and cultural globalization.

How the twin processes of economic and cultural globalization impact the L2 learners' individual identity is a subject that is waiting to be exploited for effective learning and teaching (see chapters 11 and 12 for details). Teachers and learners can start in that direction by following the five recommendations for participatory research outlined above and by just stretching their scope beyond the boundaries of the local community. In other words, they can carry the aims and activities of participatory research into cyberspace. By doing so they enter an exciting world of authentic resources that have the potential, if used properly, to help them *read* cultural artifacts and political events in ways that resonate with their individual experiences.

More specifically and in terms of the five recommendations, participants can form a *virtual* community of learners using the World Wide Web. They can contact different language schools in the country in which their target language is spoken as the first language and, through them, get in touch with learners of that particular language. The can get the Web addresses of these schools through search engines such as Yahoo or Google. They can then interact with teachers and learners at those schools through pen pal Web sites or by posting messages via chat rooms or news groups, thus sharing their joys and sorrows of encountering a new language or a new culture.

The same channels of communication can be used to interact with competent speakers of the target language as well. Participants can exchange information with other members of the *virtual* learning community and gain new perspectives on personal concerns and political events. Finally, they can select interesting reading materials on a topic but from different sources, thus broadening their critical understanding of that particular topic. Such cross-cultural materials can be collected and later used as teaching/learning materials in class. Thus, the options available on the Internet for generating learning opportunities are truly phenomenal.

Reflective task 3.6

From your perspective, is connecting with the global community to critically link the word and the world a desirable and doable activity? In responding to this task, consider the widespread belief that language teachers and learners are in a privileged position to deal with various themes and topics as long as they are appropriate and done through the medium of the target language being taught and learned.

To sum up this section on generating learning opportunities in and outside the classroom, I discussed how particular types of learner involvement and teacher questioning mediated through formal or informal collaboration can contribute to the creation and utilization of learning opportunities. I also pointed out how connecting with the local and the global community promises even greater, perhaps unlimited, possibilities for the generation of learning opportunities.

Let us now turn to sample microstrategies to illustrate how some of the ideas discussed in this chapter can be translated into classroom activities.

Microstrategies for Maximizing Learning Opportunities

The three microstrategies included here are designed to encourage learners to generate learning opportunities for themselves and for their classmates through participatory research. What follows are general guidelines. Teachers should feel free to adapt the guidelines (and even cut the project short) to suit the needs and wants as well as the linguistic and communicative abilities of their learners.

Microstrategy 3.1: Connecting with the Campus Community

3.1.0 Beyond the activities carried out inside the classroom, academic campuses offer plenty of learning opportunities to practice the still-developing target language in several communicative contexts. This microstrategy is designed to help learners explore on-campus student-related services and activities, and, in the process, benefit from informational content as well as language practice. Even if the students have already attended an orientation program during which they may have obtained information about student services, it is still worthwhile to do a more detailed project as a language learning exercise. What follows is one possible set of activities, and the teachers should modify any of them to suit the linguistic and communicative abilities of their learners.

3.1.1 Most colleges and schools offer a range of noninstructional services and activities for students. Ask your students whether they are aware of them. They may mention sports facilities, health services, student associations, counseling services, literary or artistic clubs, and the like. Try to elicit from them as much information as possible about any service they might mention. Make a list on the blackboard of available service centers or offices.

3.1.2 Divide your class into small groups, preferably not more than five students in each. Ask each group to select a particular student service, and then go to these centers, either individually or in groups, and collect informative bulletins, brochures, and leaflets. In educational settings where no such centers or offices exist, ask the students to find out for themselves where to go to get information about noninstructional services.

3.1.3 Have each group read the printed materials in class and make a list of interview questions to ask officials in those centers in order to seek additional information about the services that interest them. If no printed materials are available, ask the students to make a list of questions they would like to have answered.

3.1.4 Have students in each group go to the designated service center and request an appointment to interview an officer there for additional details about the services offered. Ask them to take notes from the conversation.

3.1.5 In class, have each group present a report about a particular service center, combining the information in the printed materials with notes from interviews with the official at that center. Conclude with a question-and-answer session. Also, ask them what kind of linguistic or communicative difficulties they encountered, and try to address those difficulties.

3.1.6 Focus on one of the student services, preferably student associations. In most colleges and schools, student associations are forever asking for members and volunteers to help with ongoing activities. Ask your students whether they would be interested in doing some volunteer work either for the student association or for any other on-campus agency that interests them. Have them state why they would or would not like to participate.

3.1.7 Find out from your students whether they are willing to invite an officer from the student association they researched (or, depending on student preference, from any other student service) to visit the class and give a structured, informational talk on what the student association does and how it benefits the student community. Encourage discussion and negotiation among the students in order to come to a consensus on the choice of topic/person.

3.1.8 On the appointed day, ask the students to listen to the guest lecturer and to take notes. If the speaker permits (most will because of the promotional nature of the talk), videotape (or, if the resources are not available, audiotape) the talk. After the lecture, encourage the students to ask questions.

3.1.9 In the next class session, play back the video (or the audio), asking the students to listen carefully for a closer examination of the structure and the content of the talk. If students have difficulty doing so, highlight the salient features of the talk in terms of pronunciation, vocabulary, etc.

3.1.10 After a month or so, ask whether any of the students have actually participated in any campus event or volunteered to do any service, and, if so, ask them to share their experience with the rest of the class.

Microstrategy 3.2: Connecting with the Local Community

3.2.0 This microstrategy is designed to bring together members of the classroom and the local community. It aims at creating opportunities for the learners to develop their oral and written communication skills as well as critical thinking and decision-making skills by following, analyzing, understanding, and reporting a news story of local interest.

3.2.1 Ask your students to read a target-language newspaper, or listen to radio news broadcasts, or watch TV news coverage focusing on stories of local interest—any act or event that excites or agitates the local community. Ask them to select any one news story that interests them, and be prepared to talk about it briefly in class (What's the story? Why is it interesting? etc.).

3.2.2 Divide your class into small groups, preferably no more than five in each. Let the members of the group listen to each other's choice of story. Ask them to negotiate among themselves and decide on one story to work on. If necessary, guide them to select stories that have the potential to develop further.

3.2.3 If two or three groups select the same news item, let them do so. But you may ask one group to concentrate on local newspaper coverage, another on radio coverage, and yet another on TV coverage.

3.2.4 Allow a week or two (depending on how the story unfolds) for each group to follow the story and develop a sense of what the story is about, why it interests or excites or agitates the local community. Encourage group work and advise each group to meet as often as possible either in the class or outside to discuss the story and to maintain a diary tracing its development.

3.2.5 Have each group plan to interview members of the community to elicit reactions to the developing story. It would be a good idea for learners as a group to come up with a list of questions they can use for their interviews. Depending on time, resources, and the nature of the story, they can talk to their family members, their teachers, their neighbors, or even city council officials. The objective here is to gather different perspectives on the same story.

3.2.6   Ask the learners to discuss within their group the full story and the reactions to it. They should then write a brief consensus report on it.

3.2.7   Have each group present its report to whole class, followed by class discussion.

3.2.8   After the class discussion is over, ask them to share with the class what they actually learned in doing the project. In addition to any linguistic items they may have learned, the focus here should be on the story itself, how it unfolded/ended, whether it unfolded/ended the way they expected, whether they had any difficulty with their negotiating, decision-making, interviewing skills, etc.

3.2.9   At higher levels of proficiency, you may ask the learners to compare how different channels of communication (newspaper, radio, and TV) shape news coverage. You may also encourage them to think critically on any bias in reporting, and how language is used (or manipulated) to present a particular point of view.

Microstrategy 3.3: Connecting with the Global Community

3.3.0   This microstrategy is designed to help learners cross the physical borders of their classroom and their local community in order to create learning opportunities. They will do so by entering virtual communities in cyberspace and by using the Internet as a tool for participatory research. In settings where access to the Internet is limited or unavailable, traditional sources of information such as newspapers, magazines, radio, and TV may be used to do a simplified version of this activity.

In this project, teachers and learners will connect with the global community to explore certain aspects of economic and cultural globalization, with particular reference to McDonald's. Yes, McDonald's! The golden arches is something that is familiar to most city-dwelling students in most countries. The reason behind selecting McDonald's for this microstrategy is to prompt the participants to think globally about something they know locally. This microstrategy can be implemented at different levels of sophistication. What follows is one possible activity that I deliberately designed to be fairly extended. Teachers should feel free to change it by deleting or diluting parts of it to suit their particular situation.

3.3.1 Begin by asking your students what they know about globalization. You might even start with different word forms: globe, global, globalize, globalization, and globalism. Touch upon how, in terms of economy, culture, and communication, the world is shrinking and is becoming more and more interdependent. Do not hesitate to use the cliche "global village." Draw from your students names of multinational corporations that have global reach. If necessary, ask leading questions to elicit names that should be familiar to them—Nike, Coca-Cola, McDonald's, etc. Zero in on McDonald's, and ask them what they know about it. Then, as homework, have them access McDonald's official Web site (www.mcdonalds.com) and find out as much as possible about McDonald's and its services around the world. Keep the assignment open-ended so that they can bring back any information they like.

3.3.2 In class, ask a few students to share the information they collected. They may have found that, for instance, McDonald's "is the largest and best-known global food service retailer" with more than 28,000 restaurants in 120 countries—or any figure displayed at the time they accessed the Web site. Ask them whether they noticed any difference in the food and the ambiance in McDonald's compared with other fast-food restaurants. Also, engage them generally on what challenges McDonald's may have to face to serve food in so many countries with so many different cultures, religions, and dietary habits.

3.3.3 Next, have them return to McDonald's home page and from there go to various links in which information about McDonald's in several countries is given. This time, ask them to focus on how McDonald's tries to be sensitive to local diet customs conditioned by cultural and religious beliefs and practices. Let them comment on its global reach and local touch.

3.3.4 In class, ask a few students to share the information they collected. Or, pair students and ask each pair to exchange information. For instance, they may have found out how McDonald's serves Kosher food in Israel, conforming to the laws of the Jewish religion; or Halal food in Saudi Arabia and other Muslim countries, following Islamic religious traditions; or vegetarian food in India, where most people do not eat meat. Ask your students to share their views on why McDonald's has to be culturally and religiously sensitive, and how it manages to do so.

3.3.5 Moving beyond the official Web site and focusing specifically on the issue of cultural and economic globalization, ask your students to find any recent news items from any part of the world where local people opposed McDonald's for cultural or economic reasons. Suggest that they can go to any search engine (such as Google or Yahoo) and enter: "globalization and McDonald's." The search will show them an overwhelming number of entries, and they can quickly browse through and select one or two items to read. Alternatively, they can go to the archives of on-line versions of leading international news agencies such as the *New York Times* (http://www.nytimes.com) or British Broadcasting Corporation (http://news.bbc.ac.uk), or any other leading news agency in their country. Ask them to make a printout of one or two items that are relevant for the assignment.

3.3.6 In class, lead a discussion on what they found. Even if only a few students obtained appropriate reading materials, share them with other students. Or, you may help them with materials you collected. Focus on the cultural factor first. If, for whatever reason, an appropriate example was not found in time, use the following:

On 24 May 2001, BBC News Online reported a news story titled "McDonald's grilled over 'veggie fries'" (http://news.bbc.co.uk/low/english/world/newsid_1348000/1348296.stm). On the same day, a similar story appeared in the *New York Times* titled *McDonald's Apologizes for Fries* (http://www.nytimes.com/aponline/business/AP-McDonald's-Fries .html).

Here's the BBC story:

McDonald's grilled over 'veggie fries'
by Steven Evans in New York

Fast food giant McDonald's has expressed regret for not giving the public what it calls "complete" information about the way its potato chips are cooked.

With a multi-million dollar court case on the way, the BBC has learned that McDonald's has conceded that it may have confused customers over whether its fries were vegetarian, and so acceptable to Hindus.

In 1990, McDonald's announced with much fanfare that it would switch to cooking its fries in vegetable oil, making them acceptable to vegetarians who will not eat food cooked in beef fat.

However, it has now emerged that this is only part of the process.

In North America, the fries are first cooked at plants using beef fat, and then frozen before being shipped to the restaurants for further frying.

American Hindus have started legal action seeking damages, which they say could run to millions of dollars.

In India the revelation caused rioting until the company assured local people that the method of cooking there was strictly vegetarian.

McDonald's has nearly 30 restaurants in India, selling chicken, lamb and vegetarian products.

Apology

McDonald's has now conceded ground. The corporation's web site on nutrition says it regrets if customers felt information was incomplete.

A spokesman for McDonald's said: "We're not too big to apologize."

The company has also clarified its policy, saying that in predominantly Muslim countries it conforms strictly to Halal standards with no beef or pork flavouring.

But the apology is unlikely to head off the lawsuit in the United States being brought by the Hindus, for whom the cow is a sacred animal.

In America, non-Hindu vegetarians are divided on the issue.

Some say they are outraged, but others say that the name of McDonald's is synonymous with beef—so what did customers really expect?

3.3.7 Use one or two texts that students brought, or use the text given above. Ask them to read and analyze the texts critically, arguing for and against the practice McDonald's followed in a particular case. In the case of the above story, ask them whether it is fair for McDonald's not to have given "complete" information to its customers. Touch upon any compromise McDonald's may have to make to balance economic compulsions, cultural expectations, and public relations.

3.3.8 Next, focus on the economic aspect of globalization, again with particular reference to McDonald's. Use text selected by students themselves as part of assignment 3.3.6 above. If necessary, use the following text.

Background information: When McDonald's opened its restaurants in India, labor unions and political activists opposed the company using catchy slogans such as *Micro chips, yes; potato chips, no.* What they meant was that the government of India should invite computer companies to make microchips in India, which would benefit the Indian economy, rather than allowing foreign companies to make potato chips, which would harm the economic interests of small farmers and restaurant owners. More strikingly, in France, Jose Bové, a leader of a farmers' union, was recently jailed for organizing the destruction of a McDonald's under construction in his town. He has since become a celebrity in France and elsewhere.

The Indian and the French examples are just the tip of the iceberg. Many labor organizations and political activists around the world regularly protest against multinational companies, accusing them of world economic domination. They also protest what they consider to be immense harm that multinational corporations inflict on small businesses in many countries. For the last few years, protesters have been marching to the venues of meetings of the International Monetary Fund (IMF), the World Bank, or the World Trade Organization (WTO), all of which, they argue, directly or indirectly aid multinational corporations in their world economic domination. Every year, they stage demonstrations on May Day (1 May) to protest economic globalization, and they usually target multinational corporations like McDonald's.

Given below are the first two paragraphs of a long essay that appeared 1 May 2001 in the on-line edition of *The Economist*, an internationally reputed magazine based in London (http://www.economist.co.uk). The essay is titled "Mayhem in May" and was written by the staff of the magazine.

Mayhem in May
1 May 2001
From The Economist Global Agenda

The first of May is one of the highlights of the increasingly demanding social calendar of anti-globalization activists. Nowadays large numbers of protesters also show up at meetings of the IMF and World Bank, the annual gathering of the World Economic Forum's in Davos, Switzerland, and any talks on trade liberalization such as this month's Summit of the Americas in Quebec. Plenty of anti-globalists were again out in force on city streets throughout the world this week for May 1st, the traditional day of solidarity for labor movements. Berlin, Sydney and Melbourne saw violent confrontations with the police. In London this year's theme was Monopoly, the capitalist board game. Scheduled events include a mass bike ride, a pigeon feed on Trafalgar Square and the building of the world's largest cardboard hotel in Mayfair.

For all their entertainment value, and despite the stupid violence which mars some of them, the anti-globalists' demonstrations cannot be dismissed as a recurring juvenile joke. How to reduce poverty in the third world—and whether globalization is a help or a hindrance—is one of the most pressing moral, political and economic issues of our times. Undeniably, anti-globalism demonstrations have moved these questions higher up the public agenda. Whether they are pushing governments towards more enlightened answers is quite another matter.

3.3.9 First, using selected texts from students or combining the background information and the text given above, help your learners understand what the basic issues are. Again, instead of telling them, ask leading questions so that they themselves can come up with answers. Then, ask them why McDonald's is targeted by anti-globalization protesters in several parts of the world. Have them form two groups and debate whether or not it is fair to target McDonald's, and what the protesters achieve by doing so.

3.3.10 Finally, ask the students to consider all the readings and the discussions, and write a brief report of what they have learned in doing this project. Ask them to focus on both language and content: any new ideas, new vocabulary, new grammatical structures, or any other notable items they may have come across.

Exploratory Projects

I present below two interrelated exploratory projects designed to help teachers do a self-assessment of their attempts to generate learning opportunities in class. The first one relates mainly to what the teacher taught and the second one to mainly what the learners may have learned. An important caveat: because it is difficult to ascertain clear evidence for the creation and utilization of learning opportunities, all we will have are *teacher perception* of learning opportunities created and *learner perception* of learning opportunities utilized. The point to remember, though, is that the feedback from this informal project, however unscientific it is, is still of immense value to the teacher (for a more systematic way of studying teaching acts, see the exploratory projects in Chapter 13). For designing these two projects, I have drawn ideas from Ellis (1995), Kumaravadivelu (1995a), and Slimani (1989).

Project 3.1: What the Teacher Taught

3.1.0 We learned that *display* questions elicit a closed set of predetermined answers, and *referential* questions elicit an open-ended set of unpredictable answers. We also learned that, compared with display questions, referential questions are likely to generate more learning opportunities. This exploratory project is designed to help you analyze your questioning pattern and its possible impact on the creation of learning opportunities.

3.1.1 Plan a lesson in which you anticipate a good deal of interactive exchanges. It would be helpful for the purpose of this project if you focus on learner comprehension of a passage with a considerable number of new words that are challenging to your students at their current proficiency level. Write a detailed lesson plan that includes the following: (a) general objectives of the lesson in terms of reading skills, and (b) specific objectives, that is, targeted items of the lesson in terms of new words, concepts, etc.

3.1.2 Arrange to videotape (if that is not possible, at least audiotape) the lesson. Teach this lesson as you normally would, that is, do not do anything special because you are videotaping or analyzing this lesson. Just be yourself!

3.1.3 Immediately after the lesson, distribute the Student Response Sheet shown in Figure 3.1 for students to complete. Explain the questions in the response sheet, if necessary, so that the students clearly understand them. Ask them to take as much time as they want and write as much as they want but to be specific in their responses. Collect their response sheets and keep them; you will need them for doing the next project. (Incidentally, consider using a suitably revised version of the Stu-

---

Student Response Sheet

Name: Class: Date:

1. What do you think the teacher most wanted you to learn from today's lesson? Be specific.

2. What are the words in this lesson that are completely new to you? List all of them.

3. What are the new words that you think you learned FULLY today?

4. What are the new words that you think you learned PARTIALLY today?

5. What are the new words that you think you still do not understand at all?

6. Other than words and their meanings, what else did you learn in class today?

7. Do you want to say anything else about today's lesson?

Figure 3.1

dent Response Sheet in all your classes. The feedback you get from your students will be useful to monitor the effectiveness of your teaching.)

3.1.4 As the students work on the response sheet, jot down any changes you may have made in your lesson plan as the lesson unfolded. Revise your list of targeted items (Go to your Specific Objectives column in your lesson plan). You may find yourself deleting some words or concepts that you did not have time to deal with, or adding new ones that came up during the lesson.

3.1.5 Watch the video (or listen to the tape). Keeping in mind the objective of this particular project, select a few episodes in which there are several occurrences of teacher questions. Transcribe only those segments; you do not need to transcribe the whole tape.

3.1.6 Now, collect instances of questions that you can easily identify as display questions or referential questions. If there are doubtful cases, ignore them for the moment.

3.1.7 Review the interactive exchanges where display questions occurred. Keeping in mind that display questions do have a place in language teaching, reflect on the suitability of the display questions you asked in the specific contexts in which they occurred. Think about whether your questions, from your perspective, created the kind of learning opportunities that you wanted to create. You may want to jot down your notes using the table shown in Figure 3.2 (or a similar one).

Episode #	Display question (turns x to y)	Learning opportunity it presumably created	Reasons to change to referential or to keep

Figure 3.2

Now, do the same for referential questions in Figure 3.3.

Episode #	Referential question (turns x to y)	Learning opportunity it presumably created	Reasons to change or to keep

Figure 3.3

3.1.8　Go over the content of your completed tables. Think about whether this particular lesson is typical or atypical of your classroom teaching in terms of the occurrence of display and referential questions. Decide on the kind of changes you will have to make in order to maximize the creation of learning opportunities in class.

Exploratory Project 3.2: What the Learners Learned

3.2.0　One of the most important challenges of classroom teaching is to assess whether the learners see learning opportunities as learning opportunities. In the previous project, you tried to self-assess the degree to which you created opportunities for vocabulary learning in the lesson you taught. It would be interesting to see what learners thought they learned from that lesson.

3.2.1　Go over the Student Response Sheets you collected for the previous project (see 3.1.3 above). Consolidate their responses to each of the following seven items in Figure 3.4 and take down key words from their responses.

Item	Key words taken from student responses	My reaction to their responses
1. What they think I wanted them to learn		
2. Words they say are completely new to them		
3. Words they say they learned fully		
4. Words they say they learned partially		
5. Words they say they do not understand even after teaching		
6. Other things they say they learned		
7. Their general comments		

Figure 3.4

3.2.2 Write down, again in key words, your reaction (your first impression) to their responses to each of the items, and complete the table.

3.2.3 For the purpose of interpretation, you may look at student responses to each of the items, and try to understand them in relation to your own teaching agenda. Or, you can form two clusters: Cluster One consisting of responses to questions 2, 3, 4, and 5, and Cluster Two consisting of responses to questions 1, 6, and 7.

3.2.4 Look at Cluster One. Think about possible reasons why they say they learned certain words completely, certain other words partially, etc. Recall your teaching, or if necessary, replay the relevant video/audio segments to see what might be the connection between how you generated learning opportunities (i.e., what you did, how you actually explained the meaning of a word, or the kind of questions you asked, etc.) and the degrees of learning perceived by the learners.

3.2.5 Now look at Cluster Two. Compare the targeted teaching items as per your lesson plan and student responses to questions 1, 6, and 7. The comparison must be very revealing. It should reveal, for instance, the gap between the teacher's agenda and the learners' understanding of it, and the gap between what is taught and what is available to learn.

3.2.6 There is yet more useful information you can draw from the data you have collected from Student Response Sheets. You have information about what every individual learner said he or she did or did not get out of this particular lesson. There will definitely be individual variations. Student responses to a couple of more lessons on different teaching items will show which student will have difficulty coping with the challenges of your classroom objectives. Think about how you can make use of that information if you wish to individualize your classroom instruction or student counseling.

3.2.7 Finally, reflect on what you learned from the process of doing this two-part exploratory project. Does it provide valuable information? Is it doable? Time consuming? Will it become easier once you do it a couple of times? Will it help if a group of teachers join together as a team and help each other collect, analyze, and interpret data? Anything else?

In Closing

I began this chapter with a series of questions on maximizing learning opportunities. There are no satisfactory answers to those questions. However, what seems to be clear is that both teachers and learners—teachers more than learners—have a responsibility to create and utilize learning opportunities in class. What is also clear is that, more than anything else, the classroom is the prime site where the success or failure of any attempt to generate learning opportunities will be determined.

The authentic classroom interactional episodes used and analyzed in this chapter are very short, and together constitute no more than a few minutes of talk between the participants in classroom events. But, even such simple and short exchanges are sufficient to show the significance of the interactive process of learning and teaching while at the same time revealing the limitations of predetermined teaching agenda, the textbook, and the syllabus. It is only through collaborative work that teachers and learners generate classroom discourse, and in generating classroom discourse, they also generate a wide range of learning opportunities. Considering their collaborative role in the classroom, "we can no longer see teachers simply as teachers, and learners simply as learners, because both are, for good or ill, managers of learning" (Allwright, 1984, p. 156).

If teachers and learners are jointly vested with the task of managing learning in the classroom, then it is imperative that there is a considerable degree of understanding between them about the aims and activities, and the processes and the procedures governing classroom learning and teaching. What could easily undermine their joint effort are potential mismatches between teacher intention and learner interpretation. We turn to that subject in the next chapter.

CHAPTER 4

Minimizing Perceptual Mismatches

Ways of seeing are also ways of not seeing.
—KENNETH BURKE, 1995, p. 70

We learned in the previous chapter that generating learning opportunities in class is the joint responsibility of teachers and learners alike, because both are co-managers of learning. Even if the
co-managers believe that they have carried out that responsibility
successfully, it is perfectly possible that they have very different perceptions about what constitutes a successful learning opportunity.
An anecdote reported by Allwright (1987, p. 99) makes this point
clear: "An ESL teacher used to handle 'conversation' classes by
going in with a dialogue which the learners first practise and then
build into a more general discussion. One day he went in with a dialogue on paper as usual, but his learners immediately started a
conversation on some topical issue. After twenty minutes or so of
lively discussion—just what the teacher always wanted but rarely
got from these learners—one member of the class put up her hand
and asked: 'Please, when are we going to start the conversation?'"

What this anecdote tells us is that teachers and learners do not
look at the same classroom event as a potential learning event. In
other words, there can be, and often are, mismatches between teacher
perceptions and learner perceptions of what is available to learn. At
least for the particular learner mentioned above, twenty minutes of
student-initiated, lively, authentic conversation did not constitute
conversational practice. She was impatiently waiting for the lesson
on conversation to start.

The gap between teacher and learner perceptions of the aims
and activities of classroom events can easily increase the gap between teacher input and learner intake. Input refers to oral and

written data of the target language to which learners are exposed
through various sources, and recognized by them as useful and usable for language learning purposes (Kumaravadivelu, 1994b). Intake, on the other hand, is "what goes in and not what is *available*
to go in" (Corder, 1967, p. 165, his emphasis). To a large extent, what
actually goes in is determined by how learners perceive the usefulness of classroom events through which they are exposed to input.
While the significance of learner perception of learning opportunities has been recognized since Corder made the distinction between
input and intake, there have been very few systematic studies on
learner and teacher perceptions in the field of classroom L2 learning and teaching. Only recently have researchers attempted to investigate it.

Studies on Learner Perceptions

Four experimental studies conducted in four different countries
involving learners of different proficiency levels have shed light on
the learner and teacher perceptions of classroom events. These studies were conducted by Kumaravadivelu (1989, 1991), Assia Slimani
(1989, 1992), David Block (1994, 1996), and Gary Barkhuizen (1998).
A common thread that runs through these studies is an unfailing
realization that one and the same classroom event is interpreted
differently by each participant.

Slimani (1989) investigated a group of first-year university students studying English as a foreign language (EFL) in Algeria. She
focused on uptake, or the students' report of their perception of what
they learned after each of six lessons she observed and recorded.
She found that "on many occasions the teacher focused on various
specific instructional features without the learners reporting them"
(p. 226) and, conversely, the learners reported to have learned several items that were different from what the teacher had planned
for them. She also found that the learners mentioned only 44 percent of the explicit focus of the lessons, and a majority of the items
unnoticed by the learners are instances of error treatment provided
by the teacher. Thus, Slimani's study confirmed beyond doubt the
widespread belief that there are perceptual mismatches between
teaching agenda and learning outcome.

In a study focusing on the similarities and differences between learner and teacher perceptions of learning purpose, Block (1994, 1996) examined the ways in which learners describe and attribute purpose to the activities that teachers ask them to do. The experiment was carried out in an EFL class for MBA students in Spain. The lesson that Block observed consisted of five activities: a brief conversation warm-up, a vocabulary review, a review of a news broadcast, a practice minitest, and an extended activity about job advertisements. Block found that while the teacher attached great importance to the job ad activity, which took the bulk of class time, the learners "tended to write it off" (1994, p. 483). On the other hand, the learners spoke most highly of the news reviewing task, which, from the teacher's perspective, "hardly deserved mention." This study points "not only to the autonomy of learner thought but also to the existence of a gap between the way teachers and learners 'see' the classroom and all that occurs within it" (Block, 1996, p. 168).

Yet another study conducted in South Africa involved high school students learning English as a second language (ESL). Barkhuizen (1998) focused on the students' perceptions of learning and teaching activities they encountered in their classes. Predictably, he, too, found that students' perception of classroom aims and events did not match those of their teachers. The teachers involved in the study were frequently surprised to learn about the thoughts and feelings of their students that, of course, were very different from theirs. For instance, the teachers "could hardly believe the high ranking given to the mechanical language skills. They were obviously not aware of the students' and their own focus on these skills in their classes and would hardly have predicted that their students see the acquiring of these skills as the most effective means of learning English" (p. 102). Based on his study, Barkhuizen advises teachers to "continuously explore their classes, particularly their learners' perceptions" (p. 104).

Reflective task 4.1

Why do you think perceptual mismatches occur in the language classroom? What does it show when learners say they learned certain items that were not at all highlighted by teachers, and did not learn certain items highlighted by teachers?

The three experimental studies reviewed above confirm our experiential knowledge that there indeed are perceptual mismatches between teaching objectives and learning outcomes, and more importantly, between the instruction that makes sense to teachers and instruction that makes sense to learners. The studies strongly support the view that "the more we know about the learner's personal approaches and personal concepts, the better and more productive our intervention will be" (Kumaravadivelu, 1991, p. 107). An important first step in knowing more about the learners' personal perspectives on classroom aims and events is to understand the possible sources that could contribute to potential mismatches between teacher intention and learner interpretation.

Sources of Potential Mismatches

More than a decade ago, Kumaravadivelu (1989, 1991) attempted to identify sources of potential mismatch between teacher intention and learner interpretation by exploring learners' and teachers' perceptions of the nature, the goals, and the demands of a selected language-learning task carried out by low intermediate level ESL learners in the United States. The task chosen for this study deals with newspaper advertisements. It focuses on the rhetorical features of comparison, and the grammatical features of *too* and *enough*. The task has two parts. Part one, "Finding an inexpensive wedding dress," presents information about a bride-to-be (her budget, her size, etc.,) and six brief classified advertisements for wedding gowns. Part two, "Finding an apartment," presents information about a renter couple (their budget, apartment specifications, etc.,) and six brief classified advertisements for apartment rentals. The learners have to decide which advertisement the bride-to-be and the renters would answer.

Two intermediate level ESL classes, taught by two different teachers, participated in this study. The teachers (TI and T2) were given the same task and were advised to follow the instructional guidelines given in the prescribed textbook. The suggested classroom management for the first part, on wedding gowns, directs the teacher to have the learners read the paragraph posing the task, elicit vocabulary concerning wedding gowns, and, finally, to have the learners read the advertisements orally to complete the problem posed by the task. The second part, dealing with renting an apartment, follows the same format.

The selected task was introduced as a paired activity, and the researcher focused his attention on two pairs of learners. One pair consisted of a Japanese male (S1) and a Brazilian female (S2), and another consisted of a Japanese male (S3) and a Malaysian female (S4). Pairing was done in such a way that learners in each pair did not share a common native language; the idea was to avoid the use of native language during paired activities.

The classroom interaction was audiotaped and transcribed. During the analysis stage, the researcher/observer talked with the teachers and the learners in order to seek certain clarifications on the questions asked and the responses given. The classroom transcripts formed the primary data, and the interview transcripts formed the secondary data. A combination of the interactional analysis of primary and secondary data, and learner, teacher, and observer perspectives of classroom events revealed insights into the mismatches between teacher intention and learner interpretation.

Reflective task 4.2

Pause here for a moment. Think about possible sources or causes behind perceptual mismatches that occur in the classroom. Try to recall specific instances of learning difficulties experienced by you or your learners, and see whether you can identify possible reasons for them.

Based on the study reported above, Kumaravadivelu identified ten sources that have the potential to contribute to the mismatch between teacher intention and learner interpretation. They are:

1. Cognitive mismatch: This source refers to the general, cognitive knowledge of the world that adult language learners bring with them to the classroom. It pertains to mental processes such as remembering, perceiving, recognizing, and inferencing. Learners use these processes to obtain a conceptual understanding of not only the physical and natural phenomena in general but also of language and language learning in particular. Consider the following episode:

Episode 4.1

S1   In United States hmm . . . what's apartments made of? Wood?

T1   Wood.

S1   Wood? In United States . . .

T1   Uh . . . if . . . if you are building new apartments, probably wood will be more expensive . . . uh . . .

This particular foreign student does not know that, in most cases, wood is used to build apartments and houses in the United States, unlike his country, where mostly brick and mortar are used. His lack of prior knowledge about building construction in the United States hinders his ability to do the task. The teacher, who lacks knowledge about how buildings are constructed in the learners' country, is not able to fully understand the reason behind the learner's query. She assumes that the learner might be thinking about the expenses involved in using wood and merely makes a comment on it. This cognitive mismatch is not intended or anticipated by the teacher.

2. Communicative mismatch: This source refers to the communicative skills necessary for the learners to exchange messages or express personal views. Because the learners have only a limited command of the target language, they struggle to convey their message.

Episode 4.2

S1   In this kind of exercise, you have to be careful and use our . . . which . . . do . . . uh . . . I forget . . . like it eliminates . . .

T1   Analyzing? It teaches you . . . you to analyze?

S1   No . . . hmm . . . through elimination of words you can find the best answer for the . . . we must use our intellect.

T1   OK . . .

The learner in this episode has the right strategy to solve a problem posed by the task through a process of elimination, but is unable to communicate his ideas clearly because of his limited communicative ability. He employs the familiar communication strategy of circumlocution to get his message across. The teacher, as my interview with her revealed, does not get the learner's intended message, but nevertheless closes the interactional sequence by saying "OK."

3. Linguistic mismatch: This source refers to the linguistic repertoire—syntactic, semantic, and pragmatic knowledge of the target language—that is minimally required to do a task, and to talk about it. In this case, the teacher correctly senses that the student has a problem and offers assistance:

Episode 4.3

T1 Do you need any help?

SI (points to something in the text)

T1 Do you know what AC is?

S1 I don't know . . . I don't know.

T1 It is an abbreviation . . . uh . . . abbreviation means to make something shorter . . . like Mr. . . . United States–U.S. . . . uh . . . it is an air conditioner.

SI Oh, air conditioner.

This is a linguistic mismatch in the sense that the teacher did not expect that a very familiar linguistic abbreviation such as AC would be problematic for the learner.

4. Pedagogic mismatch: This source refers to the teacher and learner perceptions of stated or unstated short- or long-term instructional objective(s) of language learning tasks. Consider the following attempt made by the teacher to determine the learners' perception of the main purpose of the lesson, just finished, on scanning advertisements:

Episode 4.4

T1   What do you think is the purpose of this lesson?

S3   So that we can make the right choice . . . how to buy through newspaper ads . . .

S4   Increase vocabulary . . . and learn English . . .

T1   Learn English? By what . . . by practicing? By what?

S4   By conversation . . . and writing.

T1   OK, do you think there is any one thing, one grammar thing we were working on?

S4   Yeah.

T1   What part of grammar do you think?

S4   What part?

T1   Yeah, what part of grammar do you think we were working on?

S4   Capital . . . uh . . . comma.

T1   What do you mean?

S4   No, not too much grammar . . . vocabulary.

The lesson in question was primarily a meaning-focused activity with some attention given to the grammatical features of *too* and *enough*. Clearly, the teacher was trying get the learners to identify those grammatical items. It is evident from this episode that the perception of the two learners' in terms of the purpose of the lesson do not match each other's; neither do they match that of the teacher. An intriguing part of the interaction is that S4 mentioned the use of capital letters and comma as the teaching and learning objectives of the lesson, something that was not at all mentioned by the teacher during this particular class. Interviews conducted later with the teacher revealed that punctuation was indeed the focus of a lesson taught the week before.

5. Strategic mismatch: This source refers to learning strategies: operations, steps, plans, and routines used by the learner to facilitate the obtaining, storage, retrieval, and use of information, that is, what learners do to learn and to regulate learning. In the following episode dealing with the task of finding an inexpensive wedding gown, the teacher gave the learners fifteen minutes to solve a problem. She expected that it would trigger the use of

certain specific language learning strategies that would generate discussions, disagreements, and negotiations thereby giving an opportunity for an extended conversational practice. However, consider the interaction between S1 and S2:

Episode 4.5

S1 First, one hundred ten dollars. This is costly.

S2 Yeah.

S1 Second, uh . . . size . . . five.

S2 Small.

S1 This one . . . size big.

S2 Which one . . . (laughs) . . . oh . . . yeah, that's right. No.

S1 This . . . she has only seven . . .

S2 Seventy dollars.

S1 Seventy-seven.

S2 Oh . . . yeah . . . Seventy-seven dollars.

S1 It's expensive.

S2 Yeah . . . number five.

S1 Yeah.

The learners used the simplest possible strategy of elimination and solved the problem within a few minutes and without much negotiation. The teacher's expectation of an extended dialogue did not materialize. The mismatch here is between the strategies the teacher expected the learners to use and ones they actually used.

6. Cultural mismatch: This source refers to the prior knowledge of the cultural norms of the target language community minimally required for the learners to understand and solve a problem-oriented task. Consider this:

Episode 4.6

T2   (noticed S4 looking puzzled) Do you need any help?

S4   She . . . she wants a used . . . a used wedding dress?

T2   Yeah.

S4   Why?

T2   Well, you tell me why? Why does she want to buy a used one? Hmm?

The teacher diagnoses the question asked by S4 as a problem of reading comprehension and, since the answer is rather easy to find in the text, tosses the question back to the learner. The source of S4's problem, however, is not textual but cultural. Coming from an Eastern culture, the learner, a Malaysian female, just could not believe that a bride would rent a wedding dress worn by somebody else. Her culture attaches enormous sentimental value to a wedding dress; every bride buys it, cherishes it, and keeps it forever. In her culture, a wedding ceremony is a once-in-a-lifetime event and therefore anything associated with it becomes a sentimental object to be treasured. It is not something that can be returned to the store to be reused by somebody else. The teacher is clearly unaware of the cultural nuances associated with the learner question.

7. Evaluative mismatch: This source refers to articulated or unarticulated types of self-evaluation measures used by learners to monitor their ongoing progress in their language-learning activities. Consider the following episode:

Episode 4.7

S1   Can we just say too expensive . . . or . . .

T1   Yeah, that's fine.

S1   Too expensive . . . hmm . . . to buy?

TI   Yeah.

S1   (looks confused)

At the surface, this episode shows a perfectly normal interactional exchange between the teacher and the learner. However, a detailed analysis of the intentions and interpretations of the participants reveals a different story. During this lesson, the teacher used the phrases *too expensive* and *too large* more than once. In the learner's mind, this usage conflicted with his prior knowledge of pedagogic grammar learned in previous classes, namely, that *too* plus an adjective should be followed by *to* plus a verb, as in *too expensive to buy*—a simple grammatical rule that, according to the learner, the teacher did not bother to follow. So, as part of his continual self-evaluation, he seeks feedback to confirm or reject his previous understanding of the rule. Not knowing the real intention of the learner, the teacher not only fails to clarify the learner's legitimate doubt, but creates additional confusion by responding affirmatively to both *too expensive* and *too expensive to buy*.

8. Procedural mismatch: This source refers to stated or unstated paths chosen by the learners to do a task. The procedural source pertains to locally specified, currently identified, bottom-up tactics that seek an immediate resolution to a specific problem whereas the strategic source, discussed earlier, pertains to any broad-based, higher-level, top-down strategy that seeks an overall solution in a general language learning situation. Consider this episode:

Episode 4.8

T2 (to S2) Do you have any idea?

S2 I think . . . uh . . . we have to imagine that situation, we have to find an apartment . . . so . . . I have to call them . . . ask price or something . . . I think it is better for us, this situation, so . . . uh . . . imagine you are the landlord . . . and you don't say anything . . . hmm . . . I have to ask you how much is the price or where is it or can I have a pet or something . . .

T2 (turning to S1) Do you understand?

S1 No.

T2 OK, let's try again . . .

The learner (S2) attempts a fairly detailed, bottom-up explanation of how to go about solving a problem. This procedural thinking on the part of S2 is not what the teacher expected to hear, although it is correct. She, therefore, gives up on the student without giving any feedback and decides to try another tactic.

9. Instructional mismatch: This source refers to instructional guidance given by the teacher or indicated by the textbook writer to help learners carry out the task successfully.

Episode 4.9

T2   OK . . . hmm . . . what this lesson is . . . it is called advertisement. It is supposed to help you learn to read advertisements . . . hmm . . . and they do that by . . . they give you a paragraph to read and some question . . . a task to figure out. Read and remember the items . . .

S3   (much later in the class, S3 asks a question) Do we have to memorize?

T2   No . . . no . . . you don't have to memorize.

The instructional direction given by the teacher is simple and clear enough not to be misunderstood—just read and remember the items. However, S3 was doubtful about what he was expected to do. It became clear during the postobservational interview that the word *remember* in the teacher talk had misled the learner. He associated the word with memorizing. He did not see any sense in memorizing the text and therefore asked a question that appeared to the teacher to be *silly*, as she confided later. Even straightforward instructional guidance can produce unintended effects.

10. Attitudinal mismatch: This source refers to participants' attitudes toward the nature of L2 learning and teaching, the nature of classroom culture, and teacher-learner role relationships. Adult learners, by virtue of their prior experience, have fairly well-established attitudes toward classroom management, and these preconceived notions can easily contribute to the mismatch between teacher intention and learner interpretation. Consider the following episode:

Episode 4.10

S3 This is . . .

S4 Large.

S3 Big size.

T2 Too big? Too large? OK, same thing . . .

S3 Big for her . . . and uh . . .

S4 The price . . .

S3 A little costly.

T2 Too expensive.

S3 No . . . not . . . a little costly.

T2 OK, so you won't choose that because it is too expensive . . .

S3 I think it's costly.

T2 Yeah, in English we say too expensive.

S3 I can't say costly?

T2 Well . . . (long pause). Costly is OK, yeah, but more often . . . probably we say expensive.

S3 OK, you are my teacher . . . (laughs)

T2 No, you don't have to agree with me . . .

S3 I don't have to?

This episode shows a fairly extended exchange on what the participants consider to be "standard" English. The learner has learned a particular variety of English (which, of course, is "standard" in his country) where costly is considered an appropriate usage in the given context. The teacher, a native speaker of English, spends some time trying to get the learner to accept and repeat what she considers to be the "standard" usage: expensive. What is crucial in this discourse is the fact that the learner, finally, gives up his stand invoking a norm that is largely accepted in classroom culture: the teacher is the authority figure. The teacher's generous remark on the learner's right to disagree only triggers an almost derisive response from the learner. In this episode, the mismatch relates to one's attitude toward a particular variety of English; however, there can be various types of attitudinal mismatches arising out of preconceived notions about factors such as participant expectations, classroom management, learning strategies and cultural stereotypes.

Reflective task 4.3

Assuming that these ten sources are among the underlying causes for potential mismatches in the language classroom, what are the ways in which you can make use of this information for improving teaching effectiveness?

Pedagogic Insights

There are at least three broad pedagogic insights we can derive from the above discussion. They are:

- Mismatches are unavoidable. They are a part of the practice of everyday teaching. Even highly structured and meticulously planned lessons will result in perceptual mismatches of one kind or another. In fact, given the number of participants and the varying perspectives they bring to bear on classroom events, it would be surprising if perceptual mismatches do not occur at all.

- Mismatches are identifiable. Even a preliminary study such as the one reported above has revealed ten different sources of mismatch between teacher intention and learner interpretation. These mismatches are not exhaustive, that is, further research might reveal more of them. Nor are they mutually exclusive, that is, they do not all have distinct boundaries. They are, however, distinct enough to be related to a particular source. Incidentally, the study also shows the importance of putting together learner, teacher, and observer perspectives in order to achieve a rich understanding of classroom aims and events. This is an important methodological issue we will revisit in greater detail in Chapter 13.

- Mismatches are manageable. Perceptual mismatches may be unavoidable, but they are not unmanageable. In fact, if identified in time and addressed with care, a mismatch can be converted into a learning opportunity in class. The mere recognition of the source of a mismatch could help both the learners and the teachers understand that there is an underlying reason for the difficulties the learners may have encountered in making sense of a classroom event.

Reflective task 4.4

How do any pre-service teacher education programs you are familiar with or any in-service teacher training you have undergone prepare you to deal with perceptual mismatches? In what way, do you think, can teacher education programs be restructured to impart knowledge and skill necessary to identify and minimize perceptual mismatches?

Given the importance of perceptual mismatches, it is imperative that we try to identify them, understand them, and address them effectively if we are serious about facilitating desired learning outcomes in the classroom. It is reasonable to assume that the narrower the gap between teacher intention and learner interpretation, the greater the chances of achieving learning and teaching objectives. If we wish to act on this assumption, two crucial but difficult questions have to be tackled: How can the teachers and learners identify perceptual mismatches, and how can they minimize the mismatches once they are identified? Although very little research has been conducted in the field of L2 teaching and teacher education to address these two questions specifically, there are certain steps the teacher can take to identify and minimize perceptual mismatches. I present some of them in the form of microstrategies and exploratory projects.

Microstrategies for Minimizing Perceptual Mismatches

The following two microstrategies are designed to train learners themselves to identify and express their thoughts on potential mismatches.

Microstrategy 4.1: Learner Training

4.1.0 It is reasonable to assume that some of the difficulties learners may face in understanding the aims and activities of the classroom are due to potential mismatches between their interpretation and their teacher's intention. Because mismatches are based, at least partly, on the learners' interpretations of what happens in class, they themselves can play an important role in identifying what they are. One way is to make them aware of the ten sources of mismatch introduced in this chapter. That can be done by treating the sources as a lesson in reading comprehension. What follows is one possible approach; teachers should change it to suit their particular learning and teaching environment.

4.1.1 First, talk about possible differences between teacher intention and learner interpretation of classroom aims and activities. By asking leading questions, get the learners to come up with their own explanations and examples, however tentative.

4.1.2 Introduce the ten sources of potential mismatches. Depending on the proficiency level of the learners, you might even wish to use a subset of five major mismatches—say, cognitive, communicative, linguistic, cultural, and attitudinal. Also, if necessary, simplify (see the simplified statements given for Microstrategy 4.2. below).

4.1.3 Using the sample interactional data given above to illustrate each of the mismatches (or any suitable examples you can draw from your own classes), help them understand the concept.

4.1.4 Form small groups, probably five. Allot two mismatches to each group. Have the learners talk about the allotted mismatches in their groups. Encourage them to share their understanding of mismatches and come up with examples drawn from their own classroom experiences.

4.1.5 Have a representative from each group present their examples to the class, followed by discussion. It is all right if some groups are not able to come up with examples within the limited time given to them.

4.1.6 If you judge that one more session on a similar activity will help the learners understand the concept better, select some of the interactional episodes presented in other chapters of this book (see, particularly, Chapter 13) and help your learners to identify possible mismatches in them. You may have to give them the necessary background information about these episodes.

4.1.7 Ask your learners to pay conscious attention to possible mismatches whenever they face any difficulty in understanding classroom aims and events. Suggest to them that they keep a journal or a diary in which they monitor mismatches in their various classes. Tell them this might be one way of finding out the sources of their learning difficulties before they can be addressed effectively.

Microstrategy 4.2: Learner Perception

4.2.0 This microstrategy is designed as a follow-up to the previous one. The objective here is to get learners' perceptions of a selected lesson. Do the following activity at the end of a just-completed lesson. Time is of essence here because the learners must be able to recall what happened during a lesson before they forget it.

Using Figure 4.1 as a suggested format, design a questionnaire that is appropriate to your class. You can design an open-ended questionnaire in which the learners are free to comment on any learning/ teaching item(s) they wish, or a closed questionnaire in which you establish specific items on which they must focus. If you wish to design an open-ended questionnaire, ask the learners to insert in the blanks any item or items on which they wish to give feedback. If you wish to design a closed questionnaire, insert in the blanks the specific learning/ teaching focus. It can be a particular activity within a lesson, a vocabulary item, a grammatical item, a task, an exercise, or a combination of any of these. Feel free to reformulate the statements to make them suitable to the proficiency level of your students.

Learner Perceptions

Name: Class: Date:

Please complete this questionnaire with reference to what we did in class today. Write as much as you can and give specific examples.

1. (Cognitive mismatch): I do not understand or recognize _____.
2. (Communicative mismatch): I understand _____ but I am unable to express my ideas or give an answer because I am not confident of talking in class.
3. (Linguistic mismatch): I understand _____ but I am unable to express my ideas or give an answer because I don't have enough knowledge of the language.
4. (Pedagogic mismatch): I am not clear about the main purpose of _____.
5. (Strategic mismatch): I am not clear about the overall approach I need to take in order to work on _____.
6. (Cultural mismatch): I do not have enough cultural knowledge to _____.
7. (Evaluative mismatch): I try to find out whether what I already know about _____ is correct or not.
8. (Procedural mismatch): I am not clear about what specific steps I need to follow in order to _____.
9. (Instructional mismatch): I do not understand the direction given by the teacher regarding _____.
10. (Attitudinal mismatch): I am not happy with the way the teacher did or discussed _____.

Figure 4.1

4.2.1 At the end of a lesson, distribute copies of a fully formulated questionnaire and ask your students to think about the activities just finished. Have them complete the questionnaire.

4.2.2 Go over the completed questionnaire as soon as possible, certainly before you forget the classroom events. Select a few outstanding comments from learners to mention in class.

4.2.3 In the next class, return the feedback sheets back to the students. Form small groups, and ask the members of each group to exchange their feedback sheets and read what other members have written. Have them discuss the perceptions of the members of the group, highlighting similarities and differences.

4.2.4 Ask the groups to share their group conversation with the whole class, followed by discussion.

4.2.5 Based on your reading of learners' perceptions and the group report, clear any misunderstanding not only about identifying mismatches but also about any classroom aims and events that the learners have highlighted. If necessary, re-do portions of the previous lesson to help your students learn what they are supposed to learn in that lesson.

Exploratory Projects

The two exploratory projects presented below are designed to help you understand perceptual mismatches better. The first one relates to how the learners and teachers look at the aims and activities of a particular course in general. The second relates specifically to the teacher and learner differences in the attitudes they bring to the class.

Project 4.1: Perceptions of Classroom Aims

4.1.0 This project is aimed at helping you explore possible mismatches between learner and teacher perceptions of class aims and activities. By comparing learners' perceptions with yours, you may be able to better orient your instructional goals and strategies. Using the collected information, you may also be able to negotiate the content of the course with your learners.

4.1.1 Design a survey questionnaire on the aims and activities of a particular class you are about to teach. You may adapt the questionnaire shown in Figure 4.2 to suit your specific needs, by revising, deleting, or adding to the items. This is a common questionnaire for teachers and learners.

Prioritizing Aims and Activities

Name: Class: Date:

Please read the following statements carefully and indicate your priority by circling
1 (high priority), 2 (low priority), or 3 (no priority).

I think this course is aimed at helping students to . . .

learn new words	1	2	3
use the right words in the right place	1	2	3
understand and use grammar rules	1	2	3
improve listening skills	1	2	3
speak correctly and confidently	1	2	3
improve pronunciation	1	2	3
read a lot of materials	1	2	3
read for better comprehension	1	2	3
communicate ideas in writing	1	2	3
(add any other aim not listed here)	1	2	3

I expect to achieve the aims through the following class activities:

making a list of new words	1	2	3
finding word meanings in a dictionary	1	2	3
doing grammar exercises	1	2	3
reading a textbook	1	2	3
reading newspapers and stories	1	2	3
listening to radio	1	2	3
watching TV or videos	1	2	3
practicing sounds for good pronunciation	1	2	3
speaking with classmates in pairs	1	2	3
speaking with classmates in small groups	1	2	3
role-playing dialogs	1	2	3
listening to teacher explanations	1	2	3
practicing in class	1	2	3
practicing outside the class	1	2	3
doing communicative tasks	1	2	3
paying attention to teacher corrections	1	2	3
paying attention to learner mistakes	1	2	3
(add any other activity not listed here)	1	2	3

Figure 4.2

4.1.2 Based on your curricular as well as methodological plans, prioritize the aims and activities of your class.

4.1.3 On the first day of class, or as soon as possible, administer the questionnaire and collect the completed sheets.

4.1.4 Compile the information from the completed questionnaire (both yours and the learners') and make a chart as shown in Figure 4.3:

Item	Learner priority (total for each) 1 2 3	Teacher priority	Remarks

Figure 4.3

4.1.5 Return the completed questionnaire to the students. Ask them to discuss their responses in small groups for about ten–fifteen minutes, and then report back to class on what they discussed.

4.1.6 Lead a discussion on their report. Focus on whether some students changed their expectations after talking to their classmates in their groups and, if so, why.

4.1.7 Based on the information compiled from the questionnaire and class discussion, reflect on the mismatches between teacher and learner perceptions. See whether and to what extent you are willing to modify your plans or negotiate with the learners.

4.1.8 In the next class, take your learners into confidence about any changes you contemplate. If you would rather stick to some of your own priorities, even if they are at variance with those of your learners, explain your rationale to them. Whatever the choice, it is important to make the initial expectations quite clear to everybody.

4.1.9 Monitor class progress and do not hesitate to make suitable changes in the aims and activities based on ongoing feedback from the learners.

4.1.10 Finally, at the end of the course, look back to assess whether and to what extent this process of finding out mismatches between learner and teacher perceptions of classroom aims and activities is worth the time and effort. Reflect also on how you can improve this exploratory process.

Project 4.2: Perceptions of Attitudes

4.2.0 This project is similar to the previous one except that it focuses narrowly on the teacher and learner differences in the attitudes they bring to the class. There is a wide range of classroom behavior toward which teachers and learners bring different attitudes. For the purpose of this project, you may narrow the focus to immediately relevant topics such as teacher-learner role relationship, classroom participation, teacher error correction, or learner motivation.

4.2.1 Design a survey questionnaire on possible attitudes teachers and learners may bring to class. You may adapt Figure 4.4 to suit your specific needs by revising, deleting, or adding to the items.

Perceptions About Teacher/Learner Attitudes

Name: Class: Date:

The purpose of this project is to enable you to examine your attitude to classroom learning and teaching. For each statement, indicate whether you agree (1), are not sure (2), or disagree (3). This survey is about your own opinion; feel free to express it. There are no right or wrong answers.

1. I like to join my classmates and work in groups.   1   2   3
2. I don't mind being corrected by other classmates
   who know better than me.   1   2   3
3. I am reluctant to express my views or raise questions
   in class because I fear I will make mistakes.   1   2   3
4. I hesitate to question my teachers because they
   have superior knowledge.   1   2   3
5. I can learn better if teachers explain to me
   why we are doing what we are doing in class.   1   2   3
6. I am afraid I will learn their mistakes if I work
   with other students in class.   1   2   3
7. I hesitate to disagree with teachers because
   they have authority in class.   1   2   3
8. It is the responsibility of the teachers to transmit
   knowledge in class.   1   2   3
9. I am reluctant to express my views or raise questions
   in class because of my respect for teachers.   1   2   3
10. I think teachers have the authority and knowledge
    to evaluate my learning.   1   2   3

(continues)

Figure 4.4

11. I am learning this second language because I like the culture of the people who speak the language.	1	2	3
12. I can learn better if the teachers explain to me how all the activities we do in class are connected to each other.	1	2	3
13. I think it is the responsibility of the teacher to correct students in class.	1	2	3
14. I can do tasks or exercises well if I see their practical value.	1	2	3
15. I feel motivated to do my best in class.	1	2	3
16. I believe I learn well when I actively participate in classroom conversation.	1	2	3
17. I would like to learn in my own way if I am allowed to.	1	2	3
18. I learn better by listening to what other classmates say in class.	1	2	3
19. I am learning this second language because I would like to better my job opportunities.	1	2	3
20. I like teachers who are friendly and not authoritative.	1	2	3
21. I keep quiet in the classroom because that is the way I am expected to behave.	1	2	3
22. I think the best way to learn is by listening to the teacher talk.	1	2	3
23. I feel bored in class because I don't understand why we do what we do in class.	1	2	3
24. I want the teachers to help me discover knowledge by myself.	1	2	3
25. I feel motivated when teachers ask me what classroom activities really interest me.	1	2	3

Figure 4.4 *continued*

4.2.2 Based on your prior experience with students, state your agreement or disagreement in order to identify your own attitudes toward the statements given above (change the pronouns suitably to make it a questionnaire for teachers).

4.2.3 On the first day of class, or as soon as possible, administer the questionnaire and collect the completed sheets.

4.2.4 Compile the information from the completed questionnaire (both yours and the learners') and make a chart as shown in Figure 4.5:

Item	Learner attitudes (total for each) 1 2 3	Teacher attitudes	Remarks

Figure 4.5

4.2.5 Return the completed questionnaire to the students. Ask them to discuss their responses in small groups for about ten–fifteen minutes, and then report back to class on what they discussed.

4.2.6 Lead a discussion on their report. Focus on whether students changed their attitudes after talking to their classmates in their groups and if so, why.

4.2.7 Based on the information compiled from the questionnaire and class discussion, reflect on the differences between teacher and learner attitudes. See whether and to what extent these attitudes are based on stereotypes.

4.2.8 Reflect on the extent to which you can modify the aims and activities of your class in order to be reasonably sensitive to the attitudes learners bring with them.

4.2.9 Monitor changes in the learners' attitudes, individually or collectively, during the course of a semester or an academic year.

4.2.10 Finally, at the end of the course, look back to assess whether and to what extent this process of finding out differences between learner and teacher attitudes is worth the time and effort.

In Closing

This chapter reveals the importance of minimizing perceptual mismatches in the language classroom. It also shows how challenging it is to identify and analyze them. Only a concerted and cooperative effort on the part of the teacher and the learner will bring out the gap between teacher intentions and learner interpretations. An understanding of the similarities and differences in the way the participants perceive classroom aims and events can only lead to an effective pedagogic intervention.

Perceptual mismatches are hidden; they are not easily revealed. And yet, an awareness of them is required to achieve the objectives of learning and teaching. The aim of creating an awareness of the perceptual mismatches in the language classroom can be achieved only through negotiated interaction among the participants in the classroom event. The next chapter deals with the importance of negotiated interaction in class.

CHAPTER 5

Facilitating Negotiated Interaction

> (T)he importance of interaction is not simply that it creates learning opportunities, it is that it constitutes learning itself.
>
> —DICK ALLWRIGHT, 1984, p. 9.

One of the aspects of learning to talk in an L2 is talking to learn. Studies on L2 learning and teaching point to the significance of talk in the learners' comprehension of linguistic input exposed to them. As Swain and Lapkin (1998, p. 320) recently concluded on the basis of an experimental study, dialogue "provides both the occasion for language learning and the evidence for it." A remarkably similar statement was made a hundred years ago by one of the pioneers of language teaching methods, Henry Sweet (1899–1964), when he observed that "conversation in a foreign language may be regarded from two very different points of view: (1) as an end in itself, and (2) *as a means of learning the language* and testing the pupil's knowledge of it" (p. 210, emphasis added).

As a means of language learning, conversation may not be a causal factor in language acquisition, but it is considered to be a priming device that sets the stage for acquisition to take place (Gass, 1997). The precise role of conversation in L2 development has not been sufficiently investigated. Nevertheless, many researchers believe that an L2 learning and teaching environment must include opportunities for learners to engage in meaningful interaction with competent speakers of the target language. A recurring theme in the L2 professional literature is that meaningful interaction increases the possibility of a greater amount of input becoming available, thus considerably enhancing the opportunities for the activation of fundamental processes that are essential to L2 development.

Types of Interactional Activity

In the current literature on L2 interactional studies, one comes across terms such as talk, dialogue, conversation, conversational interaction, negotiation and negotiated interaction. These terms are used sometimes interchangeably and sometimes differentially. It seems to me that one way of gaining a clear and coherent understanding of the role of interaction in language learning is by looking at it in terms of the three macrofunctions of language proposed by Michael Halliday (e.g., 1985): textual, interpersonal, and ideational. I attempt below an operational definition of these terms in the specific context of input, interaction, and L2 development.

Interaction as a textual activity refers mainly to the use of linguistic and metalinguistic features of language necessary for understanding language input. The linguistic dimension deals with phonological, syntactic, and semantic signals that enable learners and their interlocutors to understand input and transmit messages as intended. The metalinguistic dimension deals with the language awareness necessary to talk about language structures and mechanics.

Interaction as an interpersonal activity refers to the use of language to promote communication between participants. It thus involves sociolinguistic features of language required to establish roles, relationships, and responsibilities. It focuses on the nuances of interpersonal understanding, especially those necessary to open and maintain conversational channels and to identify and repair communication breakdowns.

Interaction as an ideational activity refers to an expression of the participants' own experience of the processes, persons, objects, and events of the real or imaginary world in, around, and outside the situated learning and teaching context. Specifically, it focuses on ideas and emotions participants bring with them based on their lived experiences, past and present. It also involves a cognitive awareness of, and a sociocultural sensitivity to, the external world and its impact on the formation of individual identities.

By introducing such a tripartite division of an interactional activity, I am not suggesting that these three types are equal or separate. Clearly, the three components overlap; I separate them only for the ease of analysis and understanding. As we will see below, L2 interactional studies conducted so far have been concerned more with the textual and interpersonal dimensions than with the ideational dimension. Let us consider each of these in detail.

Interaction as a Textual Activity

Most early interactional studies treat interaction as a textual activity in which learners and their interlocutors modify their input phonologically, lexically, and syntactically in order to maximize chances of mutual understanding. Such a preoccupation with textual aspects of input and interaction can best be understood in a historical perspective. A major impetus for L2 interactional studies came from research on caretaker-talk conducted in the context of child first language acquisition.

Empirical studies carried out during the 1970s (e.g., Snow and Ferguson, 1977) showed that the caretaker's speech addressed to the child contained utterances with a number of formal (i.e., linguistic) adjustments in comparison to speech used in adult-adult conversations. The formal adjustments include: short utterances; limited range of syntactic-semantic relations; few subordinate and coordinate constructions; modified pitch, intonation and rhythm; and frequent repetitions.

Extending the concept of caretaker-talk to L2 speakers, researchers studied modified speech used by native speakers of a language to outsiders with limited language proficiency. This modified speech has been referred to as foreigner-talk. Foreigner-talk has been found to be very similar to caretaker-talk (Ferguson, 1975). Specifically, it is characterized by a slow rate of delivery, clear articulation, pauses, emphatic stress, exaggerated pronunciation, paraphrasing, and substitutions of lexical items by synonyms, and by omission, addition, and replacement of syntactic features.

Moving from foreigner-talk to teacher-talk was an easy and logical step. Teacher-talk, that is, the simplified language teachers use in order to talk to L2 learners, was also found to contain characteristics of foreigner-talk. Teacher-talk, as can be expected, puts more emphasis on simplified input rather than on any extended verbal interaction between teachers and learners. Such a limited talk was considered sufficient for classroom L2 development, at least at the initial stages. A well-known hypothesis that emphasized the importance of simplified teacher-talk, and thus the textual dimension of interaction, is Krashen's input hypothesis.

INPUT HYPOTHESIS

The input hypothesis proposed by Krashen forms part of his Monitor Model of second language acquisition. The hypothesis states that "humans acquire language in only one way—by understanding messages, or by receiving comprehensible input" (Krashen, 1985, p. 2). By comprehensible input, Krashen refers to linguistic input containing structures that are a little bit beyond a learner's current level of competence. He further states that learners move from i, the current level, to $i + 1$, the next level, by understanding input containing $i + 1$. According to him, all that is needed for L2 acquisition is comprehensible input made available in an environment that does not create high anxiety for the learners.

Krashen believes that listening and reading are of primary importance and the ability to speak or write will come automatically. Therefore, he does not attach much importance to the role of interaction in L2 acquisition, arguing that it is useful only to the extent that it can be a good source of comprehensible input. He emphasizes the significance of teacher-talk that is aimed at providing comprehensible input. He asserts that when we "just talk" to our students, and if they understand our talk, then "we are not only giving a language lesson, we may be giving the best possible language lesson since we will be supplying input for acquisition" (Krashen and Terrell, 1983, p. 35).

Reflective task 5.1

Do you agree with Krashen that teachers can give "the best possible language lesson" by just talking? Imagine this scenario: a school in Wonderland gives a free TV set to each of the beginning learners of an L2 on the first day of school. Every day, the learners watch programs that use simplified language with full of visual aids to make the input comprehensible (such as children's programs). They do it with great enthusiasm and by their own will. If that's all the assistance they get in their L2, will they ever develop adequate language competence? Give reasons.

According to Krashen, providing the best possible language lesson means providing manageable, comprehensible input. One way of increasing comprehensibility of the input is to use repetitions and paraphrases, as in: "There are two young men. Two. One, two (counting). They are young. There are two young men. At least I think they are young. Do you think that they are young? Are the two men young? Or old? Do you think that they are young or old?" (Data source: Krashen & Terrell, 1983, p. 77).

Or, to use simple conversations as in the following teacher-talk based on pictures (expected responses from students follow in parentheses): "Is there a woman in this picture? (Yes.) Is there a man in the picture? (No.) Is the woman old or young? (Young.) Yes, she's young, but very ugly. (Class responds, no, pretty.) That's right, she's not ugly, she's pretty. What is she wearing? (Dress.) Yes, she's wearing a dress. What color is the dress? (Blue.) Right, she's wearing a blue dress. And what do you see behind her? (Tree.) Yes, there are trees. Are they tall? (Yes.) And beside her is a—? (Dog.) Yes, a large dog standing to her right." (Data source: Krashen & Terrell, 1983, p. 79).

Or, to use a situational role-play for the creation of what Krashen calls "original dialogs" among students: "You are a young girl who is sixteen years old. You went out with a friend at eight o'clock. You are aware of the fact that your parents require you to be at home at 11:00 at the latest. But you return at 12:30 and your father is very angry. Your father: 'Well, I'm waiting for an explanation. Why did you return so late?' You: '————'" (Data source: Krashen and Terrell, 1983, p. 101).

LIMITATIONS OF INTERACTION AS A TEXTUAL ACTIVITY

The examples given above illustrate one essential feature of interaction as a textual activity, namely, the simplified nature of language use by the teacher. Krashen has convincingly argued that comprehensible input is necessary to help the learners understand this information. However, the importance given to the input aspect of interaction is such that there is very little exchange of information one would normally associate with an interactional activity. In fact, several interactional studies (see Gass, 1997, for a comprehensive review) have questioned Krashen's claim that linguistic input can be made comprehensible without any active participation on the part of the learner. Studies show that learner comprehension can best be assisted by input as well as interactional modifications, a belief captured in the interaction hypothesis.

Interaction as an Interpersonal Activity

In light of the limitations of interaction as a textual activity, conversation and its role in language learning gained some importance. We shall elaborate by focusing on two hypotheses: interaction hypothesis and output hypothesis.

INTERACTION HYPOTHESIS

Recognizing that L2 interactional studies had hitherto focused narrowly on linguistic input, be it foreigner-talk or teacher-talk, Evelyn Hatch (1978, p. 403) pointed out that "it is not enough to look at input and the frequency of the use of a particular structure; the important thing is to look at the corpus as a whole and examine the interactions that take place within conversations to see how that interaction, itself, determines frequency of forms and how it shows language functions evolving." She further argued that it is possible to learn an L2 *through* the process of interaction. The lead given by Hatch has prompted several studies resulting in a substantial body of literature on input and interaction.

In a series of studies on the relationship between input, interaction, and L2 development spanning over a period of fifteen years, Michael Long proposed (Long, 1981) and updated (Long, 1996) what has come to be known as the interaction hypothesis. To put it simply, the hypothesis claims that oral interaction in which communication problems are negotiated between participants promotes L2 comprehension and production, ultimately facilitating language development. The term *interaction* is used restrictively to refer to a particular type of interaction in which negotiation of meaning is involved. The need for negotiation of meaning arises when participants in an interactional activity try either to prevent a potential communication breakdown or to repair an actual communication breakdown that has already occurred.

In the context of negotiation of meaning, Long makes a distinction between modified input and modified interaction. The former involves modifications of language input that has short phrases and sentences, fewer embeddings, and greater repetition of nouns and verbs, while the latter involves modifications of the conversational structure that has a considerable number of comprehension checks, confirmation checks, and clarification requests. A comprehension check is the speaker's way of finding out whether the hearer has understood what was said ("Do you understand me?" or

"Do you follow me?"). A confirmation check is the speaker's way of verifying whether his or her understanding of the hearer's meaning is correct ("Is this what you mean?" or "Are you saying you did go to Disneyland?"). A clarification request is a request for further information or help in understanding something that has been said ("Can you say that again?" or "Huh?").

Although interactional modifications do occur in day-to-day conversations among native speakers of a language, studies show (see Gass, 1997) that they occur to a greater degree in conversations involving speakers with unequal language competence, such as between native speakers and non–native speakers, or non–native speakers-non–native speakers (NNS-NNS) of different proficiency levels. The following conversation between a native speaker (NS) and a non–native speaker (NNS) shows how the participants negotiate meaning using conversational adjustments. For the immediate purpose of focusing on interactional modifications, I have simplified the transcription convention (not the content of the conversation), removing diacritic features pertaining to overlap and the time between pauses, etc.

Episode 5.1

1. NS: Well what do you think about, um, mothers, um, have their baby and they—
2. NNS: Uh-huh.
3. NS: —leave them in garbage cans.
4. NNS: Huh? What do you s—.
5. NS: They have . . . they have their baby?
6. NNS: My mom?
7. NS: No, no (laughs). Not your (laughs) m— Mothers.
8. NNS: Uh-huh—mothers—uh-huh.
9. NS: They have their baby?
10. NNS: Uh-huh.
11. NS: And then—they leave it in garbage cans.
12. NNS: Garbage?
13. NS: Garbage cans. Like big garbage cans. Outside of business—
14. NNS: Uh-huh.

15.	NS:	—and apartments.
16.	NNS:	Ahh . . .
17.	NS:	You know what I mean?
18.	NNS:	No I don't know. I d— I understand garbage.
19.	NS:	Yeah. You know dumpsters? Where—you know our garbage.
20.	NNS:	Garbage. Garbage?
21.	NS:	Uh-huh.
22.	NNS:	Ah, yeah.
23.	NS:	Yeah. And they'll have a baby and they'll leave it there.
24.	NNS:	Uh-yuh? (tone displays shock)
25.	NS:	Yeah. For someone to— to take it or for it to die.
26.	NNS:	Die? Ahh . . . Like a . . . (incomprehensible)
27.	NS:	Mm-hm.
28.	NNS:	I know. (clears throat) What do you . . .
29.	NS:	It's mean.
30.	NNS:	What's mean?
31.	NS:	No— It's mean. It's mean.
32.	NNS:	Mean.
33.	NS:	Yeah (laughs) It's bad.
34.	NNS:	It's bad. Uh- I know . . . (mumbles) . . .
35.	NS:	Mm-hm.
36.	NNS:	Because baby is not thing . . . is y'know.
37.	NS:	Baby's what?
38.	NNS:	Not thing. Baby is animal— (laughs) don't know . . . Humor.
39.	NS:	Human, yeah.
40.	NNS:	So I can't do that. I can't do that. I can't sell, I can't— I can't throw garbage.
41.	NS:	Throw it away.
42.	NNS:	Throw away.
43.	NS:	Yeah.
44.	NNS:	But—I can't kill because it's human.

(Data adapted from: Riggenbach, 1999, p. 214–5)

Reflective task 5.2

Before you proceed further, read the above interactional data again. Identify examples of comprehension checks, confirmation checks, and clarification requests. Do you think modified interactions of this kind can facilitate L2 acquisition better than the three examples of modified input given earlier (see the examples from Krashen and Terrell given above)? In what way?

Interactional modifications made possible through negotiation of meaning, like the one exemplified above, are considered to facilitate L2 development in two important ways. First, unlike any input modification that may make some of the structural features and lexical items salient by providing a lot of examples, it is the interactional modification that makes syntactic-semantic relationships transparent to the learner. In other words, input modifications may provide potentially acceptable input, but they do not help learners learn the relationship between form and meaning in order to develop the necessary capacity to use language for interactive purposes. It is the learner's interactional efforts that make form-meaning relationships in the L2 data accessible and able to be internalized. Studies by Long as well as by Pica and her colleagues (e.g., Pica, Young, and Doughty, 1987) demonstrate that learners who were exposed to linguistically unmodified input with opportunities to negotiate meaning understood it better than learners who were exposed to a linguistically simplified version of the input but offered no opportunity for such negotiation.

Second, the communicative and cognitive effort required to negotiate meaning can bring any problematic linguistic features to the learner's immediate attention—features that might otherwise go unnoticed by the learner. In fact, the negative feedback learners receive through interactional modifications might induce them to selectively pay attention to some of the problematic features. By helping learners notice the linguistic features that are problematic for them, interactional modifications can help them focus and try to produce them correctly. In that sense, negotiated interaction "connects input, internal learner capacities, particularly selective attention, and output in productive ways" (Long, 1996, p. 452).

As the above discussion shows, interactional studies have highlighted the importance of modified input and modified interaction in L2 development. They have also started focusing on the language output that learners produce as a result of input and interactional modifications.

COMPREHENSIBLE OUTPUT HYPOTHESIS

Research on learner output is fairly new because, traditionally, output has been treated as a final outcome of what has already been learned, and not as a source of learning itself. The precise role learner output plays in L2 development is as yet undetermined. The impetus for output studies came from Merrill Swain (1985), who suggested that, while comprehensible input and negotiated interaction are essential, what she called comprehensible output is equally important. She argued that negotiated interaction "needs to incorporate the notion of being pushed towards the delivery of a message that is not only conveyed, but that is conveyed precisely, coherently, and appropriately" (Swain, 1985, pp. 248–9). She further asserted that production "may force the learner to move from semantic processing to syntactic processing" (p. 249). In other words, an attempt to produce language will move learners from processing language at the level of word meaning (which can sometimes be done by guessing from the context or by just focusing on key words) to processing language at the level of grammatical structures (which requires a much higher level of cognitive activity).

In a later work, Swain (1995) identified three possible functions of output: the noticing function, the hypothesis-testing function, and the metalinguistic function. The noticing function relates to the possibility that when learners try to communicate in their still-developing target language, they may encounter a linguistic problem and become aware of what they do not know or know only partially. Such an encounter may raise their consciousness and lead to an appropriate, conscious action on their part.

The hypothesis-testing function of output relates to the possibility that when learners use the target language, they may be experimenting with what works and what does not. In fact, learner output, however deficient, can itself be an indication of the learners' attempt to test how something should be said and written. Moreover, when they participate in negotiated interaction and receive negative feedback, they are likely to test different hypotheses about a particular linguistic system.

Finally, the metalinguistic function of output relates to the possibility that learners may be consciously thinking about language and its system, about its phonological, grammatical, and semantic rules in order to guide them to produce utterances that are linguistically correct and communicatively appropriate. In fact, learners can be encouraged to think consciously about linguistic forms and their relationship to meaning when they are asked to do communicative tasks that focus on form as well as meaning (see Chapter 8 on activating intuitive heuristics). In espousing these three functions of output, Swain makes it clear that we do not yet know whether or how any of these functions really operate when learners attempt to produce the target language.

Further research on output-related studies conducted by Pica and her colleagues (e.g., Pica, Holliday, Lewis and Morgenthaler, 1989) and Gass and her colleagues (see Gass, 1997) confirms that output has the potential to provide learners with a forum for important language learning functions such as hypothesis testing, corrective feedback, and moving from meaning-based processing to a grammar-based processing. Krashen (1998, p. 180), however, questions the usefulness of comprehensible output, saying that it is "too scarce to make a real contribution to linguistic competence." While that is true, it is worthwhile to remember that comprehensible output, where available, can provide much-needed impetus for learners to notice specific features that are problematic to them and thus take corrective measures to progress toward language development.

Reflective task 5.3

Krashen has consistently argued the case of comprehensible input and has almost dismissed the role of learner interaction as well as learner output. In what way do you think the input hypothesis, the interaction hypothesis, and the output hypothesis complement or contradict each other?

LIMITATIONS OF INTERACTION AS AN INTERPERSONAL ACTIVITY

Clearly, interaction as an interpersonal activity is not as limited as interaction as a textual activity. Unlike the latter, which is concerned mostly with the linguistic aspect of modified input, the former is concerned with the relationship between modified input and modified interaction. Thus, the former is oriented to a study of the use of language structures and conversational adjustments necessary to create a coherent piece of written or spoken text suitable to a particular communicative event.

There are at least three strands of knowledge we have gained from the studies on the relationship between input, interaction, and output:

- comprehensible input is necessary but not sufficient to promote L2 development;
- negotiated interaction consisting of comprehension checks, confirmation checks, and clarification requests plays a facilitative, not a causative, role in the development of linguistic competence among L2 learners; and
- comprehensible output has the potential to provide learners with opportunities to notice the gap in their developing interlanguage, to test their hypotheses, to use corrective feedback, and to move from meaning-based processing to a grammar-based processing.

While this knowledge is indeed noteworthy, there are certain limitations to treating interaction as a textual/interpersonal activity. That input modifications and interactional modifications are crucial for L2 development has been widely recognized. However, there has not been adequate recognition that providing input and interactional modifications means much more than providing opportunities for comprehensible input or for conversational adjustments.

Treating an interactional engagement as no more than a conversational adjustment cannot but yield a distorted picture of the role of interaction in L2 development. No doubt, conversational adjustments do have a role to play in promoting communication or in resolving miscommunication. But, clearly, negotiated interaction is much broader than a mere linguistic construct. It entails a spectrum of individual, social, cultural, and political factors that create the very context and character of language communication. Therefore, in order to facilitate an effective interplay of various factors involved in language communication and language development, we may have to go beyond the narrow confines of interaction as a textual/interpersonal activity, and consider the role of interaction as an ideational activity as well.

Interaction as an Ideational Activity

Recall the operational definition given earlier for interaction as an ideational activity. Essentially, it involves a cognitive awareness of, and a sociocultural sensitivity to, the external world and its impact on the formation of individual identities. It puts a premium on the ideas and emotions participants bring with them owing to their past and present experiences both in and outside the learning and teaching environment. In short, interaction as an ideational activity focuses on the complex relationship between the individual and the social, particularly the impact of the social on the individual (see also Chapter 11).

THE INDIVIDUAL AND THE SOCIAL

As Michael Breen rightly pointed out during the early days of the interactional studies, interaction is more than a sociolinguistic process; it is "a socio-cognitive process which continually relates social action and experience to the content and capabilities of the mind, and vice versa" (1985, p. 155). What this means is that an individual's interactional behavior and its impact on the learning process can hardly be interpreted in terms of linguistic and sociolinguistic features of input and interaction alone. What also need to be seriously taken into account are the sociopsychological and sociocultural forces that shape that behavior. In drawing our attention to the sociocognitive aspect of interaction, Breen was, in part, echoing the Vygotskyan approach to language acquisition.

The Russian psychologist Lev Vygotsky emphasized the role played by social interaction in the development of language and thought. According to him (Vygotsky, 1963), meaning is constructed through social interaction. For language learners, social interaction can occur when they interact with competent speakers of the target language, and when they interact with themselves (Vygotsky called it "private speech"). It is this social interaction that shapes and solidifies learning.

Social interaction entails active participation on the part of the learners. Their participation is guided by competent speakers whose utterances should be within, what Vygotsky called, the learners' *zone of proximal development* (ZPD). He defines this zone as the distance between the actual level of language development and the level of potential development. Notice the two crucial factors emphasized here: active participation by learners in meaningful interaction, and appropriate mediational assistance from competent speakers.

It is beneficial to compare Vygotsky's ZPD and Krashen's $i + 1$. Although they may bear superficial resemblance to each other, there are significant differences. To begin with, Krashen's $i + 1$ is an input construct; Vygotsky's ZPD is an interactional construct. For Krashen, learners' movement from current level to the next level of language development marks a linear progression along a predictable order of sequence. For Vygotsky, such a movement is cyclical, organic, and unpredictable. For Krashen, the movement depends largely on the comprehensible input provided by the speaker. For Vygotsky, the movement depends largely on the richness of interactional experiences of the hearer. As Ellis (1999, p. 20) succinctly summarizes: in Vygotsky's sociocultural theory, "interaction is not just a device that facilitates learners' movement along the interlanguage continuum, but a social event which helps learners participate in their own development, including shaping the path it follows."

Reflective task 5.4

If the promotion of negotiated interaction demands serious attention to the individual and social factors, what do you think teachers have to do to re-orient their classroom input and interaction? One way of addressing this question is to think about a lesson you have been recently associated with (either as a teacher or as a student-teacher) and determine what qualitative changes would have to be made to make input and interaction in that class sensitive to the individual and social factors.

Impact on Language Teaching

Helping learners participate in their own language development and shape their own path should indeed be the prime responsibility of the classroom teacher. What can help the teacher in carrying out such a responsibility is promotion of negotiated interaction. Based on the above discussion, I would like to suggest that negotiated interaction is a matter of coming to grips with all three—textual, interpersonal and ideational—aspects of classroom discourse (see also, Kumaravadivelu, 1999b). As we have seen, interaction as a textual activity emphasizes formal concepts, interaction as an interpersonal activity emphasizes conversational signals, and interaction as an ideational activity emphasizes propositional content. Together, these three dimensions provide opportunities for teachers to create a conducive atmosphere in which learners can stretch their linguistic repertoire, sharpen their conversational capacities, and share their individual experiences.

If our objective, as it should be, is to engage our learners in a process of participation that puts a premium on their personal knowledge gained from their lived experience, then we need to re-define the concept of negotiated interaction. Moving beyond the narrow confines of conversational adjustments such as comprehension checks, confirmation checks, and clarification requests, the concept of negotiated interaction has to be extended to include the propositional content as well as the procedural conduct of participatory discourse. In other words, it has to include the creation of opportunities for the learners to share their own individual perspectives on issues that matter to them, and to share in a way that makes sense to them.

In more practical terms, this means that teachers should seek to promote negotiated interaction by yielding to the learners a reasonable degree of control over what Allwright (1981) has called the management of learning. In the specific context of promoting negotiated interaction, management of learning consists chiefly of talk management and topic management. The former may be said to refer to the management of *how* participants talk, and the latter to the management of *what* they talk about.

Talk Management

Talk management is concerned with how participants conduct their classroom conversation in order to accomplish their immediate educational goals. It represents what van Lier (1988) has called the "activity" of classroom discourse. The way in which talk is controlled and managed will be determined, to a large extent, by the structure of information exchange, or, simply, by the type of questions asked and the type of responses given. The structure of information exchange in most language classes usually signals what is called the IRF sequence, that is, the teacher initiates (I), the learner responds (R), the teacher supplies feedback (F), and the sequence continues. For example, consider the following exchange taken from a beginning ESL class:

Episode 5.2

1. Teacher: How many elephants are there in the picture? . . . How many elephants? . . . Keiko?
2. Keiko: Two.
3. Teacher: Two . . . good. What are the elephants doing? . . . Carlos, what are the elephants doing?
4. Carlos: Fight . . . fighting.
5. Teacher: They are fighting. Uh-huh . . . According to the writer, what dies when two elephants fight? What dies . . . ? Maria?
6. Maria: mm . . . grass.
7. Teacher: The grass, that's right. When two elephants fight, it's the grass that dies. (laughs) OK . . .

(Data source: Author)

As is clear, the teacher initiates the talk by asking a question (turn 1), a student responds (turn 2), and the teacher acknowledges her response by saying, "That's right" (turn 3). And, in the same turn (3), the teacher asks the next question, a student responds (turn 4), and the response is evaluated by the teacher (turn 5), and so on. This kind of IRF structure rarely provides any opportunity for the learners to ask questions or to express their views. In most traditional classes where the teacher controls talk management, the IRF structure predominates.

If teachers can hardly promote negotiated interaction by excessively adhering to the familiar IRF structure, the question then arises: what sort of talk management is necessary to promote negotiated interaction in class? In other words, how does one tell a classroom where negotiated interaction takes place from one where it does not? Consider the following episode taken from another ESL class of beginning level proficiency:

Episode 5.3

1	T:	OK. . . . All right. You know what divorce means?
2	S1:	Yes.
3	T:	What does divorce mean?
4	S1:	If finish . . . marriage . . . x
5	T:	Finish?
6	S1:	Yes.
7	S2:	No.
8	S1:	Yes.
9	T:	What do you think it means?
10	S3:	Separate.
11	T:	Separate?
12	S2:	Yes.
13	T:	OK. Why . . . why do you think people get a divorce?
14	S2:	May be . . . may be different . . . eh.
15	S1:	New . . . new.
16	T:	Let him try.
17	S2:	No . . . no . . . may be different between . . . eh . . . between . . . he like something . . . she didn't like something . . . may be . . .
18	T:	They have problems . . .
19	S2:	I go swimming . . . I eat . . . I don't eat pork . . .
20	S4:	Different idea . . . eh . . . between . . .
21	S2:	Yah.
22	T:	S5, why do you think people get divorce?
23	S5:	Eh . . . they . . . eh . . . broken . . . their love . . .
24	T:	They don't love each other . . .
25	S5:	Yah.
26	T:	Do people get divorced in Japan?
27	S5:	Yah.
28	T:	S6, Do people get divorced in China?
29	S2:	(has been consulting an Arab-English dictionary) no compatibility . . .
30	T:	No compatibility. Good. No dictionary . . . put that away . . .

31 S2: xxx.

32 T: S6, do people get divorced in China? No . . . ? (S6 turns to another student and asks something) . . . you know what divorce means?

33 S6: No.

34 T: It means . . . no more marriage . . . people are married . . . if they are married . . . then they are divorced (gestures separation) . . . they are not married any more. So . . . that doesn't happen in China?

35 S6: (nods her head)

36 T: Yes, sometimes . . . OK.

(Data source: Kumaravadivelu, 1992, p. 44)

Reflective task 5.5

Reread the interactional data given in episodes 5.2 and 5.3. What similarities and differences do you see in the way the two teachers manage classroom talk? Focus on, among other points, display questions and referential questions. Which style of talk management do you generally prefer and why? Are there specific learning and teaching situations where both (or neither) of them will be appropriate?

The contrast between episodes 5.2 and 5.3 is striking. What we have in episode 5.3 are elements of negotiated interaction in the sense that the teacher and the learners were jointly engaged in generating meaningful classroom talk. The teacher's questions were aimed at eliciting the learner's own opinions and interpretations on divorce, rather than at getting linguistic samples that could be mechanically lifted from the textbook or recalled from memory. The teacher even tried to involve a shy Chinese student whose behavior indicated that she did not fully understand what divorce means. Notice that it is only at this juncture, in turn 34, that the teacher, for the first time, explained the meaning of divorce in his words.

The teacher's management of classroom talk facilitated negotiated interaction by providing linguistic as well as paralinguistic cues that helped the low proficiency learners try to struggle with their still-developing language capacity, and in the process enhance their learning potential. In a class where negotiated interaction hardly takes place, teachers would have answered their own questions or stopped with the first correct response from a student, thereby depriving other learners of extended linguistic input and, more importantly, robbing them of a chance to stretch their limited linguistic repertoire.

There was also some information exchange taking place in episode 5.3. As we discussed in Chapter 3, one way of ensuring exchange of information is by asking referential questions that seek information and permit open-ended responses rather than asking display questions that allow teachers and learners to demonstrate their knowledge of the language only. The episode clearly shows that by asking referential questions, the teacher has succeeded in promoting negotiated interaction even in a class where the learners have very limited linguistic and communicative ability.

Employing referential questions can also become, like the use of the traditional IRF exchange structure, routinized and ritualized if no attention is paid to the actual meaning of what the learners are saying. As Scott Thornbury (1996, p. 282) points out, ritualized responses, even within a referential question-answer framework, "anchor the classroom discourse firmly in the traditional IRF camp, and suggest that 'it doesn't matter what you say so long as you pronounce it properly.'" Teachers are most likely to promote genuine negotiated interaction in class if they engage the learners on the merit of their message. In other words, they have to closely link their efficient talk management with effective topic management.

Topic Management

During the early stages of interactional studies, Hatch (1978) reported that giving the learners the freedom to nominate topics provided an effective basis for interactional opportunities. A decade later, van Lier (1988, p. 153) stressed the importance of what he has called "topicalization," a process by which "learners take up something the teacher or another learner says and (attempt to) make it into next topic." Experimental studies show several advantages to letting the learners have control over the topic: it can result (a) in the tailoring of the linguistic complexity of the input to the learner's own level, (b) in the creation of better opportunities for negotiating meaning when a communication problem arises, and (c) in the stimulation of more extensive and more complex production on the part of the learner (Ellis, 1992, p. 177).

Although insufficient work has been done on the effect of learner topic control, an oft-quoted study by Assia Slimani (1989) found that learners benefited more from self- and peer-nominated topics than from teacher-nominated topics. Investigating the notion of "uptake," which is defined as what learners claim to have learned from a particular lesson, she discovered that even in classes where the discourse initiation was predominantly in the hands of the teacher, "the topicalizations which provoked more attention and attracted more claims from more people were initiated by the learners themselves" (p. 228). Her study demonstrates that self- and peer-nominated topics are likely to create and sustain motivation among the learners, and give them a sense of freedom and achievement in taking partial control of the classroom discourse.

A significant aspect of topic control is that it allows the learners to share their individual perspectives on current topics with the teacher as well as other learners whose lives, and hence perspectives, may differ from theirs. Consider, for example, the following episode taken from a high intermediate ESL class conducted in California. The class focuses on "speaking" skills. The teacher had asked the class to read, as homework, a newspaper article on euthanasia, or mercy killing, of relatives with incurable, terminal diseases. The text is actually in the form of a debate between two speakers, Speaker A arguing for and Speaker B arguing against mercy killing.

In class, the teacher formed two groups, asking one group to focus on the arguments of Speaker A and another group on those of Speaker B. The learners were asked to work together and make a list of the arguments of their respective speaker. The groups worked together for about ten minutes and then reported to the class on their group discussion. The classroom interactional extract given below begins there. As you read, focus on the features of topic management.

Episode 5.4

1. T: OK, let's look at it together. What does Speaker A believe and what does Speaker B believe? . . . mmm . . . Somebody from Group A, can you tell me what this speaker basically believes about euthanasia?

2. S1:   Human rights.

3. T: What do you mean, "human rights?"

4. S1:   Nobody kills someone . . . mmm . . . mercy killing will be like . . . like murder. If they . . .

5. T: So, you have got words like murder (writes "murder" on the board). OK, what are some other points? mmm . . . what are some other arguments given?

6. S2:   If mercy killing . . . you are permitting . . . (reads from the text) "some people would be tempted to kill for selfish reasons" . . . It is dangerous.

7. T: OK, it's a dangerous idea (writes "dangerous idea" on the board).

8. S3:   Other point. If they . . . (reads from the text) "if the patient waits, maybe the doctor will find a way to help."

9. T: Yeah, advancement in medical science . . .

10. S4: Or a miracle can . . .

11. T: That's a really good word. It's not in the text. What does "miracle" mean, S4?

12. S4: I don't know.

13. SS: (laugh)

14. T: Miracle. That's a key word. What's a miracle?

15. S1: Miracle means . . . eh . . . very . . . eh . . . very fantastic.

16. S2: Inhuman . . .

17. T: You mean non-human . . . It has to do with superhuman or supernatural happenings. Right? Something God does is a miracle . . . For instance, Christ has performed many miracles . . .

18. S4: Because I think xx maybe something will change. Maybe some kind of energy will help . . . Miracle . . .

19. T: Ah . . . some kind of energy . . .

20. S5: Miracle xxx.

21. T: A higher power . . . like God . . .
22. S4:   No, maybe a machine or something.
23. T: That's right God can actually cause . . .
24. S4:   No, it's not God. . . . medical care . . . or nature . . .
25. S6:   Yeah, nature.
26. S7:   Nature cure . . . like . . .
27. T: You don't think it's God?
28. S4:   No, God is not a doctor (SS laugh).
29. T: True, but faith in God can cure . . .
30. S4:   I don't have faith in God . . . I'm not . . .
31. T: Well, I do. OK, we need to cut it off. It's a difficult issue. Let's turn to the other group. Group B, what did you find?

(Data source: Author)

Reflective task 5.6

Read episode 5.4 again and do a quick topic analysis. That is, what are the topics and subtopics (however loosely you define them) introduced by the learners? How would you characterize the teacher's style of topic management? Is she consistent in her style or does she change course? If you think she does change course, what might be the reason?

In terms of topic management, the teacher initially seems to be content with students recalling ideas from the text: murder, a dangerous idea, advancement in medical science, etc. But the tone and the tenor of the talk changes when S4 (in turn 10) brings up the possibility of a miracle, something that is not mentioned in the text. The teacher, to her credit, acknowledges the originality of the topic initiated by the learner and decides to pursue it. Her decision leads to an extended discussion for nearly twenty more turns involving six students.

Unfortunately, however, when an interesting debate seems to be developing between an apparently religious-minded teacher and a less-pious student (S4), the teacher decides to "cut it off." Neither did she pursue the topic of nature or nature cure initiated by learners (turns 24–26). It is unfortunate because, this being a "Speaking" class, had her topic management been a little more flexible, it would have allowed the students to continue to speak on the topics that interested them, and thus offered more opportunities for them to improve their conversational skills. Flexible topic control is so vital for promoting negotiated interaction that Ellis (1999, p. 251) sees it "as a far more important construct than meaning negotiation where language teaching is concerned."

Before closing this section, a cautionary note is in order. The emphasis on talk and topic management, however important it is, should not blind us to believe that only those students who initiate talk and topic in the classroom succeed in learning the target language. We know from the Slimani study that learners claim to have learned from the talk and topic initiated by their peers, even if they themselves have not participated. More interestingly, Slimani found that even those students who did not rank highly their classmates' contribution as a productive source of linguistic input profited from it unknowingly.

The Slimani finding, which is supported by experiential knowledge as well, is crucial because, while there are always some learners in every class who love to talk, there are also some who keep quiet because they may find speaking in their still-developing L2 very stressful. High anxiety resulting from a stressful situation may, as Krashen has cautioned us, slow the ability to process input. It is possible that "the learners who maintain silence may experience less anxiety and so be better able to 'let in' the input their fellow students have secured for them" (Ellis, 1999, p. 246).

Microstrategies for Facilitating Negotiated Interaction

Let us now turn to the kind of microstrategies that are likely to help the practicing teacher facilitate negotiated interaction in the classroom. The four interactional episodes included in this chapter and the discussion that followed each one indicate the need for teachers to engage the learners in all three dimensions of negotiated interaction: textual, interpersonal, and ideational. Therefore, as indicated earlier, microstrategies for facilitating negotiated interaction must be designed in such a way as to provide opportunities for learners to stretch their linguistic repertoire, sharpen their conversational capacities, and share their individual experiences. Here are a couple of microstrategies that illustrate such a possibility.

Microstrategy 5.1: Holiday Shopping

5.1.0 The primary objective of this microstrategy is to promote negotiated interaction through a cooperative decision-making activity that facilitates talk and topic management on the part of the learners. One possibility is to design a task centering on what people normally do during a national festival season: shopping for a gift. The unpredictable nature of interaction required by the activity and the challenges of cooperative decision making will possibly force the learners to exploit their linguistic, communicative, and cognitive resources to the maximum. Here are some possible steps, and, as usual, you might wish to adapt this microstrategy to meet your particular setting.

5.1.1 First, explain the activity: learners are to form small groups and decide which items to buy as a holiday gift for their beloved teacher (!) or for any other individual they jointly choose. To avoid misunderstanding, tell them that this is only a pretend game.

5.1.2 Explain the rules. Rule 1: Together, they can spend a total of one hundred dollars (or any specified amount of local currency) including sales tax, if any. Rule 2: They have to buy at least three items for the total amount. Rule 3: The decision has to be unanimous, that is, all the members of the group have to agree on the gift items. Rule 4: They can choose the gifts only from a published department store catalog. In several Western countries, large department stores publish catalogs listing items and their suggested price, and distribute them free of charge. In places where a catalog is not available, the teacher or a student volunteer can get a price list from a local department store, and make copies for students.

Yet another possible rule relates to the use of first language. This is a decision you have to make. Most established L2 teaching methods discourage the use of L1 in class. In a setting where the students share a common L1, I do not see any reason why L1 cannot be used in a judicious fashion (see Chapter 11 for more details). Of course, the meaning of "judicious" may vary from teacher to teacher. For instance, in this particular task, you may decide to allow the use of L1 (probably a code-mixing of L1 and L2) for conversations within small groups but insist on the group report and the ensuing class discussion being in L2. Whatever you decide, make the rules clear to your students. You may, of course, modify these rules or add new ones.

5.1.3 Explain the procedure they are to follow: They should complete the activity within the specified time limit. They need to select one of the group members as a facilitator. It is the job of the facilitator to conduct the group discussion in an orderly fashion, to take notes, and to report back to the class. Tell the facilitator to pay attention to how the members arrive at a consensus, how they negotiate communication breakdowns, and how they resolve any conflict in decision making.

5.1.4 Select any number of groups to briefly report their discussions to the class. Using leading questions if necessary, encourage the facilitators to describe the group's talk and topic management. Specifically, ask them to zero in on any linguistic or communicative difficulty they may have had to overcome.

5.1.5 After the group reports, ask the students to identify features that are strikingly common and strikingly different in the way the groups went about performing and reporting the task, followed by class discussion.

An additional activity you may want to consider is to make an audiotape or videotape of the performance of any two of the groups—one group that you expect to do well and another that you expect to do poorly. You can also transcribe portions of the discussion. Later, you can play the tapes back to the whole class and also use the transcribed data to help the learners analyze and interpret their own talk and topic management during the group discussion. This will increase their awareness of what they actually do versus what they need to do.

Microstrategy 5.2: Topic of the Week

5.2.0 This activity consists of a brief, prepared talk by students followed by an extended discussion moderated by the teacher. Depending on the class's proficiency level, one or two hours per week or month may be designated for this activity. The goal is to encourage the learners to talk about whatever interests them. The idea is to recognize their voice and their vision. Adult L2 learners bring to their class a wealth of knowledge that often remains unknown and untapped. In a multilingual and multicultural class, this knowledge may be about their culture or their community. In other settings, it may be about their passion for music or sports or their opinions about the generation gap or gender gap. If given a chance to talk about what interests them, they will be more than willing to share their knowledge with their teachers and their classmates and feel rightfully empowered.

This microstrategy can be implemented at different levels of sophistication. At lower levels of proficiency, you can launch the interaction simply by preselecting one learner per week and helping him or her prepare a brief talk in advance, and then saying in class, "Please tell us about X." At this level, you may need to allow the students to read from a prepared script, so long as it is read properly. This may be followed by a question–answer session. At higher levels, the same activity may be done more systematically and more challengingly. One possible way:

5.2.1 Have each of the students in your class select a topic of personal interest. You should approve the topics in advance to avoid subjects that might be offensive to some.

5.2.2 Ask them to do library or Internet research on the topic and prepare a talk. It is perfectly all right for more than one student to select the same or similar topic; the class can only benefit from the different perspectives.

5.2.3 Ask the presenting students to make a one-page summary of the talk with some initial questions for discussion, and distribute it to all the students before the talk. This might stimulate thinking on the part of other learners.

5.2.4 Let the presenting student talk. Encourage talking rather than reading, but do not insist. As the student talks, ask the other students to take notes on key points, examples, or any questions they might want to ask later.

5.2.5 At the end of the talk, have the class react to the talk. You may wish to start the discussion with one or two questions of your own. Encourage the students to ask questions, seek clarifications, and agree or disagree with the presenter (and state their reasons).

5.2.6 After the discussion, give the presenter a few minutes to make closing remarks.

5.2.7 Finally, as moderator, you give your informal evaluation of the talk focusing mostly on its positive aspects, but you also make suggestions for improvement. Comment also on how the other students shared their views on the topic. And, remember to appreciate the presenter for his or her effort.

Exploratory Projects

I present two exploratory projects, one dealing with talk management and another with topic management.

Project 5.1: Talk Management

5.1.0 The objective of this exploratory project is to help you make a self-assessment of talk management in your class. One way of doing that is by collecting, transcribing, analyzing, and interpreting certain selected episodes from your own teaching. Although all of us have a rough idea of what we do in class in terms of talk management, a detailed analysis of classroom discourse may offer some surprises from which we can learn and benefit.

5.1.1 Arrange to videotape (if that is not possible, at least audiotape) a lesson in which you anticipate a good deal of input and interactional modifications, a lesson in which there is a scope for information exchange. You might ask a colleague to observe and videotape your class, promising to return the favor later.

5.1.2 Watch the video (or listen to the tape) and select a few episodes or segments of classroom discourse to transcribe for analysis. You do not need to transcribe the whole tape. Again, you may wish to seek your colleague's help.

5.1.3 Do a quick discourse analysis of the episodes you selected. You will find yourself going back to the tape (and/or the transcribed version) several times, looking to analyze different items each time. To begin with, focus on instances of input modifications where you simplified your teacher-talk to make it comprehensible to your students. What features of simplification did you find—in pronunciation, grammatical structure, word meaning? What actually prompted you to decide to simplify (e.g., learners' clarification questions, their facial expressions, etc.)? Note also instances where you did not simplify, deliberately or otherwise.

5.1.4 Focus on the IRF (initiation-response-feedback) sequences. How many such sequences were there in the episodes you transcribed?

5.1.5 Select an episode with two or three IRF sequences to do a detailed analysis. It is quite possible that, for the teaching item(s) you are focused on in this episode, IRF sequences are well suited. Is that the case? If not, consider ways (such as changing question types) in which you can convert a closed IRF sequence into a more open-ended interactive exchange.

5.1.6 Turn now to learner talk. In the segments that you transcribed, how many students actually participated? What was the average length of their responses (one word, a phrase, a sentence, etc.)? How many times did the students respond to your questions and how many times did they initiate a turn on their own?

5.1.7 Reflect on your findings, relating them to the issues discussed in this chapter. Were the findings close to what you expected? Are you satisfied with the nature of your classroom discourse, particularly in terms of the number of IRF sequences and display and referential questions?

5.1.8 Based on your understanding of the lesson, reflect on aspects of talk management that you would or would not change. You might want to do this project a couple of more times at reasonable intervals to see whether any pattern emerges.

5.1.9 Finally, reflect on what you have learned about yourself as a teacher in doing this exploratory project on talk management.

Project 5.2: Topic Management

5.2.0 The purpose of this project is to help you reflect further on topic management. We learned earlier that learners benefit more from self- and peer-nominated topics than from teacher-nominated topics. As mentioned before, letting learners introduce their own topics and subtopics will certainly encourage them to share with the teacher and classmates their own perspectives on contemporary issues.

5.2.1 To do a self-assessment of how you manage topic control in your own class, you may use the same classroom data that you collected and transcribed for the previous project on talk management. This time, concentrate on topics and subtopics that came up in the lesson. Go back to your findings for 5.1.5 above. Take a look at the segments containing referential questions that are likely to prompt learner-initiated topics.

5.2.2 Analyze student responses to your referential questions and what you actually did with their responses. Try to interpret them. For instance, how many times did you pursue the topics/subtopics introduced by your learners? How many times did you, like the teacher in episode 5.4, "cut off" learner topic initiation in order to pursue your carefully prepared lesson plan, or to avoid a potentially controversial topic?

5.2.3 Speaking of controversial topics, during the lesson you transcribed did you ever feel that students were introducing unrelated or even uncomfortable topics? If so, how did you handle the situation? If no such occasion arose in your lesson, think about the following example.

5.2.4 The student-student conversation given below is taken from student conferences carried out through electronic media as part of a class taught and reported by Suresh Canagarajah (1997). He was teaching academic English to a group of predominantly African-American students just entering college in Texas. The students are discussing a lesson on recent revisions in history textbooks used in U.S. schools. In his analysis, Canagarajah points out that the students here exhibit a heightened consciousness of their ethnic identity by exploring many issues not raised in the passage, thus giving additional depth to the subject. Read this extract from a chat room discussion:

David: Yea you know it is weird how the people who write most of the history books we read in school are white. Why is that? And why does it seem that the white man in those history books are portrayed as being the better of the races?

Sonny: Exactly. Ray. Have you heard the song by BDP (I think) that talks about the black people of the Bible?

Dexter: i feel the reason for the distortion is because whites want to portray themselves as doing the right thing to their children since they are the majority.

Andrew: as in the book *1984* whoever controls the present controls the past. Since the white man is in power he can belittle the role of the Indian and black cowboys.

(break in sequence)

Amos: it's kind of funny the only Blacks mentioned in the history books are those that have been assassinated by the white man (malcom x, and martin luther king jr.)

Sonny: I think minorities would write their history if they could. How many companies want to publish "History of the Negro (igga)?"

(Data source: Canagarajah, 1997, p. 182)

5.2.5 First of all, what would be your strategy for topic management if a student exchange like the one above took place in your class? Would you politely tell the students that the issues they raise are not directly related to the prescribed text? Or, would you just let them have their say and then quietly move on to the next item on your teaching agenda? Or, would you actively pursue these issues and try to involve other students as well by asking for their opinion? Or, anything else? What would be your rationale for doing any of these?

5.2.6 Finally, in doing this exploratory project on topic management, what have you learned about yourself as a teacher?

In Closing

This chapter on facilitating negotiated interaction focused on how teachers and learners manage classroom discourse, and how such management influences the very nature and scope of input, interaction, output, and, ultimately, L2 development. An underlying thread that runs through this chapter is the joint responsibility vested with both teachers and learners. Without the willing and active cooperation of all the participants, it would be almost impossible to create a conducive atmosphere in the classroom needed to promote negotiated interaction that involves textual, interpersonal, and ideational aspects of language use. Together, the detailed discussion on the macrostrategy for facilitating negotiated interaction, the sample interactional data, the illustrative microstrategies, and the exploratory projects indicate the challenges and opportunities practicing teachers face in helping their learners maximizing their learning potential.

Any attempt at facilitating negotiated interaction can yield desired results only if all the participants feel that they have flexibility and freedom to contribute to talk and topic management. In that sense, what is also involved here is the degree of autonomy given to the learner. In the next chapter, we turn to what it means to promote learner autonomy.

CHAPTER 6

Promoting Learner Autonomy

> Learners must no longer sit there and expect to be
> taught; teachers must no longer stand up there teaching
> all the time. Teachers have to learn to let go and learners
> have to learn to take hold.
>
> —BRIAN PAGE, 1992, p. 84

The concept of autonomy, in one form or another, has long engaged the minds of people everywhere. It is grounded in a human tendency to seek control over one's life. It is displayed in different ways by different people. How it is theorized and practiced varies from time to time, context to context, and culture to culture. In its most basic form, it represents a fundamental longing for freedom of thought and freedom of action in personal, economic, social, political, and other walks of life. Individuals and societies alike have often turned to educational institutions looking for tools that can guide them toward their pursuit of autonomy.

In educational circles, autonomy is considered a worthy goal to achieve for philosophical as well as for psychological reasons. From a philosophical point of view, one of the desirable, though not easily achievable, goals of general education has always been to create autonomous individuals who are willing and able to think independently and act responsibly. In a rapidly changing world where instant and informed decision making is a prerequisite for successful functioning, helping learners become autonomous is one way of maximizing their chances for success. The psychological foundation for learner autonomy can be traced to various branches of psychology: to cognitive psychology, which suggests that learning is very effective if the learner integrates knowledge within a personal framework; to humanistic psychology, which emphasizes the promotion of learners' self-esteem through personal ownership of learning; and to educational psychology, which posits a strong connection between learner autonomy and learner motivation (Broady and Kenning, 1996).

In the field of L2 education, scholarly interest in learner autonomy received a shot in the arm during the late 1970s and early '80s
with the advent and advancement of communicative language teaching, which sought to put the learner at the center of L2 pedagogy.
A review of the literature on learner autonomy in L2 education reveals a diversity of ideas as well as terms. Some of the terms that are
widely used in the context of learner autonomy are: self-instruction,
self-direction, self-access learning, and individualized instruction. To
paraphrase Leslie Dickinson (1987, p. 11),

- self-instruction refers to situations in which learners are working
  without the direct control of the teacher;
- self-direction refers to situations in which learners accept responsibility for all the decisions concerned with learning but not
  necessarily for the implementation of those decisions;
- self-access learning refers to situations in which learners make
  use of self-access teaching material or instructional technology
  that is made available to them;
- individualized instruction refers to situations in which the learning process is adapted, either by the teacher or by the learner, to
  suit the specific characteristics of an individual learner.

As these definitions indicate, there are varying degrees of learner
involvement and teacher engagement, ranging from total learner
control over the aims and activities of learning to partial learner control to indirect teacher control in terms of methods and materials,
and place and pace of study.

Reflective task 6.1

Focusing on any one class you have taught or taken recently, consider the
degree of autonomy exercised by the learners in that class in terms of goals,
tasks, and assessment. Think about possible factors that may have contributed to total or partial or no learner control in that class.

In spite of the conceptual and terminological variations found in
the L2 literature, one can easily discern two complementary views
on learner autonomy, particularly with regard to its aims and objectives. For the purpose of analysis and discussion, I shall call

them a *narrow* view and a *broad* view of learner autonomy. In a nutshell, the narrow view maintains that the chief goal of learner autonomy is to learn to learn while the broad view maintains that the goal should be to learn to liberate.

Narrow View of Learner Autonomy: Learning to Learn

The narrow view of learner autonomy involves, simply, enabling learners to learn how to learn. This enabling process includes equipping them with the tools necessary to learn on their own, and training them to use appropriate strategies for realizing their learning objectives. The primary focus then is on the learner's academic achievement through strategic engagement. In an oft-quoted and widely used definition, Henri Holec (1981, p. 3) calls learner autonomy "the ability to take charge of one's own learning." He goes on to explain that taking charge actually means to have and to hold the responsibility for determining learning objectives, defining contents and progressions, selecting methods and techniques to be used, monitoring the procedure of acquisition, and, finally, evaluating what has been acquired.

Following the learning-to-learn approach, scholars such as Dickinson (1987), Ellis and Sinclair (1989), Little (1990), Wenden (1991), Broady and Kenning (1996) have enriched our understanding of the concept of learner autonomy. We learn from these and other scholars that promoting learner autonomy is a matter of helping learners to

- develop a capacity for critical thinking, decision making, and independent action;
- discover their learning potential, in addition to merely gathering knowledge about the learning process;
- take responsibility for learning and for using appropriate strategies to achieve their general and specific objectives;
- face heavy psychological demands that require learners to confront their weaknesses and failures;
- develop self-control and self-discipline, which lead to self-esteem and self-confidence;
- give up total dependence on the teacher and the educational system, and move beyond a mere response to instruction; and
- understand that autonomy is a complex process of interacting with one's self, the teacher, the task, and the educational environment.

While these scholars tell us what learner autonomy actually is, they also tell us what it is not:

- Autonomy is not independence, that is, learners have to learn to work cooperatively with their teachers, peers, and the educational system;

- Autonomy is not context-free, that is, the extent to which it can be practiced depends on factors such as learners' personality and motivation, their language learning needs and wants, and the educational environment within which learning takes place; and

- Autonomy is not a steady state achieved by learners, that is, autonomous learners are likely to be autonomous in one situation, but not necessarily in another, and they may very well choose to abdicate their own autonomy and look for teacher direction at certain stages in their learning.

Drawing insights from extensive research conducted during the 1990s, Anna Chamot and her colleagues have identified four processes that have the potential to enable learners to exercise control over their learning (Chamot, et al., 1999). They are: planning, monitoring, problem solving, and evaluating. These processes are better explained through their own words and through their own example:

In a typical classroom task, such as an interactive speaking interview of a classmate's leisure time activities, the good learner might begin *planning* by thinking about various activities in which people often engage in their free time. She continues *planning* by narrowing her focus to those activities for which she knows vocabulary in the target language. Depending on the extent of her knowledge, she may decide to gather additional vocabulary by asking her teacher, looking at her notes, or checking a dictionary. She thinks about how to formulate questions in the target language, and she anticipates the types of response she may get to her questions. She then writes down her questions and/or some key vocabulary pertinent to her topics. She reminds herself of language features such as pronunciation and intonation. After she begins her interview, she *monitors* herself listening to herself speak, watching the interviewee's face, and listening to the interviewee's answers such as pronunciation and intonation. She asks for clarification when she does not understand a response (*problem solving*). This good learner repeats the interviewee's main points to make sure she understands, and she gives feedback to show she is paying attention. After the interview is finished, she *evaluates* by reflecting on her use of language and any new words or phrases she acquired. She may think about whether she opened and closed interview in appropriate ways. Finally, she makes written or mental notes of what she might do differently the next time to improve her performance. In this example, the student used all four processes to successfully complete the assignment. Her strategic behavior helped her prepare for the task, actually do the task, resolve difficulties and overcome her lack of information, and reflect on her performance (Chamot et al., 1999, p. 11–12, emphases as in original).

As Chamot and her colleagues suggest, learners can use these four processes for any language learning task pertaining to listening, speaking, reading, and writing. Clearly, to what extent learners manage to do this depends on at least two factors: (a) the learners' awareness of learning strategies, and (b) the teachers' effectiveness of learner training.

Learning Strategies

Research on the learning-to-learn approach to learner autonomy has produced useful taxonomies of learning strategies (e.g., O'Malley and Chamot, 1990; Oxford, 1990) as well as user-friendly manuals (e.g., Ellis and Sinclair, 1989; Chamot et al., 1999; Scharle and Szabo, 2000). These and other researchers seek to make learners more active participants in their language learning, and to make teachers more sensitive to learner diversity and learning difficulties.

A taxonomy that offers a comprehensive system of learning strategies is the one proposed by Rebecca Oxford (1990). Her system consists of six strategy groups, three direct and three indirect. Direct strategies are those that directly involve the target language. They are composed of memory strategies for remembering and retrieving new information, cognitive strategies for understanding and producing the language, and compensation strategies for making do with the limited, still-developing proficiency in the target language. They are all considered direct strategies since they require mental processing of the target language. Indirect strategies are those that support and manage language learning without directly involving the target language. They are composed of meta-cognitive strategies for coordinating the learning process, affective strategies for regulating emotions and attitudes, and social strategies for learning and working with others. Figure 6.1 captures the salient features of the Oxford strategy system. Notice that many of the strategies suggested by Oxford are learner-centered, that is, they represent actions taken by learners to maximize their learning potential.

Taxonomies of learning strategies, such as Oxford's, have provided us with useful insights into what learners need to know and can do to plan and regulate their learning. We know from research on learning strategies that, in addition to generic metacognitive, cognitive, social, and affective strategies that learners follow, there are many individual ways of learning a language successfully and that different students will approach language learning differently. We also learn

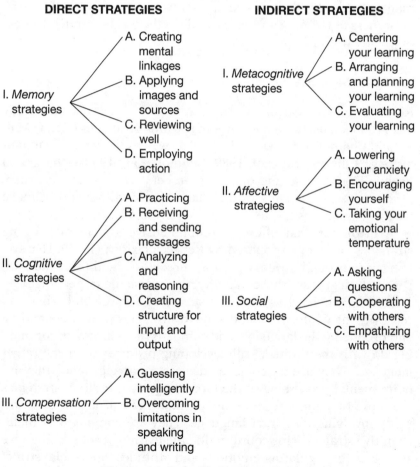

Figure 6.1 Oxford's Strategy System

that the most successful students use a greater variety of strategies and use them in ways appropriate to the language learning task and that less-successful learners not only have fewer strategy types in their repertoire but also frequently use strategies that are inappropriate to the task. The use and nonuse of appropriate strategies for appropriate tasks can easily make the difference between learning and nonlearning. It is therefore necessary to train learners in the effective use of learning strategies.

Reflective task 6.2

If the effective use of learning strategies will help learners become autonomous, in what way, do you think, can teachers contribute to the development of such an autonomy?

Learner Training

Successful learner training includes psychological as well as strategic preparation. Owing to past experience, adult L2 learners tend to bring with them preconceived notions about what constitutes learning and what constitutes teaching. They also bring with them prior expectations about the role-relationship between the learner and the teacher in the classroom. A crucial task of the teacher wishing to promote learner autonomy is to help learners take responsibility for their learning, and to bring about necessary attitudinal changes in them. This psychological preparation should be combined with strategic training that helps learners understand what the learning strategies are, how to use them for accomplishing various language learning tasks, how to monitor their performance, and how to assess the outcome of their learning.

Clearly, learners' ability to take charge of their own learning can be made possible only if they are trained to identify and use appropriate strategies. They not only have to consider the strategies that contribute to effective learning, but, more importantly, they have to discover those that suit their learning objectives and their personality traits best. Accordingly, learner training "aims to provide learners with the alternatives from which to make informed choices about what, how, why, when, and where they learn. This is not to say that they *have* to make all of these decisions all of the time. They may, indeed, choose to be teacher-dependent" (Ellis and Sinclair, 1989, p. 2, emphasis as in original). It is, of course, natural for learners to expect their teachers to train them how to use learning strategies; hence, teachers have to be ready to play a major role in learner training.

What Teachers Can Do

Gail Ellis and Barbara Sinclair (1989) and Anita Wenden (1991) offer useful suggestions for teachers in their attempts to train their learners. According to Ellis and Sinclair (1989, p. 10), teachers can play an instrumental role in learner training by:

- negotiating with learners about course content and methodology, if appropriate;
- sharing with learners, in a way that is accessible to them, the kind of information about language and language learning that teachers have but that is not always passed on to learners;
- encouraging discussion in the classroom about language and language learning;
- helping learners become aware of the wide range of alternative strategies available to them for language learning;
- creating a learning environment where learners feel they can experiment with their language learning;
- allowing learners to form their own views about language learning, and respecting their points of view;
- counseling and giving guidance to individual learners when possible.

In order to carry out these objectives and to make learner training truly meaningful, Wenden (1991, p. 105) suggests that learner training should be:

- *Informed.* The purpose of the training should be made explicit and its value brought to the students' attention.
- *Self-regulated.* Students should be trained how to plan and regulate the use of the strategy, and also how to monitor the difficulties they may face in implementing it.
- *Contextualized.* Training should be relevant to the context of the subject matter content and/or skill for which it is appropriate. It

should be directed to specific language learning problems related the learners' experience.

- *Interactive.* Learners should not be merely told what to do and when to do it and then left on their own to practice. Rather, until they evidence some ability to regulate their use of the strategy, teachers are expected to continue to work with them.

- *Diagnostic.* The content of the training should be based on the actual proficiency of the learners. Therefore, at the outset of any strategy training, information on which strategies students use and how well they use them should be collected.

Reflective task 6.3

If you wish to implement some of the learner training guidelines given above, what possibilities and limitations do you anticipate in your specific learning/teaching context? Focus, among other factors, on the attitudes of administrators, colleagues, and students.

What Learners Can Do

The wealth of information now available on learning strategies and learner training opens up opportunities for learners to monitor their learning process and maximize their learning potential. With the help of their teachers and their peers, learners can exploit some of these opportunities by:

- identifying their learning strategies and styles to know their strengths and weaknesses as language learners. Learners can achieve this, for example, by administering, or being administered, select portions of strategy inventories and style surveys and writing their own language learning histories;

- stretching their strategies and styles by incorporating some of those employed by successful language learners. For example, if some learners are "global" in their learning style, they might have to develop strategies that are associated with the analytic learning style, such as breaking down words and sentences in order to find meaning;

- evaluating their language performance to see how well they have achieved their learning objective(s). This can be achieved by monitoring language learning progress through personal journal writings, in addition to taking regular class tests and other standardized tests;

- reaching out for opportunities for additional language reception or production beyond what they get in the classroom, for example, through library resources, learning centers, and electronic media such as the Internet;

- seeking their teachers' intervention to get adequate feedback on areas of difficulty and to solve problems. This can be done through dialogues and conversations in and outside the class;

- collaborating with other learners to pool information on a specific project they are working on. This is done by learners forming small groups and dividing the responsibilities of consulting reference materials such as dictionaries and encyclopedias to collect information and sharing it with the group; and

- taking advantage of opportunities to communicate with competent speakers of the language. This can be achieved by participating in social and cultural events and by engaging in conversations with competent speakers either in person or "virtually" through Web sites.

Collectively, these activities can contribute to at least two beneficial results. Learners gain a sense of responsibility for aiding their own learning and that of their peers. They also develop a degree of sensitivity and understanding toward other learners who may be more or less proficient than they are.

As the above discussion reveals, proponents of the learning-to-learn approach to learner autonomy aim at making the learners aware of learning strategies and at training them to use those strategies effectively. Wenden (1991, p. 15) captures the spirit of this approach when she says this about learners whom she considers to be "successful" or "expert" or "intelligent": "They have acquired the learning strategies, the knowledge about learning, and the attitudes that enable them to use these skills and knowledge confidently, flexibly, appropriately and independently of a teacher. Therefore, they are autonomous." Proponents of this approach also claim that "the ideal system is one which allows the learner to take as much responsibility for his own learning as he wishes to, and which makes provision both for those who want full autonomy and those who do not want any!" (Dickinson,1987, p. 88). There are, however, critics

who point out that the learning-to-learn approach may be necessary to produce successful language learners but is certainly not
sufficient to produce truly autonomous individuals. They recommend a broader view of learner autonomy that will help learners
how to learn to liberate themselves.

Broad View Of Learner Autonomy: Learning To Liberate

The narrow view of learner autonomy treats learning to learn a language as an end in itself, while the broad view treats learning to
learn a language as a means to an end, the end being learning to liberate (cf. Benson and Voller, 1997, p. 2). In other words, the former
stands for academic autonomy, and the latter for liberatory autonomy. While academic autonomy enables learners to be strategic
practitioners in order to realize their learning potential, liberatory
autonomy empowers them to be critical thinkers in order to realize
their human potential. Liberatory autonomy goes much further
than academic autonomy by actively seeking to help learners recognize sociopolitical impediments placed in their paths to progress,
and by providing them with the intellectual tools necessary to overcome them.

The idea of liberatory autonomy has been propagated by educational philosophers such as Paulo Freire (1972), who emphasized
the development of sociopolitical consciousness as a tool for engagement in social struggle, and by social scientists such as Ivan
Illich (1971), who emphasized the need to liberate learning from
the constraints of schooling. General educationists such as Henry
Giroux (1988) and Roger Simon (1987) sought to incorporate the
idea of liberatory autonomy into the school curriculum. Similar
attempts have been made by scholars such as Phil Benson (1997,
2001) and Alastair Pennycook (1997) in the field of L2 education
(see Chapter 1 for more details).

Pointing out the inadequacy of the learning-to-learn approach,
Benson (1997) advocates what he calls a "political version" of learner
autonomy that can offer alternative political frameworks for learning purposes. Conscious of the prevalent opinion that students
may neither want nor need to be concerned with political issues,
Benson suggests a redefinition of the term *politics*. We are generally

accustomed, he argues, "to think of politics in terms of elections, parties, revolutions, and so on while neglecting the political content of everyday language and language learning practices. In proposing a political orientation for learner autonomy, therefore, we need a considerably expanded notion of the political which would embrace issues such as the societal context in which learning takes place, roles and relationships in the classroom and outside, kinds of learning tasks, and the content of the language that is learned" (p. 32).

In a similar vein, Pennycook (1997) calls for a version of autonomy that relates to the social, cultural, and political contexts of education. To become an autonomous language learner and user, he reckons, "is not so much a question of learning how to learn as it is a question of learning how to struggle for cultural alternatives" (p. 45). Accordingly, he advocates the notion of a pedagogy of cultural alternatives, an educational project that seeks to create autonomous learners by providing them with alternative ways of thinking and being in the world, a project that seeks "to open up spaces for those learners to deal differently with the world, to become authors of their own worlds" (p. 53).

What the learning-to-liberate approach to learner autonomy emphasizes is that if we are seriously committed to helping learners become autonomous individuals, then we need to take into account the sociopolitical factors that shape the culture of the L2 classroom. More than any other educational arena, the L2 classroom, where almost any and all topics can constitute the content of instructional activity, offers ample opportunities for experimenting with liberatory autonomy. Meaningful liberatory autonomy can be promoted in the language classroom by:

- encouraging learners to assume, with the help of their teachers, the role of mini-ethnographers so that they can investigate and understand how language rules and language use are socially structured, and also explore whose vested interests these rules serve;

- making them write diaries or journal entries about issues that directly engage their sense of who they are and how they relate to the social world, and continually reflect on their observations and the observations made by their peers;

- helping them in the formation of learning communities where learners develop into unified, socially cohesive, mutually supportive groups seeking self-awareness and self-improvement;

- enabling them to think critically and develop interpretive capabilities needed to contest the regulated representations of language and culture normally found in prescribed textbooks; and
- providing opportunities for them to explore the unfolding frontiers in cyberspace and the unlimited possibilities offered by on-line services on the World Wide Web, and bringing back to the class their own topics for discussion and their own perspectives on those topics.

The suggestions sketched above can easily be modified and made more relevant to suit the instructional aims and activities, and institutional constraints and resources of various learning and teaching contexts. They may be treated as foundations for promoting a full range of academic and liberatory autonomy for the benefit of the learner. Taken together, these aspects of autonomy promise the development of an overall academic ability, intellectual competence, social consciousness, and mental attitude necessary for learners to avail opportunities and overcome challenges both in and outside the classroom.

Reflective task 6.4

How do you see the relationship between academic and liberatory autonomy—as opposite concepts of autonomy or as two points on a continuum of autonomy? One way of addressing this question is to think about where they differ—in their objectives? In their methods? In their emphasis?

Degrees of Autonomy

An important challenge facing both teachers and learners is to determine the degree of autonomy that would be appropriate for their specific learning and teaching context. As partners in the pursuit of academic as well as liberatory autonomy, teachers and learners can negotiate a comfortable degree of autonomy. Several researchers, including Vee Harris (1996, p. 260), David Nunan (1997, p. 195), and Scharle and Szabo (2000, p. 9), have considered the issue of the degree of autonomy accorded to the learner. Generally, they all advocate a gradual and guided introduction of autonomy over pedagogic choices related to the aims, outcomes, tasks, and materials of learning and teaching. At the initial stage of autonomy, the emphasis is simply on raising the learner's awareness of the reasons behind the teacher's choice of goals, tasks, and materials. At the intermediary stage, the emphasis is on allowing the learner to choose from a range of options given by the teacher. Finally, at the advanced stage, the emphasis is on learner determination of his or her own goals, tasks, and materials.

It certainly makes sense to start with a modest beginning and gradually move toward greater challenges. However, it would be a mistake to try to correlate the initial, intermediary, and advanced stages of autonomy mentioned in the previous paragraph with the beginning, intermediate, and advanced levels of language proficiency of a given group of learners. In fact, teachers and learners can follow different stages of autonomy depending on the linguistic and communicative demands of a particular task in a particular class. It would also be a mistake to presuppose that academic autonomy is suitable for learners of lower proficiency levels, and liberatory autonomy for learners of higher proficiency levels. Given appropriate conditions and adequate preparations, learners at different proficiency levels will profit from an emphasis on academic as well as liberatory autonomy.

Whether one believes in the narrow or broad view of learner autonomy, what should be recognized is that autonomy is a complex construct that can be understood only through careful study, and achieved only through continual struggle. Autonomy cannot be effectively promoted in the absence of a supportive institutional environment and a conducive classroom culture. It also requires teachers who are willing to let go and learners who are willing to take hold. As Christopher Candlin wisely warns us: "Autonomy cannot be legislated, independence cannot be wished, in the curriculum as anywhere else in the social polity; what can be done is to embed their defining principles in the actions of teachers and learners and make such actions not only open for reasoned choice by both, but, much more importantly, to establish the philosophical, purposeful and language acquisitional bases of such choices themselves as part of the subject matter of the curriculum. After all, deciding what is to be done and why is one of the few genuinely communicative acts any classroom can encourage" (Candlin, 1987, p. xi–xii).

Microstrategies for Promoting Learning Autonomy

What, then, are the types of microstrategies that can embed the defining principles of autonomy in the actions of teachers and learners? I offer some possibilities below in terms of microstrategies and exploratory projects. In considering these possibilities, keep in mind that it would be a pedagogically sound practice to build exercises to promote learner autonomy into the overall language teaching curriculum rather than to devote isolated lessons on it.

Microstrategy 6.1: Learning Preferences Across Generations

6.1.0 The purpose of this microstrategy is to help your students think about learning preferences across generations. The idea is to start them on as broad a concept as "generational" learning preferences and move them toward more specific cases. You may modify the following activities, depending on the proficiency level of your students and your specific context of learning and teaching.

6.1.1 Have your students read the chart shown in Figure 6.2. It is made out of information compiled from an article by an educational administrator, Lynn Little (2000, p. 4–5). He has identified some general characteristics, including learning preferences, of leading generations of Americans.

6.1.2 Ask your students to discuss, in small groups, the general characteristics of four generations of Americans. Guide them, where necessary, to relate the generational characteristics to the history of the time period.

6.1.3 Ask them to discuss whether similar (not identical) general characteristics can be identified among people of different generations in any other society familiar to them.

6.1.4 Have them discuss the learning preferences of four generations of Americans. Guide them, where necessary, to relate the learning preferences to the generational characteristics as well as the historical development of the time period.

6.1.5 Ask them to imagine what might be the general characteristics and the learning preferences of the future generation of children born between 2000 and 2020, whose lives will be shaped by the process of globalization in terms of economy, culture, and communication.

6.1.6 Then, give them an individual task in which you ask them to think about and write down their own specific learning preferences.

Leading Generations	General Characteristics	Learning Preferences
Veterans: Born between 1922 and 1943; Many served in World War I	Believe in discipline, law and order, duty before pleasure; hard working; respect for authority; group-centered.	Prefer a stable, orderly, risk-free learning environment; respect teachers' authority; motivated to learn; focus on practice-oriented knowledge.
Baby Boomers: Born between 1943 and 1960; Children of World War II veterans	Believe in equal opportunities, personal gratification, health and wealth; optimistic; team-oriented; self-centered.	Prefer an interactive learning environment, with non-authoritarian teachers; welcome opportunities for team work, but believe in competition over cooperation. Beginning to use technology.
Generation-X'ers: Born during 1960-1980; Experienced the effects of feminist, civil-rights movements	Believe in self-reliance and independent thinking; accept diversity; pragmatic in outlook; not intimidated by authority.	Prefer a self-directed learning environment; want knowledge and skills that increase productivity; more comfortable with graphics and visual images than with print media.

Figure 6.2

Let them draw from the list of adjectives given in the chart and go beyond those, if necessary.

6.1.7   Ask them to rejoin their groups, exchange their notes about individual preferences, and identify features that are common to the members of the group.

6.1.8   Have each group of students report to the class and present the common learning preferences they have identified, followed by class discussion.

6.1.9 Where appropriate, challenge your students to discuss whether the information given in the table is too much of an overgeneralization to be of use.

6.1.10 Design a task that you might want to give them as homework (e.g., ask them to write a brief report on the learning preferences of other students that they would like to develop themselves and what they may have to do to achieve their goal).

Microstrategy 6.2: Inferencing as a Learning Strategy

6.2.0 This microstrategy is designed to help your students know whether and how well they use inferencing as a strategy for improving their reading comprehension. You may design similar microstrategies focusing on other learning strategies appropriate to your students. Keep in mind that, in this and in any similar microstrategy on learner autonomy you may design, your task is to probe the *how* rather than the *what* of learners' responses, that is, focus on the thought processes underlying their answers rather than on the answers themselves.

6.2.1 Put the following passage on an overhead transparency and ask your students to read it quickly. Tell them not to be bothered, at this stage, by any new words they may come across. The passage is taken from *Runaway World*. It was written by Antony Giddens, director of London School of Economics and Political Science.

> A friend of mine studies village life in central Africa. A few years ago, she paid her first visit to a remote area where she was to carry out her fieldwork. The day she arrived, she was invited to a local home for an evening's entertainment. She expected to find out about the traditional pastimes of this isolated community. Instead, the occasion turned out to be a viewing of *Basic Instinct* on video. The film at that point hadn't even reached the cinemas in London.
>
> Such vignettes reveal something about our world. And what they reveal isn't trivial. It isn't just a matter of people adding modern paraphernalia—videos, television sets, personal computers and so forth—to their existing ways of life. We live in a world of transformations, affecting almost every aspect of what we do. For better or worse, we are being propelled into a global order that no one fully understands, but which is making its effects felt upon all of us. Antony Giddens (2000, p. 24–25)

6.2.2 Have your students read it again, this time jotting down all new words.

6.2.3 Ask a few students to share with the class some of the words that are new to them. As they respond, write the words down on the board, or on a separate transparency.

6.2.4 Call upon a couple of students to explain the strategies they might use to find the meanings of some of the listed words that are new to them.

6.2.5 Then, introduce or elaborate (depending on the level of your students' awareness) inferencing as a learning strategy. Encourage them to think by asking questions such as: What is inferencing? Do you use it for language learning purposes? What do you actually do when you use it? Do you find it useful? Etc. Lead them to understand that inferencing as a strategy involves the use of textual clues (such as knowledge of their L1 and their still-developing L2) or contextual clues (such as background knowledge), and has been found to be very useful in guessing the meaning of unknown words.

6.2.6 Focusing on the first paragraph, ask the students to guess the meaning of, for example, the word *remote*. If students give a partially correct answer, ask them questions such as: How do you know? How did you guess? If they don't do it themselves, draw their attention to two other related words—*village life* and *isolated community*—that offer clues to the meaning of *remote*. Also, ask them to guess the profession of Giddens' friend. Find out whether they are able to make use of textual information such as *studies village life* and *fieldwork*. If necessary, draw their attention to the difference between what a sociologist does and what an anthropologist does.

6.2.7 Taking the discussion to a higher level of inferencing, have them read the last sentence again: *The film at that point hadn't even reached the cinemas in London.* Zero in on the word *even*. Concentrate on whether and how they are able to understand the irony of a just-released American movie finding its way to a remote village in central Africa even before it had reached a European Capital city like London. Similarly, ask them to read the sentence, *She expected to find out about the traditional pastimes of this isolated community*. Ask them to think about what it means when an outsider—whether a tourist or an anthropologist—goes to places like central Africa "expecting" to find something.

6.2.8 Now focus on the second paragraph, which contains some challenging words. Ask your learners, for instance, to guess the meaning of *vignettes, trivial,* and *paraphernalia* and to tell the rest of the class how they did it. See whether they are able to make use of all the semantic redundancies in the paragraph (e.g., the word *paraphernalia* is followed by a list of items). Focus on their process of meaning-making, prompting them with questions such as, How did you come up with that?

6.2.9 Follow a slightly different procedure in helping your learners understand the author's choice of words like *transformation* and *propel*. For instance, rewrite *We live in a world of transformations* to read *We live in a changing world* and see whether your learners notice any difference. Similarly, replace *we are being propelled into a global order* with *we are moving into a global order* and ask them if and how they see the difference in meaning.

6.2.10 Finally, in order to help your students reflect on their knowledge and use of inferencing as a learning strategy, ask them to write a brief report recalling the thought processes that were going through their mind while working on this task in class.

Exploratory Project 6.1: Where Am I and Where Do I Want To Be?

6.1.0 As the title suggests, the objective of this project is to help you reflect on where you are right now as an individual wishing to promote learner autonomy, and where you want to be within a time period you set for yourself (one semester? one year? two years?).

6.1.1 Select any one class you recently taught. Try to recall the degree of learner autonomy you promoted in that class. Consider the entire semester (or academic year), not just one class session. Think in terms of an interrelated GAME plan:

- *G*oals: general as well as specific instructional goals and objectives,
- *A*ctivities: the type of classroom activities needed for realizing the goals,
- *M*aterials: the selection of appropriate instructional materials, and
- *E*valuation: methods of assessing desired learning outcomes.

6.1.2 Note down your random thoughts about what you did to promote learner autonomy in terms of the GAME plan. A possible format for your note-taking is shown in Figure 6.3.

Year/Semester:		Class:	
Goals	Activities	Materials	Evaluation

Figure 6.3

6.1.3 Read the following twenty statements, and, using your random notes as a guide, rate yourself on a 5–1 (5 = no promotion of learner autonomy; 1 = substantial promotion of learner autonomy) to estimate where you stand now. Check the statements that reflect your current status.

Goals

5: I start with and follow a set of instructional goals I have pre-pared (or given to me) for all the classes I teach.

4: I discuss my instructional goals with my students, and modify them suitably based on their feedback.

3: I present my students with a set of instructional goals for them to choose from.

2: I ask my students to tell me what they expect to learn from my class and try to incorporate their goals in my teaching agenda.

1: I honor my students' needs and wants, their goals and objec-tives that I identify by administering a questionnaire specially prepared for a particular class.

Activities

5: I achieve my instructional goals by presenting language items clearly, and by providing ample opportunities for students to practice.

4: I determine the type of activity (individual task, pair-work, group work, whole class) that best suits my instructional goal.

3: I encourage my students to adapt the content, the goal and the method of an activity within limits acceptable to me.

2: I let my students work independently on tasks and, when neces-sary, help them get back on track.

1: I invite my students to create a task and accomplish it at their own pace, in their own way and reach a jointly determined goal.

Materials

5: I use commercially produced textbooks that are selected and prescribed by me or by my school authorities.

4: In addition to using prescribed textbooks, I prepare supplementary materials that I believe will interest my students.

3: I involve my students in the final selection of textbooks by asking them to choose from a range of options I consider appropriate for their level.

2: I start with prescribed textbooks and prepared materials, and then encourage my students to modify or adapt the tasks and exercises the way they think interesting and appropriate.

1: I invite my students to read the local newspapers, surf the Internet, and go to other sources to bring materials that they think are interesting and appropriate.

Evaluation

5: I evaluate the learning outcome of my students by using common tests, that is, tests given in the textbook or those designed by my school.

4: I assess my students' performance using a combination of common tests and those I design for learners in a particular class.

3: I give my students a range of test formats (essay, multiple choice, yes/no, etc.) to choose from, and I try to honor their choice as much as possible.

2: I ask my students to assess their own performance using specific and clear guidelines I give them. I normally keep their assessment in mind when I do mine.

1: I ask my students to assess their performance using their own guidelines, which I ask to specify. I then allow their self-assessment to inform my own.

6.1.4 Take a different color pen or pencil and go over the statements again, this time checking where you wish to be within a specified period of time, considering your specific context and level of teaching responsibilities.

6.1.5 Think about all the resources that are available to you to help you get where you wish to be. Also, think about how you can make use of them. Use the format shown in Figure 6.4 to take notes:

Item (from GAME plan)	Available resources	How to use resources
. . .	. . .	. . .

Figure 6.4

6.1.6 Think about all the constraints (e.g., lack of resources and time, administrative hurdles, learner apathy, etc.) that you think will frustrate you from getting where you wish to be. Also think about how you can cope with them. Use the format shown in Figure 6.5 to take notes:

Item (from GAME plan)	Possible constraints	How to cope with them
. . .	. . .	. . .

Figure 6.5

6.1.7 Finally, think about what you learned from doing this project, and how your attitude toward learner autonomy has or has not changed.

Exploratory Project 6.2: Learner Profile

6.2.0 One of the first steps in promoting learner autonomy is to identify who your learners are, what learning strategies and styles they bring with them, and what they hope to learn in your class. Accordingly, this project is designed to help you create a learner profile at the beginning of a course.

6.2.1 Use the questionnaire shown in Figure 6.6 to conduct a survey among your learners. Keep in mind that what follows is a generic questionnaire. You should feel free to modify, add, or delete any statement in order to make the survey more relevant to your specific learning and teaching context.

6.2.2 Collect the completed survey from your students. Have an individual conference with each student to discuss their individual aims, strategies, and styles. You can also use the information to individualize your instruction as much as possible.

Name: Class: Date:

Note: This is not a test. This is a survey to seek your opinion about yourself. This survey will help me understand what you expect to learn in this class, and what you normally like to do in order to learn. Please read the following statements carefully and circle 1 if you agree, 2 if you disagree, or 3 if you are not sure. Do not think too much; your first impression is always the best.

1.0 Aims

1.1	I want to improve my listening skills	1	2	3
1.2	I want to improve my speaking skills	1	2	3
1.3	I want to be able to read well and read fast	1	2	3
1.4	I want to be able to write well	1	2	3
1.5	I want to improve my critical thinking skills	1	2	3
1.6	I want to improve my grammar	1	2	3
1.7	I want to increase my vocabulary	1	2	3
1.8	I want to learn to pronounce words correctly	1	2	3
1.9	I want to be able to participate in class discussions	1	2	3

2.0 Strategies

2.1	I know how to read well in my first language	1	2	3
2.2	I know how to write well in my first language	1	2	3
2.3	I use my first language knowledge to learn the second	1	2	3
2.4	I compare the grammar rules of the languages I know	1	2	3
2.5	I use what I already know to learn something new	1	2	3
2.6	When I read, I focus on pictures, subtitles, and key words	1	2	3
2.7	I think about grammar rules when I speak and write	1	2	3
2.8	I associate new information with images and pictures	1	2	3
2.9	I monitor and judge my progress in language learning	1	2	3
2.10	When I read, I use a dictionary to understand new words	1	2	3
2.11	I think about strategies that will help me learn better	1	2	3
2.12	I identify the problems that slow down my progress	1	2	3
2.13	I use the library, the Internet, and other sources to learn	1	2	3
2.14	I seek out conversation partners to improve my skills	1	2	3
2.15	I do not like to make mistakes when I speak or write	1	2	3
2.16	When I read, I try to guess the meaning of new words	1	2	3
2.17	I like to find out grammar rules myself	1	2	3
2.18	I don't think I can evaluate my own learning	1	2	3

3.0 Styles

3.1	I like working with a partner in class	1	2	3
3.2	I participate actively in whole-class discussions	1	2	3
3.3	I like to work on topics and themes that I select	1	2	3
3.4	I learn best when my teachers explain grammar rules	1	2	3
3.5	I think I do better when I work alone	1	2	3

(continues)

Figure 6.6

3.6	I like to learn from my teachers, not from my classmates	1	2	3
3.7	I hesitate to participate because I fear I'll make mistakes	1	2	3
3.8	I share with my class interesting readings from the Internet	1	2	3
3.9	I think working in a small group is a waste of time	1	2	3
3.10	I feel frustrated when I work with classmates	1	2	3
3.11	I participate actively in a small group	1	2	3
3.12	I read newspapers daily to increase my vocabulary	1	2	3
3.13	I don't like telling my teachers what to do in class	1	2	3

Figure 6.6 *continued*

6.2.3 Consolidate and tabulate the information from your students to get a general idea of the class profile. You may use the format shown in Figure 6.7.

Class:	Total number of students:		Date:
Item	No. of learners who agree	No. of learners who disagree	No. of learners who are not sure

Figure 6.7

6.2.4 Distribute the completed table to your class, and use it as you would use any other instructional material. For instance, ask the students to study the table and discuss the class profile. Initiate a class discussion in which the learners, in pairs or in small groups, determine where the aims, strategies, and styles overlap, and where they diverge. Encourage them to think about how the class profile can be used to develop a coherent classroom community.

6.2.5 Think about how, and to what extent, you can incorporate the needs and wants, and the strategies and styles, of your learners into your instructional agenda. To start, it would be a useful exercise to select any one lesson you have planned to teach and see what changes you may have to make in your lesson plan in terms of specific objectives, type of activities, and classroom management in order to be sensitive to the learners' profile.

In Closing

It is clear that any serious promotion of learner autonomy involves the willing cooperation of teachers as well as learners. They are required to jointly determine the degree of autonomy that would be appropriate for their specific learning and teaching context, and the right path to reach their goals. This might call for a fundamental attitudinal change on their part. In practical terms, what this means is that teachers have to determine the degree of control they are willing and able to yield to their students in terms of curricular aims and objectives, selection of tasks and materials, and assessment of learning outcomes. Conversely, this also means that learners have to decide, with some guidance from their teachers if necessary, the degree of responsibility they are willing and able to take in those areas of learning and teaching.

CHAPTER 7

Fostering Language Awareness

> As you are reading these words, you are taking part in
> one of the wonders of the natural world. For you and I
> belong to a species with a remarkable ability. . . . That
> ability is language. . . . The ability comes so naturally
> that we are apt to forget what a miracle it is.
>
> —STEPHEN PINKER, 1994, p. 15

Language is intricately woven into the fabric of human life. It is
closely linked to the relationship between mother and child, between
self and society, between thought and action, between war and
peace. It is all-pervasive. We use it, misuse it, and abuse it. And yet,
we seldom think about it. We hardly notice its presence around us.
We rarely recognize when people use it to control others. We barely
notice when politicians manipulate it to manage public opinion.

It is no wonder, therefore, that educational centers seek to play
a pivotal role in fostering students' awareness of the role played by
language in the development of individuals as well as institutions.
The relevant literature in the fields of education and language
teaching presents various strands of thought about how language
awareness can be fostered. These thoughts may be classified under
the rubric of (a) general language awareness and (b) critical language awareness. The former treats language awareness primarily
as an awareness of linguistic and sociolinguistic features governing
language usage, while the latter treats it primarily as an awareness
of social and political factors governing language use. Let us consider both in relation to L2 classroom teaching.

General Language Awareness

Educational philosophers all over the world have long emphasized
the role of general language awareness in human development.
However, it is only recently that concerted efforts have been made

in educational circles to relate language awareness directly to educational policies. Two prominent movements that have recently contributed to such efforts in the West are the Language Awareness movement in the United Kingdom and the Whole Language movement in the United States.

The British Movement

The origin of the current Language Awareness (LA) movement in Britain can be traced to a 1975 report of the Bullock Committee set up by the British government to go into "the teaching of reading and other uses of English." The report was titled *A Language for Life*, which succinctly captures the essence of LA. It generated serious debates among educationists, leading eventually to several curricular reform proposals. While they differ in emphasis, they all adhere to a rather broad definition of LA: "a person's sensitivity to and conscious awareness of the nature of language and its role in human life" (Donmall 1985, p. 7, cited in van Lier, 1996, p. 79).

Reflective task 7.1

Think, in very specific terms, about the role played by your teacher(s) (or anybody else) in promoting your sensitivity to language and its role in your life. If possible, compare your thoughts with those of one other person.

Following the generally agreed upon definition of LA, educationists and language teachers in Britain attempted to develop pedagogic principles and practices with the view to promoting language awareness among school-children. They sought to bridge the gap between primary and secondary school expectations of language related work, and the gap between first- and second-language teaching objectives and activities. In addition, they were also interested in promoting linguistic tolerance among learners coming from mainstream as well as from minority language backgrounds. As Eric Hawkins (1984, p. 6), one of the leading proponents of LA, declared: "We are seeking to light fires of curiosity about the central human characteristic of language which will blaze throughout our pupils' lives. While combating linguistic complacency, we are seeking to arm our pupils against fear of the unknown which breeds prejudice and antagonism."

The American Movement

As the LA movement was spreading in Britain, a similar effort was undertaken in the United States under the label Whole Language movement. It was aimed at providing rich language experience for school-children by integrating the four language skills of listening, speaking, reading, and writing, and by introducing language related activities in content areas across the school curriculum. Supporters of the movement argued that various components of language such as sounds, words, phrases, and sentences should be taught holistically using authentic materials and meaningful activities that resonate with learners and their daily life.

In addition, the Whole Language movement wanted to recognize the diverse linguistic resources that learners bring to the class—resources that include dialectal variations in L1 as well as L2. As Ken Goodman (1986, p. 27), one of the leading supporters of the Whole Language movement, observed: "Whole language is whole. It does not exclude some languages, some dialects, or some registers because their speakers lack status in a particular society. Every language form constitutes a precious linguistic resource for its users. This does not mean that whole language teachers are not aware of the social values assigned to different language varieties and how these affect people who use them. But they can put these social values in proper perspective."

Reflective task 7.2

If the educational institution you are associated with has an official policy of promoting a "standard" variety as opposed to a "nonstandard" variety of a language, what are the ways in which you can be sensitive to those students who may speak a "nonstandard" variety at home? How can you make use of the linguistic resources such learners bring to your class?

A common theme stressed by both American and British educators relates to the integration of language experience across the curriculum at elementary as well as secondary school levels. Since elementary school teachers deal with all the subjects taught at their level, they already are considered to conceive of their task in terms of integrated rather than subject-oriented teaching. That is not the case in departmentalized secondary schools. The American and British educators, therefore, emphasize the need for secondary school subject teachers to think of the language of math, or the language of science, or the language of history, as something that should be explicitly taught along with mathematical problems, scientific concepts, or historical events. They therefore suggest that secondary school teachers, regardless of their subject specialization, should be trained in areas such as the nature and function of language, language and thought, and language and culture (Hawkins, 1984, p. 28). In other words, they should be equipped with the knowledge and skill necessary "to consider how language is used in their fields and then think of their curriculum as a dual curriculum with a double agenda it implies" (Goodman, 1986, p. 31).

General Language Awareness in Action

While there are minor variations between the British and American approaches to actual classroom practices aimed at promoting language awareness, they largely focus on the properties of language structure and language usage with particular reference to literacy skills (reading and writing). Furthermore, in spite of their well-intentioned emphasis on language across the curriculum, their efforts were mostly directed at language classes since these classes, whether L1 or L2, easily lend themselves to metalinguistic activities through which participants can objectify a language and talk about it. They showed that there are interesting ways in which learners' attention can be explicitly drawn to the logic of a linguistic subsystem be it spelling, intonation, or grammar.

It is only natural for language learners to expect some logic in the way a language operates. The fact that certain language subsystems defy logic can itself be considered an opportunity for creating language awareness. The English language is a prime candidate if one is looking for a language full of what appear to be irregularities. Calling it "a zany logic-defying tongue," Stephen Pinker (1994, p. 18) reminds us that English is a language in which "one drives on a parkway and parks in a driveway, plays at a recital and recites at a play." Nothing perhaps testifies to the "zaniness" of the English language more than its spelling system. As Hawkins (1984, p. 118) points out, there are at least nine different spellings for the sound of the vowel [I:] in English: bel*ie*ve, rec*ei*ve, p*eo*ple, k*ey*, l*ea*ve, ma*chi*ne, q*ua*y, b*e*, and s*ee*). Similarly, one is often reminded of the well-known complaint by British playwright George Bernard Shaw that *fish* could just as well be spelled *ghoti* (*gh* as in tou*gh*, *o* as in w*o*men, *ti* as in na*ti*on).

Simple examples like the above can provide an interesting way of fostering general language awareness among learners, particularly about the regularity or the irregularity of linguistic systems. The same examples can also be used creatively to help learners analyze and understand whether there is underlying logic behind apparent irregularities. For instance, Stubbs (1980, p. 48, cited in Hawkins, 1984, p. 118–9) observes that Shaw's fish-*ghoti* example is actually a clear case of a misunderstanding of the English spelling system because *gh* cannot represent the sound *f* in initial position in any word in English. Other sounds in *ghoti* also have restrictions about whether they can occur in the initial, middle, or final position of an English word.

Reflective task 7.3

How can you make use of just this one example (fish-*ghoti*) to teach some of the basics of the spelling system in English?

Subtle nuances of stress and intonation are yet another area of L2 learning and teaching where any attempt at explicit language awareness will be of immense help. Several studies on discourse strategies of everyday communication between native and non-native speakers of a language reveal the importance of proper use of prosodic features. John Gumperz (1982), for instance, has studied communicative tensions between London residents and immigrants from India, Pakistan, and the Caribbean islands. He found that the mistrust and miscommunication prevalent among these communities arise in part because of faulty use of stress and intonation features by non-native speakers of English, and he has provided several interesting examples to support his claim.

One such example deals with a London bus driver, an immigrant from the West Indies. When a passenger boarded the bus and presented a large bill to buy a ticket, the driver said, "Exact change, *please*," putting extra emphasis on *please* and with falling intonation. Walking down the aisle, the passenger wondered aloud, "Why do these people have to be so rude and threatening?" (Gumperz,

1982, p. 168). Gumperz explains that, according to the conventions of British English, the polite way of marking this directive would be to put the stress on *change* and not on *please*, the reason being that *change* is the new information that needs to be highlighted. Or, the driver could have used *please* with a rising intonation, signaling a polite question.

A strong stress on *please* with a falling intonation would be equivalent to giving an order—a convention that would be appropriate only if the speaker is in a position of authority, as in the case of a parent who might firmly say to a child: "Clean up the mess . . . *please*." Gumperz goes on to say that the driver did not intend to be impolite, and that putting emphasis on *please* in this context, even with a falling intonation, would indicate politeness according to speech conventions used by West Indian speakers. From a classroom point of view, raising the learners' awareness of subtle nuances of intonation patterns would be beneficial particularly if the learners' L1 does not possess prosodic features similar to those in their L2.

Sometimes, even without teacher initiative, learners themselves might raise questions that provide opportunities for teachers to create explicit language awareness in class. But teachers may not be always ready and attentive as shown in the following classroom dialogue on renting a house. A learner is curious about the expression *a three bedroom house*:

1　S:　Why three bed, er, three bedroom? Why we don't say three bedrooms?

2　T:　Ahhm, oh, I don't know.

3　S:　Is not right.

4　T:　We don't say it. We don't say it. There's no explanation. But we often do that in English. Three bedroom house.

5　S:　(Another student) Don't ask for it.

6　S:　Yes.

7　T:　Well, do ask why, ask why and 99 percent of the time I know the answer. One percent of the time nobody knows the answer. If I don't know it, nobody knows (laughter). Ah, no, I don't know the answer.

(Data source: Nunan, 1989, p. 181–2.)

While, as Nunan observes, the teacher's reply is "hardly encouraging," it highlights the need for incorporating a focus on language awareness in teacher education programs.

Reflective task 7.4

Do you approve of the way the teacher handled the student's question in the above episode? Why/why not? What are the different ways of responding to this question—if your objective is to create general language awareness?

Language Awareness of Language Teachers

A conscious awareness of the way the language they are teaching works and the way it is used is absolutely essential for teachers whether they are native speakers or non-native speakers. Most native speaking teachers, having unconsciously mastered their L1 in their childhood, may know the underlying system of their language intuitively, but they may lack explicit knowledge needed to give a proper explanation. Most non-native speaking teachers may have consciously learned their L2 and learned about it as well, but still may lack adequate competence and confidence in it.

Emphasizing the need for creating language awareness among language teachers, Scott Thornbury (1997, p. xii) correctly cautions that teachers' limited knowledge of language may result in "a failure on the part of the teacher to anticipate learners' learning problems and a consequent inability to plan lessons that are pitched at the right level; an inability to interpret course book syllabuses and materials and to adapt these to the specific needs of the learners; an inability to deal satisfactorily with errors, or to field learners' queries; and a general failure to earn the confidence of the learners due to a lack of basic terminology and ability to present new language clearly and efficiently." In order to address these concerns, Thornbury (1997) has written a book, *About Language: Tasks for Teachers of English*, consisting of nearly three hundred tasks starting with phonemes and progressing through words, phrases, sentences, and complete texts.

Taking a different approach, Leo van Lier (1996) has called for Language Awareness in Teacher Education (LATE) based not on additional courses in linguistics or grammar, "not on sweeping changes or reforms of great magnitude, but on one small moment in the educational process: teachers and students talking to each other" (p. 85). He would like a LATE course for teachers that would "examine the reality of language use in relevant educational settings, preferably incorporating classroom observation and gathering of data by students" (p. 88). He suggests three things a LATE course should do:

- *Take an experimental approach to LA*, one that acknowledges that teachers have a great deal of knowledge and know-how of language, and which systematically draws upon that experiential base.

- *Reject language-as-product*, i.e., focus not on language as a body of content matter that can be transmitted piecemeal to an audience, but rather as a living thing that shapes our existence and that we use to make sense of our world and our work.

- *Study language critically*, i.e., emphasize that language study is not only relevant to teacher education and classroom practice, but that it is essential to human growth and self-fulfillment.

(van Lier, 1996, p. 88–9)

Van Lier argues that within each of these three components, teachers should explore issues that are of interest to them and to their learners, and he believes that linguistic features of phonology, syntax, discourse, etc., will automatically become a part of that larger exploration.

Reflective task 7.5

To what extent, do you think, has the teacher education program you are associated with helped you to "examine the reality of language use in relevant educational settings" in order for you to develop language awareness?

It is clear from the above that American and British educators have made serious attempts to promote general language awareness among language teachers in particular and among teachers in general. For most part, however, they narrowly focused on language structures and literacy skills rather than on the broader role language plays in shaping and reshaping human lives. In addition, as van Lier (1996) rightly points out, they also dissipated their energy by indulging in endless arguments about the importance of phonics (as American educators did), or the imposition of "standard English" (as their British counterparts did).

I am not suggesting that the work on general language awareness has been useless or unnecessary, only that it has been insufficient. In other words, in spite of their lofty ideals about creating awareness of language and its potential to liberate the human mind, supporters of general language awareness shied away from sociopolitical aspects of language, especially aspects of the relationship between language and power. A widespread dissatisfaction with the limitations of the general language awareness movements led to the emergence of another school of thought that emphasizes what is called *critical* language awareness.

Critical Language Awareness

The principles and practices of Critical Language Awareness (CLA) can be traced to the contributions made by, among others, Norman Fairclough (1992, 1995) and his colleagues in Britain, and later by Allan Luke (1996, 1997) and his colleagues in Australia. Without dismissing the basic linguistic and sociolinguistic aspects of general language awareness, advocates of CLA seek to consider the sociopolitical nature of language use as well. They particularly wish to acknowledge and act upon the fact that language, any language, is implicitly linked to the exercise of power. Therefore, given that "power relations work increasingly at an implicit level through language, and given that language practices are increasingly targets for intervention and control, a critical awareness of language is a prerequisite for effective citizenship, and democratic entitlement" (Fairclough, 1995, p. 222).

Like critical pedagogists (see Chapter 1), CLA advocates, too, assert that a critical awareness of the word is essential to develop a critical awareness of the world. They also see language education as a prime source for sensitizing learners to social inequalities that confront them and for developing necessary capabilities for addressing those inequalities. CLA, therefore, should be fully integrated not only with the development of language practices across the curriculum but also with the development of the individual learner's intellectual capabilities that are required for long-term, multifaceted struggles in various sociopolitical arenas (Fairclough, 1992).

One way of integrating CLA with the development of learners' intellectual capabilities is to help them understand how power is produced, maintained, and also resisted with the help of different language forms. This is not an easy task because, as Allan Luke (1996) reminds us, what lends controlling power to language is the way it is used and interpreted in specific sociopolitical contexts. Therefore, he and his colleagues suggest that the teaching of CLA should begin by putting any textual material used in the class "up for grabs, for critical debate, for weighing, judging, critiquing." Such a critical analysis of texts "also requires classroom frames for talking about how and in whose interests social institutions and texts can refract and bend social and natural reality, manipulate and position readers and writers" (Luke, O'Brian, and Comber, 1994, p. 141).

If we wish to encourage L2 learners to do the kind of critical analysis of language use suggested by CLA advocates, then we should take into account the ideological markers of a text in addition to its propositional message. Only then will we be able to help our learners understand how language is used by some as a tool for social, economic, and political control. If we refrain from taking such a critical approach, we will knowingly or unknowingly contribute not only to the marginalization of our learners but to our own marginalization as well. What James Gee (1994, p. 190) says about teachers of English is also true of all language teachers: "English teachers can cooperate in their own marginalization by seeing themselves as "language teachers" with no connection to such social and political issues. Or they . . . accept their role as persons who socialize students into a world view that, given its power here and abroad, must be looked at critically, comparatively, and with a constant sense of the possibilities for change."

Reflective task 7.6

Do you agree with Gee that, if your language teaching is not connected to social and political issues, you are cooperating in your own marginalization? In what way is this true or not true?

Critical Language Awareness in Action

There are several ways of fostering CLA in the L2 classroom. A beginning can be made by paying attention to the selection of textbooks and supplementary materials. Rather than selecting textbooks for the strings of grammatical structures and vocabulary items that provide much needed linguistic input to the learner, they should be selected for their potential to challenge the intellectual capabilities of the learner as well. Whether centrally prescribed or self-selected by teachers, textbooks can be excellent resources for critical reading aimed at sensitizing learners to subtle meanings, concealed assumptions, and hidden attitudes embedded in a text.

As suggested by CLA practitioners (see, for example, Catherine Wallace, 1992; Kristine Brown, 1999), a critical dimension to reading can be easily added to usual classroom practice by

- incorporating open-ended questions to the ones already given in the textbook;
- shifting from an emphasis on one right answer to multiple interpretations, as long as plausible reasons are provided;
- encouraging learners to recognize and respect a variety of viewpoints;
- asking learners to discuss how topics could be dealt with differently, from the point of their own linguistic and cultural perspective;
- helping learners to critically reflect on taken-for-granted views and aspects of language;
- encouraging learners to regularly keep diaries or journals in which they note and comment on social practices and language use that particularly strike them—something they read or heard on the bus, or on the street, or at the mall.

Such a critical approach can actually lend a motivating dimension to texts that are normally no more than a bland, boring collection of linguistic input.

Reflective task 7.7

The ideas given above pertain mainly to critical reading. In what way can CLA be promoted through speaking, listening, and writing activities as well?

While a critical reading of passages included in most L2 textbooks can provide opportunities for fostering CLA in the classroom, perhaps nothing is more useful for that purpose than supplementary materials such as government reports or newspaper articles. They have a tendency to use deceptive language to hide real intentions particularly when dealing with sensitive cultural or political issues. In his perceptive essay *Politics and the English Language*, George Orwell (1946) observed that the "great enemy of clear language is insincerity. When there is a gap between one's real and one's declared aims, one turns as it were instinctively to long words and exhausted idioms, like a cuttlefish squirting out ink."

The language of insincerity results in what is called doublespeak. According to William Lutz (1989, p. 1), doublespeak "is language that makes the bad seem good, the negative appear positive, the unpleasant appear attractive or at least tolerable." A detailed discourse analysis of newspaper and news magazine articles will yield telling examples of doublespeak that can be used in class for creating critical language awareness. Brian Morgan (1998), for instance, cites a British newspaper article that printed a collection of terms used by the British media to describe the 1991 Gulf War. Here are some examples.

They have a war machine.	We have army, navy and air force.
Their men are brainwashed.	Our boys are professional.
They have propaganda.	We have press briefings.
They destroy.	We take out.
They kill (enemies).	We neutralize (enemies).
They are ruthless.	We are resolute.
Their missiles cause civilian casualties.	Our missiles cause collateral damage.
Their planes are zapped.	Our planes fail to return from missions.

As these examples show, doublespeak is the result of a deliberate attempt to mislead and misinform. A critical engagement with political discourse appearing in newspapers and news magazines can go a long way in helping learners realize that language can conceal as much as it can reveal. Doublespeak is not limited to times of war; newspapers carry political discourses full of doublespeak other times as well (see the microstrategy 7.2 below).

Reflective task 7.8

Do you think helping learners analyze and understand the language of current affairs in the L2 classroom is a good way of fostering critical language awareness? How would you respond to those who may believe that such discussions can come only at the expense of the important task of developing basic language skills?

To sum up our discussion so far, language is an integral part of the practice of everyday life. Therefore, any educational enterprise must include the teaching of language awareness. A general awareness of the way in which a language operates in terms of phonology, syntax, semantics, and discourse is necessary but not sufficient. What is also needed is the fostering of critical language awareness that can enrich one's understanding of how a language is often used to control people economically, culturally, and socially. It is therefore important for teachers, language teachers in particular, to design activities that foster both general and critical language awareness in the classroom.

Microstrategies for Fostering Language Awareness

This section presents two microstrategies—one dealing with general language awareness and another with critical language awareness.

Microstrategy 7.1: Language Use and Levels of Formality

7.1.0 This microstrategy is designed to foster general language awareness about levels of formality involved in interpersonal communication. One example of formal-informal language use pertains to the way in which we address people at home, in school, or at our workplace. Therefore, a useful microstrategy may be to ask L2 learners to explore how different cultural communities require different levels of formality in addressing people. Here's one way of doing it. Make changes to suit your specific learning/teaching situation.

7.1.1 Write the following (or similar) forms of address on the board:

Madam President
Mr. Chairman

Your Honor

Sir

Hello Darling

Hey

Divide the class into small groups and ask each group to discuss in what context(s) and with whom would it be appropriate to use these forms of address. Also, ask them to discuss whether more than one of these forms can be used to address the same person in different contexts, and if so, in which contexts.

7.1.2 Have representatives from groups briefly share their discussion with the entire class. Let them also talk about any disagreements within their groups.

7.1.3 Have individual learners make a list of terms they use to address family members (grandfather, grandmother, father, mother, elder brother, younger brother, elder sister, younger sister, etc.,) in their cultural communities. Specifically, ask them to think about when and where they use the address forms they listed, and when and where (and if) they use actual names to address family members. Allow them to use their L1 script if they wish, but advise them to give English gloss as well. If they normally use any honorific terms, ask them to write these, too.

7.1.4 Divide the class into small groups (or form pairs, depending on your convenience). Ask the learners to share their list with others and compare how forms of address work within a family in different linguistic or cultural communities.

7.1.5 Have them talk about how factors such as setting, age, and gender of participants affect forms of address, and in what contexts boundaries may be crossed.

7.1.6 Again in small groups, ask them to compare how forms of address are structured in their L1 (or in various L1's represented in class) and in L2. Depending on the proficiency level and cultural knowledge of your students, you may have to give them different forms of address in L2.

7.1.7 Ask the students to share some of their salient points with the class. Lead a detailed discussion on any selected issues that came up in small groups.

7.1.8 Help them (if necessary, through leading questions) reflect on how different forms of address may actually reveal cultural values and beliefs, and how these are reflected in language use.

Microstrategy 7.2: Language Use and Doublespeak

7.2.0 This microstrategy aims at fostering critical language awareness in learners by drawing their attention to doublespeak, that is,
deceptive language that is widely used to mislead people—whether in
a democratic society or in a totalitarian regime. For illustrative purposes, I will be using the first paragraph from a book that was devoted
to doublespeak. It was written by William Lutz in 1989 and titled
*Doublespeak: From "Revenue Enhancement" to "Terminal Living": How
Government, Business, Advertisers, and Others Use Language to Deceive
You*. Here's a possible classroom activity:

7.2.1 Write the full title of Lutz's book on the board. Ask your students to focus on the key words in the title and give them some time to
think about how (a) government, (b) business, and (c) advertisers use
language to deceive the general public. Let them share their thoughts
and examples with the class.

 Write the following paragraph on the board or, if you have prepared
a transparency, project it on the OHP screen. Ask your students to read
it carefully.

> There are no potholes in the streets of Tucson, Arizona, just "pave-
> ment deficiencies." The Reagan Administration didn't propose any
> new taxes, just "revenue enhancement" through new "user's fees."
> Those aren't bums on the street, just "non-goal oriented members
> of society." There was no robbery of an automatic teller machine,
> just an "unauthorized withdrawal." The patient didn't die of medi-
> cal malpractice, it was just a "diagnostic misadventure of a high
> magnitude." The U.S. Army doesn't kill the enemy anymore, it just
> "services the target." (Lutz, 1989, p. 1)

7.2.2 If there are any difficult vocabulary items, deal with them first,
so that the students fully understand the text before proceeding further.
If necessary, make a two-column table highlighting only the juxtaposed
lexical items (potholes/pavement deficiencies, etc.).

7.2.3 Form small groups and allot one or two sentences to each
group for a detailed analysis. Ask them to think about critical questions
such as: What is achieved by the use of such doublespeak? At what
cost? At whose cost? Who benefits from such doublespeak and how?

7.2.4 Ask a representative from each group to present a brief report,
followed by class discussion.

7.2.5 Help them (with leading questions, if necessary) to think why many people fail to notice doublespeak even though it is so common in public discourse and in private conversations.

7.2.6 Help them (again with leading questions, if necessary) to think of ways in which a critical awareness of doublespeak and its function can help them in their role as language learners, and in their role as educated citizens.

7.2.7 Give them a suitable take-home assignment. For instance, have them read a newspaper or a news magazine of their choice for one week. Ask them to make a list of what they consider to be instances of doublespeak, and bring this list to class on a specified day.

7.2.8 In class, form pairs and have them exchange their list with their partner's. After a brief conversation between partners, ask them to share some of their interesting examples with the class.

7.2.9 Based on the class discussion, ask them to draft a letter to the editor of the newspaper or the news magazine, drawing the editor's attention to doublespeak. Help them revise the draft, and encourage them to actually send the letter to the editor.

Exploratory Projects

I present ideas for a two-part exploratory project focusing on general and critical language awareness. Both parts deal with the concept of speech acts—what people actually do with language, like ordering, persuading, informing, instructing, negotiating, insulting, soothing, etc. Specifically, the project pertains to apologizing as a speech act, because the way people apologize differs from context to context, language to language, and culture to culture. This project then is aimed at creating language as well cultural awareness among L2 learners about the language of personal and political apologies.

Project 7.1: The Language of Personal Apologies

7.1.0 The objective of this part of the project is to design a classroom activity to make learners explore the language of personal apology in formal and informal contexts. Here are some suggestions for designing such an activity:

7.1.1 Imagine a couple of scenarios where people normally tender an apology, one in a formal context and another in an informal context—such as, a job-seeker apologizing to a potential employer for being late for a job interview, or a teenager apologizing to parents for returning home very late after a date on a Saturday night. Or, think of other scenarios that are suitable to your learning and teaching context.

7.1.2 Make a brief lesson plan about what the scenarios will be and how you will implement your plan.

7.1.3 Think about how you will introduce the scenarios. Would it be appropriate to start with a set of pre-activity questions to elicit from your students their own idea of an apology? If yes, what might be the actual questions?

7.1.4 Anticipate some possible student responses. What would be a good transitional strategy that can relate student responses to the two scenarios you have planned to use in class?

7.1.5 Think about the best way of carrying out the activity—through group work? Pair work? Role play? What would be the justification for your choice?

7.1.6 What are the ideas and issues you expect your learners to come up with during class discussion? And, how would you relate them to your objective of creating language awareness?

7.1.7 What are the ways in which you can explicitly draw your learners' attention to how English usage varies between formal and informal contexts for apologizing?

7.1.8 What are the ways in which you can help learners consciously think and talk about probable variations in the realization of apology as a speech act in L1 and L2 speech communities?

7.1.9 Think about difficulties—linguistic, conceptual, or communicative—you may have to anticipate and deal with in order to achieve your classroom objectives.

7.1.10 Finally, design an appropriate take-home writing assignment on linguistic and cultural variations in tendering a personal apology.

Project 7.2: The Language of Political Apologies

7.2.0 The objective of this part of the project is to design a classroom activity to make learners explore the language of political apology between nations or within a nation between various groups of people.

7.2.1 Recently, we have been witnessing a global phenomenon: official apologies emanating from political as well as religious leaders of the world for real or perceived human rights abuses of the past. Examine the archives of the on-line edition of a national newspaper (or a news magazine) of your choice. Go to any search engine on the Internet (such as Yahoo, Google) to find the web address of the newspaper or the news magazine you are interested in. Look for information on recent political apologies.

7.2.2 Your research may have revealed several instances of political apologies of a sensitive nature: (a) the Pope apologizing to Jews for the Vatican's indifference during the Holocaust, (b) Switzerland apologizing to Jews for the loss of their money deposited in Swiss banks during the Holocaust, (c) the United States apologizing to Japanese-Americans for their internment during the Second World War, (d) Japan apologizing to some of its Asian neighbors for treating enemy women as "comfort women," and (e) Australia trying to reconcile its past with an apology to the aboriginals in that country, and so on.

7.2.3 Select any one of the above five cases or any other similar case that you came up with in your archival research. Then, write an outline of a classroom activity—a step-by-step teaching strategy to make your learners aware of the complex factors (e.g., historical, political, national, cultural, linguistic) involved in political apologies, keeping in mind the proficiency level of your students.

7.2.4 Think about the best way of carrying out the classroom activity—through group work? Pair work? Role play? How to steer class discussion to achieve the major objective of creating critical language awareness?

7.2.5 Plan how to start the activity in class—for instance, how you would extend the earlier discussion on personal apologies to the concept of national or international apology.

7.2.6 If it is difficult to do archival research on the Internet, focus on current newspapers or news magazines and select stories of political apologies that are linguistically and conceptually appropriate to your class. I present below one such story; you may find several others.

In early April 2001, a Chinese interceptor plane and a U.S. intelligence plane collided off China's southern coast, killing the Chinese pilot, Wang Wei. The American spy plane with its twenty-four-member crew made a safe emergency landing on Hainan Island without formal approval from the Chinese control tower. The Chinese government demanded a formal apology from the American government. After a prolonged negotiation between the two countries, the matter was resolved. Here's how the on-line edition of the *Washington Post* reported the story (www.washingtonpost.com/wp-dyn/articles/A6425-2001Apr11 .html). Only one-third of the story is reproduced below, unedited.

Resolving Crisis Was a Matter of Interpretation
By John Pomfret
Washington Post Foreign Service
Thursday, April 12, 2001; Page A01
BEIJING, April 11—In the end, it was a matter of what the United States chose to say and what China chose to hear.

The letter that U.S. Ambassador Joseph W. Prueher handed to Chinese Foreign Minister Tang Jiaxuan today asked Tang to "convey to the Chinese people and to the family of pilot Wang Wei that we are very sorry for their loss." And it said, "We are very sorry the entering of China's airspace and the landing did not have verbal clearance."

The word "apology" did not appear in the English-language document handed to Tang. But in announcing the U.S. move and describing the letter to the Chinese people, China chose to translate the double "very sorry" as "shenbiao qianyi," which means "a deep expression of apology or regret."

And the deal was done, with both sides proclaiming they got what they wanted.

"In Chinese, you don't use that phrase unless you're admitting you're wrong and accepting responsibility," said Mei Renyi, director of the American Studies Center at Beijing Foreign Studies University. "If they're translating it that way, especially in the context of a formal letter, it means the U.S. is admitting it was wrong."

But a translation into Chinese released by the U.S. Embassy used other language. For "very sorry," it used the Chinese words "feichang wanxi," which linguists described as an expression of great sympathy but not an apology. It also used "feichang baoqian," or extremely sorry.

7.2.7 Write a detailed lesson plan using this or a similar news story of your choice. Think about how you can use a topical text like this to foster general as well as critical language awareness.

7.2.8 Plan how you will conduct your classroom activity in terms of group work, whole class discussion, etc.

7.2.9 Plan how you would highlight the use of translation between English and Chinese languages in this delicate diplomatic negotiation. If there are students in your class who know the Chinese language, plan how you can make use of their linguistic and cultural knowledge to enrich class discussion

7.2.10 Design an appropriate take-home writing assignment for your students on any aspect of political apologies.

7.2.11 Finally, reflect on the desirability or the difficulty of discussing topics such as political apology in your class—in other words, what difficulties you anticipate if you do decide to take up such topics for discussion in class. Later, compare your anticipated difficulties with how the students actually reacted to the classroom activity.

In Closing

An unmistakable lesson we learn from this chapter is that language awareness, general as well as critical, should form an integral part of language education as well as content education. Language awareness is essential for the realization of an individual's full potential and, through that, for the realization of a nation's democratic ideals. Fostering general and critical language awareness is one way of connecting the curricular agenda of a teaching program with the learning purpose of an individual learner, and both with contemporary sociopolitical order.

While language awareness activities are commonly associated with the development of advanced skills in critical thinking, reading, and writing, they are useful for grammar learning and teaching as well. Clearly, language awareness facilitates the process of noticing or consciousness-raising on the part of the learners. It is then possible that such a process of noticing could activate the learners' intuitive heuristics, ultimately enhancing their state of readiness to internalize the grammatical system of their L2. We will explore that possibility in the next chapter.

CHAPTER 8

Activating Intuitive Heuristics

> . . . give free play to those creative principles that
> humans bring to the process of language learning . . .
> (and) create a rich linguistic environment for the intu-
> itive heuristics that the normal human being automati-
> cally possesses.
> —NOAM CHOMSKY, 1970, p. 108

In educational contexts, *heuristics* refers to the process of self-discovery on the part of the learner. It also refers to a particular method of teaching—"a method of teaching allowing the students to learn by discovering things by themselves and learning from their own experiences rather than by telling them things" (*Cambridge International Dictionary of English*, 1995, p. 666). When applying it to language learning and teaching it means that an important task facing the language teacher is to create a rich linguistic environment in the classroom so that learners can activate their intuitive heuristics and discover the linguistic system by themselves. The concept of language awareness we discussed in the previous chapter is closely linked to intuitive heuristics. That is to say, one can increase one's language awareness by attempting to discover the rules and patterns of the linguistic system, and, conversely, one can enhance one's capacity to discover the linguistic system by increasing one's language awareness.

It is common knowledge that language is systematic and rule-governed. There are phonological rules that deal with the nature of sound systems in a language. There are syntactic rules that deal with the grammatical construction of morphemes and words into larger units of phrases, clauses, and sentences. There are semantic rules that deal with the way in which meaning in a language is structured. While all the systems and subsystems of a language are rule-governed, the one that teachers and learners readily associate

rigid rules with is grammar. I shall therefore discuss the macrostrategy of activating intuitive heuristics with particular reference to the
teaching of L2 grammar.

The primacy of grammar in language teaching has been recognized from time immemorial. However, an informed consensus on
how to teach grammar is yet to be reached. In his analysis of twenty-
five centuries of language teaching, Louis Kelly points out that "since
the beginning of language teaching the manner of learning the syntax
and flexions of language has been disputed. Accepted methods have
ranged from the inductive, by which the pupil himself arrives at rules
from examples, to the deductive whereby one proceeds from rules
to knowledge. At all periods of language teaching both have existed,
but never on an equal footing" (Louis Kelly, 1969, p. 34).

In spite of the historical truth that both inductive and deductive
methods have coexisted for a long time, scholars have reminded the
language teaching profession of the virtues of learner self-discovery,
and they have done so with remarkable consistency. Long before
Chomsky expressed his views in the above quotation, Henry Sweet
(1899–1964) had suggested that "the pre-grammatical stage may be
utilized to convey a good deal of grammatical information not directly through rules, but indirectly through examples, so that when
the learner comes to the rule, he finds that he knows it already, or,
at any rate, has advanced half-way towards knowing it" (p. 128).
Even stronger views were expressed by Otto Jesperson (1904), who
advocated what he called an "Inventional Grammar" created by
learners themselves as they gained insights into the underlying patterns of grammar based on their discovery process.

The refrain of learner self-discovery has continued unabated in
recent times as well. William Rutherford (1987), for instance, uses
the term *grammaticization* to focus more on the psycholinguistic
processes governing the relationship between grammatical products
such as the passive, the relative clauses, etc., than on the grammatical products themselves. Through the process of grammaticization
"the learner is constantly engaged in reanalysing data, reformulat-
ing hypotheses, recasting generalizations, etc." (Rutherford, 1987,
p. 159). Diane Larsen-Freeman (2000) uses an even more elegant
term, *grammaring*, to focus more on reasoning than on rules. Both
grammaticization and grammaring seek to help learners discover
powerful patterns underlying the linguistic system. The persistent
emphasis on a process-oriented approach to grammar teaching has

serious consequences to the learning and teaching of L2 grammar because, as Eric Hawkins (1984, pp. 150–1) concludes: "Grammar, approached as a voyage of discovery into the patterns of the language rather than the learning of prescriptive rules, is no longer a bogey word."

Reflective task 8.1

Based on your experience as a language learner (and teacher), consider the usefulness of self-discovery in learning/teaching the grammatical system of an L2. Compare your thoughts with those of another person, if possible.

The logic of preferring reasoning over rules appears to be fairly simple. What is not so simple is the way such logic can be translated into the practice of everyday teaching. Let us turn to that complex issue.

Grammar in Action

In the true spirit of heuristics, let us first try to discover what the teachers in the following interactional episodes actually do in the classroom to help their learners understand the pattern underlying certain grammatical rules. The interactional episodes are taken from two different grammar classes taught by two different teachers. The classes consisted of high intermediate to low advanced ESL learners.

The teacher in episode 8.1 was focusing on adverbial clauses. The day before the class, she had asked her students to read one unit of a lesson in the prescribed book. The unit presented definitions of *clause, dependent clause, independent clause*, etc., followed by a series of fill-in-the-blank-type questions. The students were supposed to have read the lesson and come prepared with the answers. Study the classroom interaction:

Episode 8.1

1   T: Who wants to try number one?

2   S: (reads from the text) A clause is a group of words containing a subject and a verb.

3   T: All right. Does everybody agree? Is that all right? hmm . . . All right. Look at number two and fill in the blanks. Who wants to try number two? . . . Yes . . .

4   S: (reads from the text) A dependent . . . independent clause is a complete sentence. It contains the main subject and verb of sentence. It is also called a main clause.

5   T: Right, everybody agrees? Let's try to do number three.

6   S: A dependent clause is not a complete sentence.

7   T: All right.

8   S: The dependent clause?

9   T: The dependent clause . . . right.

10   S: Must be connected to the independent clause.

11   T: All right. Is that clear? . . . OK. eh . . . let's see now . . . number four. What would be your answer, S1?

12   S1:   Yah . . . main clause . . .

13   T: Main clause. Agreed, everybody? OK?

14   Ss: Yah.

15   T: Right. Now, answer this question: does a dependent clause have a subject and a verb?

16   Ss: Yah.

17   T: Yes, fine. Can it stand alone as a sentence?

18   Ss: Yes.

19   T: eh . . . mmm. Now, let's go to the dependent clause. Same question. Does it have a subject and a verb?

20   S: No.

21   S: Yah.

22   S: Yah.

23   S: No.

24   T: (in a very authoritative tone) Who said no?
25   Ss: Yes.
26   T: a . . . ah . . . (showing strong approval)
27   S: Yes.
28   T: Right. Now . . .

(Data source: Kumaravadivelu, 1992, p. 46)

Reflective task 8.2

Consider the teacher's instructional method. Is it good enough to foster language awareness? Is it good enough to activate intuitive heuristics? What would you have done differently?

Now consider episode 8.2. The teacher in this class was focusing on complex sentences with cause and effect relationships. She did not use any textbook in this episode. Instead, she distributed a humorous cartoon with the caption "a modern way to eat your apple." It pictured a rat jumping on a piece of cheese, a candle, a rope, a fifty-pound weight, an apple, and a human face with a wide-open mouth. The initial action of the rat jumping on the cheese triggers a series of actions that will ultimately pop the apple into the person's mouth. Here is a part of the interaction:

Episode 8.2

1   T: What happens if the rat or the mouse doesn't jump on the cheese?
2   S1: The man . . . doesn't eat the apple.
3   T: Doesn't eat the apple?
4   S2: The man has to use his hands.
5   T: Yes, imagine the man doesn't want to use his hands. The man . . .
6   S1: Will not eat the apple xxx

7	T:	What happens if the candle doesn't burn the rope?
8	S3:	The weight . . . the weight will not fall down . . .
9	T:	OK, the weight won't . . . (writes on board)
10	S3:	Won't fall down.
11	T:	What happens after the candle burns the rope?
12	S:	The weight will . . .
13	T:	The weight will fall down. eh . . . use a consequence. Connect one action to another action . . . using a word like . . . eh . . .
14	S4:	If . . .
15	T:	If . . . that might be good example. S4?
16	S4:	If rat does not eat the cheese the candle won't . . . won't burn the rope . . .
17	T:	OK, the candle won't burn the rope. Use another word like . . . "when" . . .
18	S3:	When the rat eats the cheese, the candle will burn.
19	T:	A . . . hmm. Use another word like eh . . . "after."
20	S5:	After the weight fall down, the apple will throw up . . .
21	T:	Throw up? S6? Will . . .
22	S6:	Will be thrown up.
23	T:	Will be thrown up. Right. And use another one like . . . "unless" . . .
24	S:	The 50-pound weight won't fall down unless the rope is burned.
25	T:	Good. Yes . . . (writes on the board) You can connect any of these two actions with any of these words. What do you notice about this part?
26	S:	will xxx
27	T:	Yes . . . it is always going to have something to do with "will." Do you notice over here . . .
28	S:	Present xx
29	T:	Always present tense. This is our new unit. We will start with complex sentences of this nature using relationships that involve cause and effect, OK?

(Data source: Kumaravadivelu, 1992, p. 45)

Reflective task 8.3

Pause here for a moment and think about what the teacher in episode 8.2 has been able to achieve that the teacher in 8.1 has not. And, how did she manage to do that?

Let us compare the two episodes. The teacher in episode 8.1 is interested mainly in eliciting grammatical descriptions that can be easily lifted from the handout, with either no or partial understanding on the part of the learner. With her mode of presentation, she has not only minimized the creation of learning opportunity in class but has resisted any attempt on the part of the learner to seek any clarification. For instance, in turn 8 a student has doubts about the answer given by another student (turn 6) and says with a rising intonation: "the dependent clause?" The teacher, instead of clearing the learner's confusion, merely asserts: "the dependent clause . . . right" (turn 9) and moves on. On another occasion, two learners (turns 20 and 23) say "no" to the question whether a dependent clause has a subject and a verb. Their incorrect response prompts no more than a stern disapproval (turn 24: "Who said no?") from the teacher, which triggers a choral "yes" from the class.

In the end, neither the teacher nor the those two learners seem to understand what each other is trying say. If the teacher had given a few examples and asked the learners to analyze them, they would have had an opportunity to find out more about how dependent and independent clauses are structured in English. The teacher's preoccupation with grammatical description may have even been an obstacle to grammar learning. What seems to be clear is that in her enthusiasm to deal with the grammatical rules governing dependent/independent clauses in English, the teacher missed an opportunity to create the kind of linguistic environment that is necessary to activate the learners' intuitive heuristics.

In sharp contrast, the teacher in episode 8.2 asks a series of questions for which the answers cannot be lifted from the distributed material. Her method of presentation seems to actively engage the learners' minds. Like the teacher in the previous episode, she, too, focuses explicitly on grammar (turn 17: "use another word like . . .

'when'"; turn 19: "Use another word like eh . . . 'after'"; turn 23: "use another one like . . . 'unless'") and error correction (turn 23: "will be thrown up"). However, she does not even mention the teaching item of grammatical relations involving cause and effect for the first twenty-eight interactional turns. She gradually and logically leads the learners to think and talk about that relationship. She successfully elicits from them the main grammatical item that she wants to highlight (see turns 26 and 28) before she herself mentions it in turn 29.

Even in an explicitly grammar focused class, the teacher in this episode has involved the learners in a meaningful conversational exchange. She appears to have created learning opportunities, promoted interaction in class, and fostered general language awareness. In the process of doing all this, she also appears to have succeeded in activating the intuitive heuristics of her learners.

Evidently, the two teachers have followed two different methods of teaching grammar. The first one has followed a deductive method and the second an inductive method. Let us consider these two methods of grammar teaching in relation to their usefulness for activating intuitive heuristics.

Deductive Teaching and Intuitive Heuristics

In a typical deductive method of teaching grammar, the teacher presents learners with a set of grammatical rules, offers explicit explanations of those rules, and then provides opportunities for learners to practice them. After adequate practice, the learners are expected to use those rules in their speech and writing. Although such a method of grammar teaching is widespread, there are concerns about its feasibility as well as its desirability.

The suitability of a deductive method of grammar teaching has been called into question by theoretical as well as applied linguists. The preeminent linguist Chomsky firmly believes that one does not learn the grammatical structure of a second language through "explanation and instruction" beyond the most rudimentary elements, for the simple reason that no one has enough explicit knowledge about this structure to provide explanation and instruction (Chomsky, 1970). What he implies is that the linguistic system of a language, any language, is so complex that even theoretical linguists who spend their lives trying to describe, explain, and understand it have not been able to do so satisfactorily. Therefore, it is too much to expect either the language teacher or the language learner to do so.

Of course, it could be argued that, unlike theoretical linguists who are concerned with the principles and parameters of an overall grammatical system in order to derive a comprehensive theory of syntax, language teachers are interested only in what is called *pedagogical grammar* that has been selected and simplified to meet the needs of L2 learners. But even that simplification is not as simple as it seems. As Rutherford (1987, p. 17), echoing Chomsky, asks: "The most brilliant linguists can as yet come nowhere near knowing fully what constitute the proper generalizations and the correct formulations of the rule of English syntax, then, how can anything of this sort, in whatever 'simplified' form, be profitably 'taught' by any teacher or 'learned' by any learner?" The pedagogical grammar of even a language like English—one of the most analyzed and studied languages in the world—remains unsatisfactory, prompting a prominent pedagogical grammarian to conclude: "Pedagogical grammar is not static: Many problems remain to be understood, and until they are, second language teaching will depend on guesswork" (Terence Odlin, 1994, p. 11).

In spite of persistent questions about the feasibility of explicit grammar description and instruction, the deductive method of grammar teaching has long been a desired method for many teachers and learners. They see certain advantages to it. For example, many adult L2 learners, particularly those who bring an analytical approach to language learning, would like explicit description and instruction of grammatical rules so that they can consciously analyze them to understand how the linguistic system works. They can also use the explicit grammar rules for language practice and for error correction. Some learners may even use explicit rules to work out the similarities and differences between their L1 and L2.

The deductive approach with its explicit description and explanation of grammar rules may have its advantages for teaching grammar to adults. However, with regard to the specific purpose of activating learners' intuitive heuristics, it has only limited use. The reason is simple: it encourages very little teacher-learner interaction and almost no learner-learner interaction that is necessary to create an environment conducive to self-discovery. Once a grammatical rule is explicitly stated, the natural tendency of the learners will be not to think about its underlying rationale—a tendency that might lead to a superficial knowledge rather than a sound understanding of the rule. This might be one reason why we often come across learners who can supply the correct grammar on a class test but cannot use it for communicative purposes outside the class.

Reflective task 8.4

With reference to your specific L2 learning and teaching situation, what features of the deductive method would you keep and what features would you give up or modify? Why?

Inductive Teaching and Intuitive Heuristics

The inductive approach is based on the premise that the essence of grammar teaching lies in helping learners discover what the grammatical rules are. Teachers present their learners with contextualized oral and written samples of a grammatical element, draw their attention to it in different ways, and guide them to see and hear the underlying pattern. They avoid explicit description and explanation, and minimize the use of technical terms, at least at the initial stages of teaching a particular grammatical item. Learners analyze the samples provided to them and try to develop a working hypothesis that can later be confirmed or rejected based on additional information and experience.

It is easy to see why the inductive method of teaching is well suited to activate the intuitive heuristics of the learner. In inductive teaching, learners have an opportunity to encounter a grammatical structure or a language expression "several times in contexts where its relationship to the design of the language may be observed, and its meaning (structural, lexical, and socio-cultural) inductively absorbed from its use in such varying situations" (Rivers, 1964, p. 152). Such encounters can help them infer the underlying rules and principles governing the communicative use of grammatical structures. It can also help them see grammar "as a comprehensive conglomerate, uniting all the levels of structure or rule complexes of a language, viz. the structure of words and phrases, the structure of sentences, the structure of texts and the structure of interaction"

(Dirven, 1990, pp. 7–8). Thus, the inductive teaching of grammar has the potential to activate the learners' intuitive heuristics and stimulate their working hypotheses not only about a grammatical subsystem but also about the L2 system as a whole.

It is then fair to assume that learning through self-discovery rather than learning from teacher explanation will favorably affect grammar learning in particular and language learning in general. If the teachers have the ability to devise creative exercises and if the learners have the ability to derive probable generalizations based on the presented data and classroom interaction, then the inductive method will prove to be highly beneficial. After all, learners will be able to comprehend and retain better if they themselves discover the grammatical rules.

The emphasis on the inductive mode of presentation is not meant to prohibit the use of explicit explanation through form-focused activities. Instead, what needs to be seriously considered is whether the presentation of definitions and rules should be preceded by the presentation of relevant data, promotion of negotiated interaction, and fostering of language awareness; and, whether a judicious combination of the inductive and deductive methods of teaching will be more effective. Developments in research on L2 grammar learning and teaching indicate that with suitable instructional modifications, teachers can strike a balance along the inductive-deductive continuum. I shall discuss these developments under the rubric input enhancement and intuitive heuristics.

Reflective task 8.5

What difficulties do you anticipate if you wish to follow the inductive method of grammar teaching? Consider factors such as your own teacher preparation, textbooks, learner attitudes, etc. How would you overcome some of the difficulties you've identified?

Input Enhancement and Intuitive Heuristics

Input enhancement can be considered to encompass two interrelated acts of *consciousness-raising* and *noticing the gap*, both of which have a direct bearing on activating learners' intuitive heuristics. Although the term *input enhancement* is originally used in the L2 literature to refer more to consciousness-raising activities than to noticing the gap activities, for reasons that will become clear I use it here as a cover term to refer to both.

Consciousness-Raising

Put simply, consciousness-raising (C-R) refers to a deliberate attempt to draw the learner's explicit attention to features of the target language, particularly to its grammatical features. This may look deceptively similar to traditional grammar teaching, but, as Rutherford points out, C-R differs from it in fundamental ways. First, C-R "is a means to attainment of grammatical competence . . . whereas 'grammar teaching' typically represents an attempt to instill that competence directly" (Rutherford, 1987, p. 24). Second, C-R treats an explicit focus on grammar as necessary *but not* sufficient for developing grammatical competence whereas traditional grammar teaching treats it as necessary *and* sufficient. Third, C-R acknowledges the learner's active role in grammar construction; traditional grammar teaching considers the learner *tabula rasa*, a blank slate. Finally, traditional grammar teaching is concerned mainly with syntax, while C-R is concerned with syntax and its relation to semantics, discourse, and pragmatics.

Because the term *consciousness* does not lend itself to a clear-cut definition, Sharwood Smith (1991) suggested *input enhancement* in the place of *consciousness-raising*. The new term correctly shifts the attention from an internal process related to what happens in the mind to an external operation related to input and interaction. According to Rutherford and Sharwood Smith, there are simple ways in which input enhancement can be effected. They include color coding or bold-faced type for selected linguistic features in reading texts, pointing out an error in speech or writing, and asking learners to unscramble sentences of a paragraph and provide their reasons for reordering.

Classroom interactional episode 8.2 discussed above, for instance, illustrates how input can be enhanced through negotiated interaction in class. In that episode, what was made salient was not just the grammatical product of cause-effect relationship but the process of grammaticization, that is, the ability to handle form-meaning relationship with particular reference to grammatical clauses in English. The process of grammaticization also involves making the connection between propositional content and syntactic forms within a communicative context. The episode also shows that through proper management of classroom interaction, teachers can help learners notice the gap between their current level of knowledge and the target level they wish to achieve.

Noticing the Gap

Learners' ability to notice the gap between what they already know and what they need to know is, of course, crucial for making progress in language learning. Schmidt and Frota (1986, p. 311), who proposed what is called the "notice the gap principle," categorically state that "a second language learner will begin to acquire the target-like form if and only if it is present in comprehended input and 'noticed' in the normal sense of the word, that is consciously." In order to notice the gap, learners have to first recognize that there is something to be learned. Susan Gass (1997, p. 4) calls this *apperception*— "an internal cognitive act in which a linguistic form is related to some bit of existing knowledge (or gap in knowledge)." By making the selected linguistic features noticeable or recognizable, teachers can aid learners in their cognitive act of connecting the known to the new.

Both consciousness-raising and noticing the gap activities sensitize learners to the way linguistic systems work. The act of consciousness-raising is largely external to learners, that is, teachers can create the conditions necessary for raising learners' consciousness about aspects of linguistic properties. They can do that by providing sufficient linguistic data for their learners to formulate their own working hypotheses about a particular grammatical rule. They can also do that by promoting meaningful classroom interaction centering on the selected linguistic features. Of course, learners themselves can raise their own consciousness to some extent. The act of noticing the gap, however, is entirely internal to learners, that is, they have to make an effort to notice the gap in their developing linguistic knowledge. Thus, by making learners become aware of the need to pay attention to various aspects of language use, input enhancing activities contribute to the activation of their intuitive heuristics.

Reflective task 8.6

What type of classroom activities do you think will help you raise your learners' consciousness and prompt them to notice language features?

Input Enhancement in Action

Current literature on L2 grammar learning and teaching presents several types of activities to achieve the goals of input enhancement. I shall highlight two of them: grammar tasks advocated by Rod Ellis and his colleagues, and pedagogic tasks advocated by Michael Long and his colleagues.

GRAMMAR TASKS

Based on a series of studies, Ellis and his colleagues (see Ellis, 1997, 1999 for comprehensive reviews) suggest the use of what they call grammar tasks or grammar discovery tasks to help learners gain cognitive understanding of grammar. They argue that it does not really matter whether grammar discovery tasks are inductive or deductive so long as these tasks are designed to offer a range of data options and a range of learner operations that can be performed on them.

The data options include:

- Authentic vs. contrived (whether or not the data consist of text prepared by competent speakers for other competent speakers for purposes other than language teaching).
- Oral vs. written (whether the data represent spoken language or written language). Spoken language data can be made available to the learner in the form of a recording or, more likely, by means of a transcription.
- Discrete sentences vs. continuous text (whether the data consist of a series of disconnected sentences or continuous discourse).
- Well-formed vs. deviant (whether the data conform to the norms of the target variety or whether they include deviations from these norms, as, for example, in grammaticality judgment tasks).
- Gap vs. non-gap (whether the data are distributed among the learn-

ers in such a way that the information contained in the data has to be shared or whether each learner has access to all data).

(Ellis, 1997, p. 161)

The learner operations that can be performed on the data include:

- Identification (the learners are invited to identify incidents of a specific feature in the data by, for example, underlining it).
- Judgment (the learners are invited to judge the correctness or appropriateness of features in the data).
- Completion (the learners are invited to complete a text, for example, by filling in blanks as in a cloze passage or by selecting from choices supplied).
- Modification (the learners are invited to modify a text in some way, for example, by replacing one item with another, by reordering elements in the text, by inserting some additional item into the text, or by rewriting part of it).
- Sorting (the learners are invited to classify specific items present in the data by sorting them into defined categories).
- Matching (the learners are invited to match two sets of data according to some stated principle).
- Rule provision (in the case of inductive tasks learners may or may not be asked to give a rule to account for the phenomena they have investigated; the rule can be presented verbally or nonverbally).

(Ellis, 1997, p. 161)

A close reading of these data options and learner operations clearly indicates that they can be used in teacher-directed classes as well as in pair or group interactive settings.

Reproduced in Figure 8.1 is a task designed by Fotos and Ellis taken from Ellis (1999, pp. 207–8), which illustrates how to activate the learners' intuitive heuristics about an aspect of L2 grammar. It focuses on the use of dative verbs in English. Designed as a pair or small group work, it consists of (1) task cards (Appendix A in the original text) with a list of grammatical and ungrammatical sentences illustrating the use of dative verbs, specifying which are correct and which are incorrect; and (2) a task sheet (Appendix B in the original text) with some grammatical information about dative verbs and a chart to fill in for each of the verbs for which data has been supplied. It also gives directions asking the learners to formulate three rules about the use of dative verbs. Study the task in detail.

It can be easily seen that the above task skillfully combines the elements of a purely grammar-focused instruction with possibilities for meaningful interaction. It makes grammar the topic of class-room communication. As Ellis (1999, p. 206) points out, grammar tasks "provide opportunities to communicate in the L2 in groups or pairs, and they encourage an active, discovery-oriented approach on the part of the learners." Grammar tasks, then, are aimed at rais-ing the learners' consciousness about the grammatical properties of the L2 thereby facilitating the process of noticing the gap, and ulti-mately activating their intuitive heuristics.

Appendix A: Task cards

Students in groups of 4—one different card to each member
Students in pair—two different cards to each member

1.	Correct:	I asked my friend a question
1.	Incorrect:	She asked a question to her mother
2.	Correct:	Kimiko reviewed the lesson for John
2.	Incorrect:	Kimiko reviewed John the lesson
3.	Correct:	The teacher calculated the answers for the students
3.	Incorrect:	The teacher calculated students' answer
4.	Correct:	The secretary reported the problem to her boss
4.	Incorrect:	The student reported the teacher the matter
5.	Correct:	I offered her a cup of tea
5.	Correct:	I offered a cup of tea to the president
6.	Correct:	The teacher pronounced the difficult word for the class
6.	Incorrect:	The teacher pronounced the class the difficult word
7.	Correct:	I bought many presents for my family
7.	Correct:	I bought my family several presents
8.	Correct:	She cooked a delicious dinner for us
8.	Correct:	She cooked us a wonderful meal
9.	Correct:	She suggested a plan to me
9.	Incorrect:	She suggested me a good restaurant
10.	Correct:	The teacher repeated the question for the student
10.	Incorrect:	The teacher repeated the student the question

Figure 8.1

Appendix B: Task Sheets

There are verbs in English that can have two objects. One of the objects is called the direct object. The other is called the indirect object. An indirect object names the person for whom the action of the verb is performed.

Indirect object   direct object
She   wrote   Susan   a letter.

  Different verbs may have the objects in different order, and this is often a problem for students of English. The following exercise will help you understand some confusing verbs.

Directions: In groups, you are to study correct and incorrect sentences using different verbs. You all have different sentences. You must read your sentences to the rest of the group. Do not show your sentences to the other members. Read the sentences only as many times as necessary. Work together as a group and decide on the basis of the correct and incorrect sentences where the indirect objects should be located. Fill out the rest of this page. Choose one student to report your results to the rest of the class. Please speak only in English during this exercise.

Verbs: Possible correct order of direct and indirect object
asked:
reviewed:
calculated:
reported:
offered:
pronounced:
bought:
cooked:
suggested:
repeated:

Conclusion: Write 3 rules concerning the possible order of objects.
Rule 1: _____
Verbs which follow this rule: _____
Rule 2: _____
Verbs which follow this rule: _____
Rule 3: _____
Verbs which follow this rule: _____

(Data source: Ellis, 1999, p. 207–8)

Figure 8.1 (continued)

Reflective task 8.7

If you believe that grammar tasks are relevant for your learning and teaching context, what constraints do you anticipate in designing and using them in your class? Lack of resources? Lack of time? Lack of training? Some other restraint? And, how can you try to overcome some of the constraints?

PEDAGOGIC TASKS

Pedagogic tasks, like grammar discovery tasks, aim at input enhancement in terms of consciousness-raising and noticing the gap, but seek to achieve that aim in a very different way. Unlike grammar discovery tasks, which focus primarily and explicitly on the grammatical form, pedagogic tasks draw the learners' attention to it if and only if it is absolutely necessary to carry out the communicative activities and negotiation of meaning in class.

In this context, Long and his colleagues (see Long, 1991, and Doughty and Williams, ed., 1998) make a distinction between *focus on form* and *focus on formS (plural)*. The former refers to meaning-focused activities in which an attention to form is secondary and implicit, whereas the latter refers to grammar-focused activities in which an attention to form is primary and explicit. Focus on form "overtly draws students' attention to linguistic elements as they arise incidentally in lessons whose overriding focus is on meaning or communication" (Long, 1991, pp. 45–6). It entails a prerequisite engagement in meaning before attention to grammatical forms can be expected to be effective, that is, the meaning of an utterance must be evident to learners before their attention is drawn to the grammatical features embedded in that utterance. It constitutes an occasional shift of attention to grammatical forms by teachers or learners when they notice problems with comprehension or production (Long and Robinson, 1998, p. 23).

While stressing their preference for activities that focus on form over activities that focus on formS, Long and his colleagues stress that "focus on formS and focus on form are *not* polar opposites in the way that *form* and *meaning* have often been considered to be. Rather, focus on form *entails* a focus on formal elements of language; whereas focus on formS is *limited* to such a focus, and focus on meaning *excludes* it" (Doughty and Williams, 1998, p. 4, all italics as in original).

The basic principles of focus on form can be implemented through any of the communicative activities that make the learners preoccupied with meaning rather than form. These activities include attending a job interview, making an airline reservation, reading a journal abstract, writing a lab report, or locating a book in the library. To give a specific activity suggested by Long and Robinson, (1998, pp. 24–5), learners may be asked to work in pairs or in small groups on a problem-solving task that requires them to collect and synthesize information on economic growth in Japan. They may be required to read published reports on economic trends for different sectors of the Japanese economy.

Long and Robinson point out that, in doing this task on economy, learners are likely to come across terms such as rose, fell, grew, sank, plummeted, increased, decreased, declined, doubled, deteriorated, and exceeded. The frequent occurrence of these lexical items in the input makes them salient, and so increases the likelihood of being noticed by learners. A subsequent speaking or writing task may encourage the learners to incorporate them in their speech or writing. Certain grammatical items can be dealt with in an appropriate manner if there is an expressed need for it.

Reflective task 8.8

Are pedagogic tasks designable and doable in your specific learning and teaching context? If not, and if you wish to design them and use them, how can you make use of the resources (however limited they are) you may already have at your disposal?

To sum up this section, it is fair to assume from the above discussion that grammar tasks and pedagogic tasks offer two complementary types of input enhancement. Together, they can help teachers to meet the needs of learners with different learning styles and learning purposes. They carry the potential to assist teachers in their attempt to activate their intuitive heuristics by raising learners' awareness of linguistic features and language use. Gliding comfortably along the inductive-deductive continuum, they offer several options for teachers to design and implement microstrategies that are appropriate to the needs and wants of their learners.

Microstrategies for Activating Intuitive Heuristics

The grammar of a language consists of a number of systems such as time and tense, prepositions, articles, interrogatives, etc., and several subsystems within each. For the purpose of designing microstrategies for activating the learner's intuitive heuristics, teachers can select any of the grammatical subsystems suitable to the proficiency level of their students. In designing microstrategies, teachers may find it useful to consult a good pedagogic grammar book such as *A Communicative Grammar of English* (Leech and Svartvik, 1980) or *The Grammar Book* (Celce-Murcia and Larsen-Freeman, 1983). Also useful are learner resource books such as *Grammar Practice Activities* (Ur, 1988) and teacher resource books such as *About Language* (Thornbury, 1997). The activities and tasks given in these grammar-based books can be easily adapted to suit the needs and wants of a specific group of learners. Given below are two illustrative microstrategies on different aspects of the English grammatical system.

Microstrategy 8.1: Articles of Trouble

8.1.0 The article system in English is one of most troublesome aspects of English grammar for L2 learners to learn to use satisfactorily. In this microstrategy, I focus on a subset of the article system dealing with basic features of the definite (*the*) and the indefinite (*a, an,* and ∅ [zero]) articles, and present one way of teaching them. You may wish to modify the suggested steps depending on what your learners already know or do not know. Keep the main objective in mind, i.e., creating conditions for activating learners' intuitive heuristics (conditions that also promote negotiated interaction and foster language awareness).

8.1.1 Write on the board (or project on the OHP screen) two or three clusters of simple sentences to illustrate singular count nouns with indefinite/definite references. Here's a sample cluster:

There is *a* table in this classroom.

There is *a* book on *the* table.

The book belongs to me.

8.1.2 Ask the learners in pairs or in small groups to study the sample sentences and suggest possible rules governing the use of *a* and *the* in these sentences. Depending on their responses, ask leading questions and/or give more sample sentences till they reach a reasonable degree of understanding.

8.1.3 By way of testing their understanding, give a cluster of sentences like

John bought——book and——calculator yesterday.

He returned——book but kept——calculator.

with all the articles deleted. Ask them to supply the missing articles and justify their response.

8.1.4 Write on the board (or project on the OHP screen) clusters of simple sentences like the ones given below:

There is *an* apple on the table.

There is also *an* orange on the table.

The apple is fully ripe but *the* orange is not.

8.1.5 Have your students study the data and generate the rules governing the use of *an* and *the*. Ask them to explain their reasoning. Then give clusters of sentences deleting the articles and ask them to supply the missing ones and justify their response. Follow up their work with a class discussion.

8.1.6 Using leading questions and appropriate sample data, help your learners understand that we use the definite article when the speaker(s) and the hearer(s) know what is being talked about, which is not the case when we use the indefinite articles. Turn now to other contexts in which the definite article is used. Give sample data such as

The stars; the earth; the moon
(where the reference is to only one object or the group of objects that exists or has existed);

The press; the media; the parliament
(where the reference is to an institution shared by the community);

The president; the queen
(where the reference is understood to be unique in the context);

The tiger is a beautiful animal
(where the reference is to what is general or typical of a whole class of objects);

and ask the learners in pairs or in small groups to find out and explain the rules governing these usages. Discuss their response suitably.

8.1.7 Now, extend the focus to include use of the zero article before first mentions of plural countable nouns and uncountable (mass) nouns. Again, provide your learners with a cluster of appropriate examples, such as

> There are ∅ apples on the table;
>
> There are ∅ books on the table;
>
> There is ∅ grass in my garden;

and ask them in pairs or in small groups to find out and explain the rules governing these usages.

8.1.8 Ask your students to bring a newspaper to class. In pairs, have them select a few headlines, insert suitable articles into the headlines, and then rewrite each of the headlines in complete sentence form. Have them also focus on any variation of meaning if the article usage is varied.

8.1.9 Select a short text that is linguistically and conceptually appropriate to your learners, one which also has a variety of article usages. Delete each of the articles and insert a blank of equal length (——). Remember to insert a blank wherever the ∅ article occurs. Ask your learners to fill in each blank with *a, an, the*, or ∅ on their own in class. Then they should form pairs, exchange their completed work, and discuss each other's responses. Then, ask each pair to talk before the class about one item that they were not able to agree on. Ask other students in class to resolve the differences; you should step in only if they are not able to do it by themselves.

8.1.10 Finally, reflect on (a) the degree to which this kind of activity achieves your objective of activating the learners' intuitive heuristics, and (b) the feasibility and the desirability of designing and implementing a microstrategy like this, in terms of your time, effort, and the result. Also think about which part of the activity you will keep, which part you will modify, and why.

Microstrategy 8.2: Dictating Grammar

8.2.0 *Dictogloss* as a grammar task was originally popularized by Ruth Wajnryb (1990). It encourages learners to communicate about grammar and, through the process of communication, makes them "confront their own strengths and weaknesses" (1990, p.10) and find out what they need to know. A dictogloss task has the potential to result in a context-sensitive knowledge of grammatical rules because form, function, and meaning are so intimately linked in the way this task is normally done (Swain, 1995). It basically involves listening to a short text dictated by the teacher, taking notes, reconstructing the text, and identifying the gap between the reconstructed and the original text in addition to all the negotiated interaction that goes with the process. The following microstrategy reflects the general thrust of a dictogloss task.

8.2.1   Select (or write) a short but dense text (just a short paragraph will do) dealing with any topic that is being discussed in class. It should include grammatical features just introduced or about to be introduced. Make sure that the linguistic level of the text is at or slightly above the current level of your students.

8.2.2   In class, give clear directions as to what you expect the learners to do. At this stage of the task, they need to listen to your dictation carefully and take notes as fast, and as much, as they can. Read the text twice at normal speed, which should prevent them from taking down the text verbatim.

8.2.3   Have them work together in small groups and reconstruct the text as accurately as possible, putting together notes from all the members of the group. Ask them to think aloud and talk about the content as well as the grammatical features of the text they just heard. As a group, they have to arrive at a consensus version of the text.

8.2.4   Write the short text on the board (or project it on the OHP screen). Ask your learners, once again in their groups, to analyze and compare their version with the original version, in terms of content as well as grammar.

8.2.5   Ask each group to report back to class. Let them first focus on the message as well as the grammatical features they got right.

8.2.6   Do 8.2.5 again, this time focusing on the message they missed as well as the grammatical features they did not get right.

8.2.7   In class discussion, first focus on the message of the text and help them understand it. Do it inductively or deductively as you deem appropriate given the response of your students.

8.2.8   Now, focus on the grammatical features. Highlight what you need to highlight, that is, their success or failure in noticing what they are supposed to notice.

8.2.9   Finally, ask the learners what they were able to learn from the process of doing the dictogloss task. By asking leading questions, try to find out whether the task achieved its purpose of raising their language awareness, of helping them notice the gap, etc.

Exploratory Projects

With some basic exploratory research projects, teachers should be able to design microstrategies like the ones illustrated above. I present below two such projects, one dealing predominantly with focus on formS and the other predominantly with focus on form, but both attempt to activate the learner's intuitive heuristics.

Project 8.1: Focus on FormS

8.1.0 The purpose of this project is to help you explore how to plan for teaching a grammatical subsystem keeping in mind the overall objective of activating the learner's intuitive heuristics. Luckily, you do not have to reinvent grammar; all you need to do is to consult the resources that are already available (see above for a sample list of four books) and make use of them for designing grammar tasks. For the purpose of illustrating a doable project, I focus on a deceptively simple grammatical item in English: present progressive (also called present continuous). You may do this project individually or with another colleague.

8.1.1 A common textbook explanation for present progressive is that it is used to describe an action in progress. Taking this explanation at the face value, write down a couple of sentences to exemplify present progressive.

8.1.2 Study the following six different uses for the present progressive and write down at least one example for each.

1. To describe events/situations in progress at the moment of speaking
2. To describe temporary situations in the present, though not necessarily at the moment of speaking
3. To describe changing or developing situations in the present
4. To describe repeated events or situations (with always, constantly, forever, etc.)
5. To describe the background to an event in the present
6. To describe a present arrangement for a future event

(Data source: Thornbury, 1997, p. 80)

8.1.3 Keeping in mind the proficiency level of your students, select one or a combination of these six uses and think of possible ways of introducing them to your students in such a way as to prompt them to guess the general rules governing their use.

8.1.4 Having been told repeatedly that the present progressive is used to describe an action in progress, L2 learners of English, at least at the initial level of grammar learning, wonder why a sentence like *I am leaving for Washington tomorrow* is considered grammatically correct. Think about ways of helping them reflect on the connection between the present progressive and future time reference.

8.1.5 Read the following:

> We all know that the present continuous tense is used to describe actions that are taking place now. However, native speakers do not use this tense to describe people's actions all the time. We don't spend our time saying "Look. I'm opening the door. I'm drinking a cup of tea . . . etc." That's not how we use the present continuous. We actually use it when there is some point, some value in commenting on people's actions. So we might ring home and say "Oh, what's John doing at the moment?" It's a reasonable question since we can't see him and don't know the answer to the question.
>
> (Data source: Harmer, 1991, p. 56)

Think of a couple of other scenarios in which present progressive can be used in a communicatively appropriate sense. Having told your students that the present progressive is used to describe an action in progress, how would you help them understand the absurdity of a sentence like *Look, I'm opening the door*? In other words, how would you help them connect communicative appropriateness with grammatical correctness in this particular grammatical context?

8.1.6 A general rule prevents the use of the present progressive in English with stative verbs such as *see, love,* etc. However, read the following:

> For example, the following verb form would appear to violate a rule in English which says the *-ing* of the progressive aspect cannot be attached to a stative verb such as love:
>   I am loving every minute of my class.
>   And yet, most English speakers would agree that combining the progressive aspect with a stative verb, as has been done in this example, accomplishes the special effect of intensifying the emotion expressed by the verb, which makes it at least conversationally acceptable, and meaningful, in English.
>
> (Data source: Larsen Freeman, 2000, p. 10)

Write down a few more examples of this kind. If, as per the prescriptive rules of English grammar, the *-ing* of the progressive aspect cannot be attached to a stative verb, how would you explain what is "conversationally acceptable" in English? Would it be necessary to bring up the issue of style and language variety here? Would it be necessary to discuss how people are supposed to speak and write and how they actually speak and write?

8.1.7 Think about what kind of out-of-class assignment you can give your students to strengthen their understanding of the use of the present progressive. For instance, would the running commentary of a sports event broadcast over the radio be a good source of data containing several instances of the present progressive in a communicative context? If yes, how would you design an assignment based on that?

8.1.8 Go back to what you have done so far and see to what extent your classroom plans and procedures can actually raise your learners' language awareness, promote meaningful interaction, and, ultimately, activate their intuitive heuristics.

8.1.9 At the earliest opportunity, try to implement your plan (or parts of it) in the classroom and see how it actually works. When the students are working in pairs or in small groups, use the time to jot down your impression of how the activity develops in class. Based on your classroom experience, reflect on what part to keep and what part to change in order to achieve your goals.

8.1.10 Finally, critically reflect on the process of doing this project. Specifically reflect on the usefulness of exploratory projects like this for designing appropriate microstrategies.

Project 8.2: Focus on Form

8.2.0 Recall the earlier discussion on pedagogic tasks, which focus on form attempting to draw the learners' attention to grammar only if it is needed to carry out the tasks. Their main focus then is on communicating to solve a problem or to perform an activity. One of the objectives of pedagogic tasks, however, remains grammar construction on the part of the learner. This project is aimed at helping you experiment with a pedagogic task. Here's one way of doing it.

8.2.1 Select a communicative activity appropriate to the level and interest of your learners. It may deal with social and/or academic communication such as getting acquainted with classmates on the first day of class, responding to a newspaper ad, deciding on a birthday gift, taking a stand on a current social or political event, etc. At higher levels of challenge, the activity may require the learners to collect information from different sources (through, for instance, library or the Internet) or gather opinions from different people, synthesize and interpret the information, discuss the information in small groups, make a presentation to class, and do an out-of-class writing assignment. The activity can be made more or less difficult by simplifying or complicating the collaborative decision making learners have to do to complete the activity.

8.2.2 Break down the activity into as many small steps as possible. Identify which of the steps can be done individually, in pairs, or in small groups. Write clear directions to make sure that learners know what they are expected to do every step of the way.

8.2.3 Introduce the activity to the class. Depending on time, focus on as many steps as possible in class. Have them jot down any difficulty they may face in completing the activity. Ask them to be very specific and to be attentive to three possible areas of difficulty: linguistic difficulty, that is, they struggle with words and grammatical structures needed to do the activity; or communicative difficulty, that is, they are not able to communicate what they want to communicate; or conceptual difficulty, that is, they do not fully understand the concepts and ideas involved in the task. Tell them that you will collect their notes at the end of the session. If possible, and if students give you permission, audiotape the learner activity as it unfolds in one particular group.

8.2.4 At a convenient stopping point, ask a select number of groups to share with the class what they have accomplished. Have a detailed discussion, drawing as many students as possible to respond and react. Highlight the multiplicity of routes the learners may have taken to solve the problem and multiplicity of results they may have arrived at.

8.2.5 Then, ask them to consult the notes they have taken about the three types of difficulties and share them with the class. Deal with their conceptual and communicative difficulties first. Let learners themselves resolve some of the difficulties, because what was difficult for one group might not have been difficult for another.

8.2.6 Zero in on their linguistic difficulties. Let your learners talk about the lexical and grammatical difficulties they encountered. As they share their experiences, try to look for any patterns that may emerge, that is, specific vocabulary items or specific grammatical structures that were problematic and needed explicit attention.

8.2.7 To the extent possible, deal with the emerging pattern of lexical and grammatical difficulties then and there. Do it either inductively or deductively, depending on the circumstances.

8.2.8 Collect the notes that the learners have taken down. At your leisure, but as soon as possible so that you don't forget the class discussion, read their notes. After reading the notes and listening to the audiotape (if you did tape the conversation in one group), decide what additional classroom instruction is needed to help your learners understand the rules governing some of the linguistic features that came up during the class activity.

8.2.9 As always, reflect on the process of doing this exploratory project. What did you learn? Is a project like this worth pursing? If yes, with what modifications? If not, why not?

In Closing

Based on the discussion in this chapter, it is fairly reasonable to conclude that (a) activating the intuitive heuristics that every learner naturally possesses is a worthy goal to pursue, and (b) there are several options available to those L2 teachers who wish to pursue that worthy goal. It is clear that linguistic input that is carefully structured, accompanied by classroom interaction that is suitably managed, can provide a rich amount of sample data necessary for L2 learners to search for and understand the pattern underlying L2 grammatical systems.

In order to help learners with their process of self-discovery, they should be helped to see grammar "as a rational, dynamic system that is comprised of structures characterized by the three dimensions of form, meaning and use" (Larsen-Freeman, 2000, p. 10). This chapter provided conceptual arguments, illustrative microstrategies, and exploratory projects to help the teacher treat grammar as a dynamic system with multiple dimensions. Embedded within that multidimensional system is the notion of context. We will see in the next chapter how contextualizing linguistic input and classroom interaction can maximize the learning potential in the L2 classroom.

CHAPTER 9

Contextualizing Linguistic Input

> (L)anguage takes place in social contexts and makes con-
> nections with the realities that make up those contexts.
> —HALLIDAY AND HASAN, 1976, p. 305

Language communication is inseparable from its communicative context. Taken out of context, language communication makes little sense. What all this means to learning and teaching an L2 is that we must introduce our learners to language as it is used in communicative contexts even if it is selected and simplified for them; otherwise, we will be denying an important aspect of its reality.

The reality of language is represented in some of the terms used recently to refer to language: language as text (Halliday, 1974), language as communication (Widdowson, 1978), language as context (Goodwin and Duranti, 1992), and language as discourse (McCarthy and Carter, 1994; Celce-Murcia and Olshtain, 2000). These terms, taken from the fields of theoretical linguistics, applied linguistics, and anthropology, are used interchangeably and have one thing in common: they all treat language as something that invokes context as well as something that provides context (Goodwin and Duranti, 1992, p. 7).

In spite of the importance given to context in linguistic and anthropological circles and in spite of its widespread use, the term context eludes a clear definition. In fact, as anthropologists Charles Goodwin and Alessandro Duranti (1992, p. 2) point out: "It does not seem possible at the present time to give a single, precise, technical definition of context, and eventually we might have to accept that such a definition may not be possible." They also point out that the term comes from the Latin *contextus*, which means a joining together. The opening quote from Michael Halliday and Ruqaiya Hasan mentions the joining together of realities that make up a context. What are those realities? For the limited purpose of L2 learning and teaching, we can talk about four realities: linguistic, extralinguistic, situational, and extrasituational. In the following pages, I briefly discuss each of these contexts and then connect the discussion to possible microstrategies and exploratory projects aimed at contextualizing linguistic input.

Linguistic Context

Linguistic context, as I use the term here, refers to the immediate linguistic environment that contains formal aspects of language required for the process of meaning-making. The formal aspects include pronouns, articles, conjunctions, ellipses, substitutions, and other features of the linguistic code. Such a linguistic environment pertains mainly to the grammatical and lexical levels within a sentence or between sentences in a text.

At the sentence level, the linguistic environment may contain adequate contextual clues for understanding the meaning of grammatical or lexical items. For instance, consider the meaning of the word *table* in the following sentences:

1. There is a large *table* in the dining area.
2. The *table* of contents shows what this books is all about.
3. I use a multiplication *table* to do my math problems.
4. The *table* reveals our company's profit and loss.
5. The Prime Minister will *table* a motion in Parliament today.

The common meaning of the word is, of course, what is given in sentence 1, referring to a flat surface usually supported by four legs. However, the linguistic environment surrounding the word *table* in other sentences (e.g., "multiplication" and "math" in sentence 3) provide adequate clues for determining its meaning in those specific contexts. While it is true that even decontextualized lexis can carry meaning in the sense that a word does have a canonical meaning (as in sentence 1), noticing the linguistic environment in which it occurs can ensure a proper understanding of the item in other contexts.

At the intersentential level, linguistic context relates mainly to the notion of cohesion. Halliday and Hasan (1976, p. 18) define cohesion "as the set of possibilities that exists in the language for making text hang together." It refers to relations of semantic meaning between sentences in a text (by the way, the term *text* stands for any passage with more than one sentence). It occurs where the understanding of one element of the text is dependent on that of another. One cannot be decoded without the other. For instance, the exchange

  A: Have the kids gone to bed?
  B: No, they haven't.

is cohesive because B's response is dependent on and is communicatively appropriate to A's question. In addition, the pronoun *they* cohesively refers back to *the kids*. In contrast, the exchange

  A: Have the kids gone to bed?
  B: Roses are red.

is not cohesive because B's response is a separate propositional statement not connected to A's question. When we read a text, grammatical and lexical cohesive features help us recognize whether it is a unified whole or just a collection of unrelated sentences.

Extending the Hallidayan notion of cohesion, Henry Widdowson (1978, p. 26) points out that cohesion also "refers to the way sentences and parts of sentences combine so as to ensure that there is propositional development." What he means is that the sentences

  A: What happened to the crops?
  B: The crops were destroyed by the rain.
  A: When were the crops destroyed by the rain?
  B: The crops were destroyed by the rain last week.

may appear to be related, but they are not considered cohesive because they all represent separate and independent statements. The sentences

  A: What happened to the crops?
  B: They were destroyed by the rain.
  A: When?
  B: Last week.

are indeed cohesive because they have been fused together "by removing redundancies so that propositional development is carried forward" (ibid., p. 26).

As the above examples show, the appropriateness of linguistic forms is one of the realities that make up the context of language behavior. Appropriate cohesive features provide the necessary syntactic and semantic connections within and between sentences.

Reflective task 9.1

What would be a good way of helping L2 learners of lower level proficiency to exploit the linguistic context to understand the meaning of the word *spring* in the following sentences?

The mattress has lost its *spring*.

Their anxieties obviously *spring* from their past experience.

The *spring* semester starts on January 5th.

If Winter comes, can *Spring* be far behind?

Extralinguistic Context

Extralinguistic context, as I use the term here, refers to the immediate linguistic environment that contains prosodic signals such as stress and intonation. They may also include the relative loudness or duration of syllables, and changes in the pitch of a speaker's voice. They carry subtle information beyond what is expressed through syntactic and semantic features of the language. In a conversation, they signal, among other things, what information has been or needs to be foregrounded for emphasis or for attention.

Using or understanding the use of extralinguistic features such as stress and intonation is not easy even for advanced L2 learners, particularly if their L1 has features that are very different from their L2. Improper use of such features can challenge mutual intelligibility. For instance, English is *stress-timed* in that primary stress is placed on particular words in a sentence for purposes of emphasizing new or important information. In contrast, languages such as Spanish or Chinese are *syllable-timed*, with each syllable receiving nearly equal length, pitch, and volume. Stress in these languages, therefore, does not play as much a role in conveying meaning as in English.

Consider the following examples given in Bean, Kumaravadivelu, and Lowenberg (1995, pp. 109–10). In responding to the questions below, conventions of English require primary stress on the word or phrase providing the new information requested in the question.

1.   Who did you give the tickets to?
1a. I gave the tickets to *him*.
2.   What did you give him?
2a. I gave the *tickets* to him.
3.   Who gave the tickets to him?
3a. *I* gave the tickets to him.

Users of English who are unaware of such a convention might answer the same questions with the following stress pattern:

1.   Who did you give the tickets to?
1b. I gave the tickets to *him*.
2.   What did you give him?
2b. I gave the tickets to *him*.
3.   Who gave the tickets to him?
3b. I gave the tickets to *him*.

Such responses could be confusing because they do not adhere to the convention that the most heavily stressed words in the answers would signal the information requested. A lack of knowledge of such a convention may easily lead to miscommunication.

In addition to emphasizing pieces of information, extralinguistic features also show a speaker's intended or unintended attitudes toward the message or the messenger. Participants in a conversation provide what Gumperz (1982) has called *conversational cues* through the use of extralinguistic features. The cues in turn help them with their conversational inference "by means of which participants in an exchange assess others' intentions, and on which they base their responses" (Gumperz, 1982, p. 153). According to Gumperz, contextualization cues operate at different levels ranging from prosodic features of stress and intonation to lexical formulations.

We saw in the previous chapter how a London bus driver of West Indian origin was perceived to be rude because he put the stress on the wrong word. Providing yet another example, Gumperz (1982, p. 173) showed how Indian and Pakistani women serving in a cafeteria at a British airport were perceived as "surly and uncooperative" because they did not get their intonation right. According to the conventions of English, when customers who had chosen meat were asked whether they wanted gravy, the Asian assistants would say *gravy* using falling intonation, instead of saying *gravy?* with rising intonation. Saying the word with a falling intonation is likely to be interpreted as a statement giving a piece of information as if to say, "Hey, this stuff here is called gravy." The proper way is to say it with a rising intonation that would indicate a polite offer.

Reflective task 9.2

Can you recall any instance you may have observed or experienced in which a misplaced stress or wrong intonation led to misunderstanding? And, how did you handle the situation?

Linguistic context with its cohesive features and extralinguistic context with its prosodic features are, in a sense, internal constructs built into the system of many languages. The two contexts certainly contribute to the process of meaning-making. However, they play only a limited role in helping us interpret and understand the real or intended meaning of messages that speakers and writers may wish to convey in a communicative event. For that we need to go beyond the language system and consider the situational context in which the communication takes place.

Situational Context

In an influential essay on the problem of meaning, Bronislaw Malinowski (1923) proposed that any linguistic analysis must take into account what he called *the context of situation* and *the context of culture*. The two are clearly intertwined, but, for the purpose of discussion, I shall take up the former in this subsection and the latter in the next subsection. In a nutshell, Malinowski argued that language is embedded within a context of situation and that the situation in which utterances are made cannot be ignored. In other words, words and utterances can have different meanings and functions in different contexts. Therefore, a true analysis and understanding of language communication is possible only if one goes beyond the linguistic and extralinguistic contexts in which it occurs and considers the situational context as well.

Malinowski's context of situation has been further expanded by several scholars, including John Austin (1962) and Dell Hymes (1970, 1972). Proposing what he called *a speech act theory*, Austin pointed out that we use language in order to perform speech acts such as requesting, ordering, complaining, and promising. The intended meaning—to use his phrase, the illocutionary force—of a speech act is entirely dependent on the social conventions attached to it. For instance, a statement like "I now pronounce you man and wife" has its intended communicative value only if it is uttered in a proper context (e.g., a church) and by a proper person (e.g., a priest). Obviously, the same statement uttered by a clerk in a department store will not render two customers a married couple. The statement gains its illocutionary force only because of the situational context in which it is uttered and not because of its linguistic properties.

The situational context of a communicative event is shaped by a combination of several factors. Hymes (1972) has identified and described eight of them using the acronym SPEAKING:

> *S*etting: the place and time in which the communicative event takes place.
>
> *P*articipants: speakers and hearers and their role relationships.
>
> *E*nds: the stated or unstated objectives the participants wish to accomplish.
>
> *A*ct sequence: the form, content, and sequence of utterances.
>
> *K*ey: the manner and tone (serious, sarcastic, etc.) of the utterances.
>
> *I*nstrumentalities: the channel (oral or written) and the code (formal or informal).
>
> *N*orms: conventions of interaction and interpretation based on shared knowledge.
>
> *G*enre: categories of communication such as lecture, report, essay, poem, etc.

According to Hymes, these factors, which are essentially nonlinguistic in nature, constitute a frame of reference for interpreting and understanding a speech event.

Reflective task 9.3

What are all the possible situational contexts in which the following brief exchange could be considered appropriate?

    A: Not now, darling.

    B: Then when?

Following Austin and Hymes, Widdowson (1978, p. 29) argues that, more than the linguistic and extralinguistic contexts, it is the situational context that makes an interactive exchange communicatively coherent. Consider his oft-quoted example:

    A: That's the telephone.

    B: I'm in the bath.

    A: O.K.

Widdowson explains that the three utterances in this communicative act mark a complete absence of cohesion. But still, given a plausible situational context, we can perceive this as a coherent discourse. For instance, if we visualize a household consisting of A and B, we can recognize A's first remark as a request, B's remark as an excuse for not complying with the request, and A's second remark as an acceptance of B's excuse as well as an undertaking to attend to the phone call.

The above example shows that embedding a conversational exchange in an appropriate situational context can make it communicatively coherent even if it lacks linguistic cohesion. The following example, however, shows that a communicative exchange may be both cohesive and coherent, but still may not be considered contextually appropriate given the setting in which it takes place and the role relationship between the speaker and the listener. During his first term in office, President Clinton appeared before a live audience in a program sponsored by the music channel MTV. Here is an exchange between an unidentified female member of the audience and the president:

Question: Mr. President, the world is dying to know. Is it boxers or briefs?

Clinton: Usually briefs.

Several newspapers in the United States criticized the woman for asking such a question and the president for responding to it the way he did. They considered this exchange highly inappropriate.

Reflective task 9.4

What is or is not appropriate about this exchange? How would you use this or a similar example to teach the concept of appropriateness to L2 learners?

Extrasituational Context

The problem of what is and what is not appropriate becomes even more acute in an extrasituational context, or the context of culture, to use Malinowski's term. Communicative appropriateness depends on the social, cultural, political, or ideological contexts that shape meaning in a particular speech event. It depends largely on the norms of interpretation, which varies from culture to culture. Acquiring knowledge of how extrasituational factors contribute to the process of meaning-making implies acquiring knowledge of how language features interface with cultural norms. Such a cultural view of language and language use, as McCarthy and Carter (1994, p. 150) point out, explores "the ways in which forms of language, from individual words to complete discourse structures, encode something of the beliefs and values held by the language user."

More than the mastery of linguistic features, it is the mastery of cultural norms of interpretation that poses a severe challenge to L2 learners and users. Margie Berns (1990, p. 34) narrates a typical cross-cultural encounter in which a statement made with good intentions could easily lead to misunderstanding. One day a valued friend of hers from Zambia greeted her with "Hello, Margie. How are you? Oh, I see you've put on weight," an utterance that is linguistically well formed and situationally well framed. But, as an American speaker operating within American cultural values and expectations, Berns considered it inappropriate. She initially interpreted the remark as a rude and thoughtless one.

When confronted, her friend explained that his intention was nothing more than to express his pleasure at her apparent good health and the prosperity it signified. Recalling the incident, Berns says: "In the context of a greeting in Zambia, where a healthy, robust appearance is valued more highly than a lean, slender figure, my friend's observation would have been recognized as appropriate to the situation by other Zambians. However, when said to an American unfamiliar with Zambian norms of the greeting situation and with the cultural values reflected in these norms, miscommunication and a clash of conventional patterns resulted" (Berns, 1990, pp. 35–6).

Norms of interpretation vary so much across speech communities that what is considered a compliment in one cultural context can be a cause for complaint in another. A study of extrasituational contexts governing communication, therefore, can provide a rich source of information. Understanding the role of the extrasituational context will help L2 learners use the target language in a manner that is consistent with the conventions of its speech community and thus minimize potential misinterpretation.

Reflective task 9.5

The way someone is complimented for his or her good appearance varies from context to context, culture to culture. Conduct a quick, informal survey among people of different backgrounds in terms of language, culture, age, and gender and find out how they would compliment someone for his or her good looks. Think about how you would sensitize your L2 learners to possible variations (and misinterpretations) in the realization of this speech act.

To sum up the discussion so far, successful language communication is a matter of realities coming together that make up linguistic, extralinguistic, situational, and extrasituational contexts. The above discussion, along with the illustrative examples, show that linguistic and extralinguistic features are largely structural devices that signal semantic relationships that are, in turn, governed by situational and extrasituational factors. Using language for effective communication integrates contextual factors, and, therefore, teaching it for effective learning must invoke contextualization of linguistic input.

Contextualizing Linguistic Input

In spite of the paramount importance of context in language development, not much work has been done to investigate the precise manner in which various components of language use interact with each other in the acquisition of a language. However, even the limited number of studies that have been conducted show the importance of contextual features in comprehension and production. In a series of studies, Elizabeth Bates and Brian MacWhinney (1982) provided evidence to show that sentence comprehension and production involve a rapid and simultaneous integration of semantic, pragmatic, and discourse phenomena. In a study to determine how L2 learners resolve the problem of competing factors of syntax, semantics, and pragmatics in processing L2 utterances, Gass (1986, p. 35) concluded that "syntax, semantics and pragmatic acquisition cannot be understood as isolated grammatical components with a unidirectional information flow."

While insights from L2 acquisition research has been sparse, experiential knowledge has helped language educators realize that linguistic input to learners should be presented in units of text, or what we now call discourse, so that learners can benefit from the interactive effect of various components and contexts. Nearly a century ago, Henry Sweet intuitively argued that "the main foundation of the practical study of language should be connected texts" (1899/1964, p. 100). Before Sweet, Wilhelm Vietor (1882, cited in Howatt, 1984) had stated that words should be presented in sentences, and sentences should be practiced in meaningful contexts and not be taught as isolated, disconnected elements. Introducing isolated sentences will result in pragmatic dissonance, depriving learners of necessary contextual clues, thereby rendering the process of meaning-making harder.

The idea of presenting language as text or discourse got a boost during the late 1970s and 1980s with the widespread acceptance of communicative approaches to language teaching. During the early days of communicative language teaching, attempts to contextualize linguistic input were directed more toward grammar-oriented, mechanical drills that were embedded within an artificially created text and context than toward fostering authentic communication in class. Teachers were advised to use three classes of drills—mechanical, meaningful, and communicative—and proceed sequentially and systematically (see, for example, Christina Paulston, 1974). Mechanical drills permitted only a controlled student response with only one way of saying it; meaningful drills permitted a controlled response with more than one way of saying it; and communicative drills permitted an open-ended response with new information. Some of these activities and the strict sequence in which they are supposed to be introduced to the learner imposed "a false reality or situations that are contrary to fact, thereby contradicting any notion of authentic communication" (Joel Walz, 1989, p. 164).

Starting with the later days of communicative language teaching and continuing into the present are attempts that incorporate some of the linguistic, extralinguistic, situational, and extrasituational features in learning and teaching. These attempts include teaching through proficiency-oriented activities (Omaggio, 1986), interactive scenarios (Di Pietro, 1987), problem-solving tasks (Prabhu, 1987; Nunan, 1989a), simulation games (Crookall and Oxford, 1990), or discourse activities (McCarthy and Carter, 1994; Riggenbach, 1999; Celce-Murcia and Olshtain, 2000). Earlier attempts at contextualizing linguistic input start with grammar moving gradually toward discourse, treating language mostly as atomized products, whereas discourse-based activities start with discourse as "the overall driving force" engaging "language as *process* and meaning as negotiated and contextual" (McCarthy and Carter, 1994, p. 182, italics as in original).

One way of engaging "language as process and meaning as negotiated and contextual" is to present the linguistic input within thematic contexts that reflect the natural use of language. Illustrating such an engagement, Marianne Celce-Murcia and Elite Olshtain (2000, p. 195) suggest that the English past tense, for example, "can be learned and taught most effectively within a real or a 'fictional' narrative where the simple past form is central to the development of the main plot and the present tense and progressive aspect typically describes the background. Relative clauses, on the other hand, can best be learned and taught within a context that requires identification and specification of nouns (defining characteristics): the need to single out individuals within a group or to select items with special characteristics." This kind of discourse engagement, Celce-Murcia and Olshtain rightly point out, relies heavily on contextual analysis "in an attempt to pair up grammatical form with meaningful sociocultural context" (p. 195). And, a language curriculum based on this kind of discourse engagement "can be viewed as a reflection of the postmethod and postcommunicative era, as a document where form and function need to be reconciled with communication needs and social contexts" (p. 199).

One way of contextualizing linguistic input, therefore, is to reconcile form and function with communicative needs and social contexts. Let us now turn to illustrative microstrategies and exploratory projects that seek to do precisely that.

Microstrategies for Contextualizing Linguistic Input

Some of the authors cited in the previous two paragraphs offer several instructional suggestions to create meaningful contexts for language learning and teaching activities in class. These suggestions can be easily adapted to suit the linguistic and communicative levels of a specific group of learners. Drawing insights from them, I present below two microstrategies.

Microstrategy 9.1: Travel Matters

9.1.0 The following microstrategy is based on language learning scenarios proposed by Di Pietro. He suggests that we treat the language classroom itself as a kind of speech community that can provide the setting for interactive language use. The idea is to design a series of communicative scenarios in which learners are encouraged to role-play to use and, in using, expand their developing linguistic repertoire. One of the scenarios Di Pietro presents is what might happen to a traveler at an airport. Here's an adapted version.

9.1.1 To begin with, ask your learners about any long-distance travel they may have undertaken by plane, train, or bus to visit other places in or outside their country. Have some of them share their travel experiences—any pleasant surprises or unexpected hassles involving, for instance, their tickets, luggage, etc., and how they handled them.

9.1.2 Then, present the following scenario to your students: they are at the airport (or train/bus station) for a return trip home. They are told that, because of a clerical mistake, their flight (or train/bus) has been overbooked. A supervisor is requesting ten of the passengers to take a flight (or train/bus) scheduled for the following day. If they do, they will be suitably compensated, including a free hotel room for the night. Your students are among the passengers and they have to make a quick decision.

9.1.3 Form three groups. One group plays the role of the supervisor, another the role of passengers willing to accept the offer, and a third the role of those not willing to accept the offer. Ask each group to discuss and prepare a script for arguing its case. They should be able to anticipate the case of the other two groups and be prepared for a counterargument. Ask each group to designate one member to represent the group in a later role-play.

9.1.4 As the group discussion proceeds, move from group to group, monitoring any communicative or linguistic difficulty the participants may encounter. Look for any pattern of difficulty (in terms of vocabulary or grammar) that may emerge, and take notes. If possible, tape (audio or video) the conversation in one group for later analysis.

9.1.5 At the end of the group discussion, ask the designated members (one from each group) to role-play their parts for the class. Let the role-play lead where it may.

9.1.6 After the performance, lead a class discussion on how well the decisions were made, how well they were articulated, and how the decision-making process and the presentation could be improved.

9.1.7 At this point, you might wish to offer your comments, both positive and negative. You might highlight some of the communicative and linguistic difficulties you may have noted during the group discussion.

9.1.8 Based on your notes (and on an analysis of the conversation you may have taped), you might decide to treat in detail any grammatical and lexical features by designing focused exercises to be done in class later.

9.1.9 Finally, reflect on the usefulness of this kind of an activity for your group of learners, and your readiness to design such microstrategies.

Microstrategy 9.2: Time Traveling

9.2.0 This microstrategy aims at providing an opportunity for L2 learners to combine form and function within a coherent, communicative context that puts a premium on their personal life history. More specifically, it deals with the use of time expressions in its past, present, and future tenses. A time-tested instructional strategy that several teachers and textbook writers have effectively exploited for this purpose is the timeline. Here's one possibility; you may wish to modify it to suit your learning and teaching situation.

9.2.1   First, ask your learners whether (and how often) they think about the life they have traveled so far and about the future course of action.

9.2.2   Distribute two copies of a time chart like the one shown in Figure 9.1. Change the years to suit the age group of your learners. Include at least ten years before and after the current year.

1990	1992	1994	1996	1998	2000	2002	2004	2006	2008	2010

Figure 9.1

Explain to them how they are supposed to use this chart. Give them some time to think. Ask them to use one copy to take notes about their past, present, and future, focusing on major areas like school, sports, travel, job, family, etc., Ask them to highlight any interesting and surprising events in life.

9.2.3   Form pairs. Have each student find out information about his/her partner and take notes to complete the second copy of the chart. Circulate as they converse, listening to monitor their use of tenses and time expressions. Take notes to help you focus on certain grammatical features later. If possible, tape (audio or video) the conversation in one group for later analysis.

9.2.4   Then, depending on time, ask every student to talk about their partner using the notes they took. Encourage them to talk rather than read. In addition to giving information about their partners, let them highlight any information that was surprising or noteworthy.

9.2.5   After the presentations, ask the students to say what surprised or interested them about their classmates. Allow the class to seek additional information or more details about any information already shared.

9.2.6   Now it is your turn to comment on what you heard about your students. It may not be a bad idea for you to share your own timeline with your students at this point.

9.2.7   Next, you might wish to focus explicitly on the students' use of time and tenses, and on any communicative or linguistic difficulties you may have noted during their conversations.

9.2.8 Based on your notes (and on an analysis of the conversation you may have taped), you might decide to treat various aspects of tense and time expressions followed by focused exercises to be done in class later.

9.2.9 And, as before, reflect on the usefulness of this kind of an activity for your group of learners, and on your readiness to design such microstrategies.

Exploratory Projects

The following exploratory research projects are suggested to help you design your own microstrategies like the ones illustrated above. The first one focuses on linguistic and extralinguistic context and the second on situational and extrasituational context.

Project 9.1: Cloze Encounters

9.1.0 Cloze procedures refer to a method of deleting every fifth, sixth, or nth word from a prose selection and evaluating the response learners make as they supply the words deleted. They require "attention to longer stretches of linguistic context. They often require references about extralinguistic context" (John Oller, 1979, p. 42). They assess whether a person has the basic syntactic, semantic, and rhetorical skills necessary to understand a piece of discourse. One type of cloze is constructed deleting every nth word; other types involve deleting specific grammatical items such as articles, prepositions, pronouns, etc. While cloze procedures are generally used for testing purposes, "they must be sensitive to any of the things that teachers are trying to accomplish in the way of instructional objectives" (Oller, 1979, p. 362). In addition to teaching and testing reading skills, cloze procedures can be used effectively for teaching and testing discourse grammar as well.

9.1.1 First decide which of the discourse grammar items (e.g., articles, prepositions, pronouns, logical connectors, etc.) will be your focus. For illustrative purposes, say you opt for pronouns. Select a passage suitable to the proficiency and interest level of your students. Make sure the passage has several instances of different types of pronouns.

9.1.2 Keeping a copy of the original for your reference, delete all the pronouns in that passage and replace them with blanks of equal length. You may also number the blanks for easy reference. Write clear directions telling your students what you expect them to do. Here's a sample:

220

Contextualizing linguistic input

Please read the following passage two or three times and fill in each blank with a suitable noun or pronoun (like he, she, etc.). Do not supply more than one word for each blank. If you think no word is needed for any blank, write a zero (∅).

An attack on the family

John, the eight-year-old son of Mary and Larry Prescott, grew very fond of the scorpions in the garden wall. ____(1) found them to be pleasant, unassuming creatures with, on the whole, the most charming habits. One day, ____(2) found a fat female scorpion in the garden wall, wearing what at first glance appeared to be a pale brown fur coat. Closer inspection proved that this strange ____(3) was made up of a mass of tiny babies clinging to the mother's back. ____(4) liked this family of scorpions, and ____(5) made up his mind to smuggle them into the house and up to his bedroom so that ____(6) might keep them and ____(7) watch them grow up. With infinite care ____(8) moved the mother and family into a matchbox, and then ____(9) hurried to the house. It was rather unfortunate that just as ____(10) entered the door, his mother and father were already at the dining table. His mother said ____(11) was ready to serve lunch and ____(12) wanted ____(13) to join them immediately. ____(14) placed the matchbox carefully on the shelf in the drawing room, so that the ____(15) could get plenty of air, and ____(16) made his way to the dining room and ____(17) joined the family for the meal. Eating his food slowly and listening to the family arguing, ____(18) completely forgot about his exciting new captures. At last, Larry, his father, having finished his lunch, brought the cigarettes from the drawing room, and slipping back in his chair ____(19) put one in his mouth and ____(20) picked up the matchbox ____(21) had brought. Unaware of the coming danger ____(22) watched him interestedly as, still talking happily, ____(23) opened the matchbox.

____(24) maintains to this day that the female ____(25) meant no harm. ____(26) was agitated and annoyed at being shut up in a matchbox for so long, and so ____(27) seized the first opportunity to escape. ____(28) climbed out of the box with great speed, her tiny babies clinging on to her desperately, and ____(29) crawled on to the back of Larry's hand. There, not quite certain what to do next, ____(30) paused, her sting curved up at the ready. Larry, feeling the movement of her claws, glanced down to see what it was, and from that moment things got increasingly confused. (Authorship of the passage unknown)

9.1.3 Distribute copies of the passage to your students and ask them to do the exercise in class, individually.

9.1.4 Have the students exchange their completed exercise with the person sitting next to them. You call out the answers for the blanks and have the students put a check mark next to each, if correct, and then have the students return the sheets.

9.1.5 Then, have a discussion on the use of pronouns with particular reference to their occurrence in this passage. This can be done in several ways. One way is to take up the correct answer to each of the blanks, ask one or two students who got it right to explain their choice. Focus also on any wrong answer. Encourage the class to say why the answer is wrong. You step in with your explanation only if necessary.

9.1.6 Depending on the performance of the class, you may wish to take up a few items for detailed treatment. For instance, it is possible that some of the students may have supplied a full noun where a pronoun is sufficient, or some may have supplied a pronoun where none (∅) is required. Help your learners derive the rule(s) by themselves, wherever appropriate.

9.1.7 In order to make sure they have satisfactorily learned the use of pronouns, you may select another passage, follow the same deletion procedure, and test what they have learned.

9.1.8 Finally, reflect on the practicality of doing this kind of exploratory project in helping you achieve your immediate goal of contextualizing linguistic input.

Project 9.2: Be Patriotic, Have Sex!

9.2.0 As we learned in this chapter, language as discourse is shaped by the linguistic, extralinguistic, situational, and extrasituational realities. One way of sensitizing the L2 learner to those realities is to introduce to them contextualized input that connects form and function with communicative needs and sociocultural contexts. Newspapers (or the Internet) provide a rich source of contextualized language for designing classroom activities.

9.2.1 Select a short news story that is appropriate to the linguistic and communicative level of your students. Make sure that it is interesting enough to capture their attention. Consider, for instance, a news story like the following taken from the on-line edition of the *New York Times* (www.nytimes.com/2001/04/21/world/21SING.html).

April 21, 2001
Singapore, Hoping for a Baby Boom,
Makes Sex a Civic Duty
By Seth Mydans

Singapore, April 15—Here in strait-laced Singapore, it's the new patriotism: have sex.

Alarmed by its declining birthrate, this tiny city-state of just four million people is urging its citizens to multiply as fast as they can.

"We need more babies!" proclaimed Prime Minister Goh Chok Tong last fall. The world, he said, is in danger of running short of Singaporeans.

And, Singapore being Singapore, a campaign has begun that focuses more on people's financial calculations than on that strange, hard-to-quantify thing called romance.

A government office, the Working Committee on Marriage and Procreation, has developed monetary and workplace incentives that go into effect this month. The idea is to persuade people that having children is a better deal than going without.

In what it calls the Baby Bonus Scheme, the government is offering cash to couples who have second and third children. It is extending maternity leave and adding a brief paternity leave for government workers. It is experimenting with flexible working hours to make child rearing easier. It is offering special deals on apartment rentals to young couples.

The local press has enthusiastically gotten with the program, filling its pages with encomiums to the joys not only of parenthood but of sex. "Let's Get on the Love Wagon," urged a headline in *The Straits Times* not long after Mr. Goh's speech.

It meant that literally. The article gave tips for having sex in the back seat of a car complete with directions to "some of the darkest, most secluded and most romantic spots for Romeos and Juliets." It suggested covering the windows with newspapers for privacy.

The problem with this, some Singaporeans pointed out, is birth control. Having sex in the back of a car does not necessarily mean helping the city-state to improve its demographic profile by having babies.

Like citizens of other nations with rising living standards, Singaporeans have been choosing for two decades now to have smaller families. The birthrate has fallen to 1.5 children per woman of childbearing age—far below the 2.5 needed to maintain the population level. (Incomplete).

9.2.2 First, think about how you can help your learners relate the text and the context; more specifically, explore the linguistic, extralinguistic, situational, and extrasituational factors that help them with the process of meaning-making. What kind of questions do you need to raise and address in order to help you design a series of tasks?

9.2.3 How can you set the stage for your task? How best to start them thinking about all the possible contexts in which some of the utterances taken from the text such as "We need more babies," or "Let's Get on the Love Wagon," will be considered appropriate?

9.2.4 What might be the social and cultural contexts in which it will be considered appropriate for the prime minister of a country to say what he said?

9.2.5 How can you help your learners make the connection between the title of the story, the prime minister's statement, the setting up of a Working Committee on Marriage and Procreation, and the social context described in the last paragraph?

9.2.6 How can you help them focus on the features of cohesion and coherence in this text?

9.2.7 Once you design your microstrategy, try to implement it in the classroom. Monitor how well the students respond and how well it helps you achieve your instructional goals.

9.2.8 Finally, see whether the feedback you get from class performance indicates any need for revising the content as well as the implementation of your microstrategy.

In Closing

This chapter on contextualized discourse and its significance in the development of communicative competence can be summed up in the words of Evelyn Hatch (1992, p. 318): "Communicative competence is the ability to manipulate the system, selecting forms that not only make for coherent text but also meet goals and fit the ritual constraints of communication. That is, communicative competence is the ability to create coherent text that is appropriate for a given situation within a social setting." What helps the L2 learner and user is the realization that an appropriate and coherent text—whether spoken or written—can be created only if the realities that make up linguistic, extralinguistic, situational, and extrasituational contexts are taken into serious consideration.

Teaching language as discourse, therefore, demands contextualization of linguistic input. It must, however, be recognized that contextualization of linguistic input that begins with a focus on discourse challenges the traditional way of language teaching. For teaching can no longer depend on a decontextualized set of linguistic items preselected and presequenced by syllabus designers and textbook writers. It has to be consistent with the chief characteristics of language communication, which relies on a variety of contextual factors.

The emphasis on contextualizing linguistic input has a direct bearing on yet another aspect of language teaching—the teaching of language skills of listening, speaking, reading, and writing—to which we turn next.

CHAPTER 10

Integrating Language Skills

> "It's like dividing water; it flows back together again."
> —DIRECTOR OF A LANGUAGE INSTITUTE,
> on separating language skills (Cited in Selinker
> and Tomlin, 1986, p. 229)

In the previous chapter, we learned that there exists a deep and inseparable connection between language use and the context in which it is embedded. A different kind of connectedness exists in the way we use the primary skills of language identified traditionally as listening, speaking, reading, and writing. In the practice of everyday life, we continually integrate these skills. Rare indeed is the day when we only listen, or only speak, or only read, or only write. Just think how artificial and tiresome it would be if, for some peculiar reason, we decide to separate these skills and use only one for a specified period of time.

Such an artificial separation of language skills, however, is quite normal in most language schools. In North America, as in several other countries, language institutes in colleges and universities offer classes based on isolated skills and proficiency levels with course titles such as Beginning Reading, Intermediate Listening, or Advanced Writing. Curriculum designers and textbook writers have long been using the separation of skills as a guiding principle for syllabus construction and materials production. They even try to narrowly link a particular skill with a particular set of learning strategies. They thus talk about reading strategies, listening strategies, speaking strategies, and writing strategies. Such a linkage is misleading; for, as Oxford (2001, p. 19), who has done extensive research on learning strategies, asserts, "Many strategies, such as paying selective attention, self-evaluating, asking questions, analyzing, synthesizing, planning and predicting are applicable across skill areas."

There is, luckily, a clear disjunction between what curriculum designers and textbook writers prescribe, and what teachers and learners actually practice in the classroom. If we step into any normal language classroom, we rarely see teachers and learners in a reading class only read, or in a writing class only write, or in a speaking class only speak. That, of course, would be impossible. Faced with a set of predetermined curricula and prescribed textbooks, what most teachers do is to place extra emphasis on a specific skill designated for a specific class while helping learners freely use all the skills necessary for successfully carrying out a classroom activity. In other words, even if the class is supposed to focus on one specific skill at a time, teachers and learners do the inevitable, namely, follow an integrated approach.

Reflective task 10.1

Think about any recent L2 class you may have taught or observed. Recall how or whether the teacher in that class integrated or segregated language skills and to what effect.

A History of Separation

Skill separation is, in fact, a remnant of a bygone era and has very little empirical or experiential justification. It is based on a particular belief in language, language learning, and language teaching. During the1950s and '60s, before the advent of communicative approaches, proponents of audiolingual method believed that language is basically aural-oral. That is, speech is primary and constitutes the very basis of language. They also emphasized the formal properties of grammatical usage more than the functional properties of communicative use. Given such an emphasis, it appeared reasonable to separate language skills. However, as Widdowson (1998, p. 325) observes, "We can talk of skills in respect to usage, but if we talk about language use, we need a different concept, and perhaps a different term." Not only did the audiolingualists divide the language into four skill areas but they also recommended a strict sequencing of them: listening, speaking, reading, and writing, in that order. That is, they believed learners should not be allowed to attempt to speak before they learn to listen, or to write before they learn to read. This order was suggested partly because that is the order in which children learn their first language. Clearly, such a suggestion ignores the apparent dissimilarities between children learning their first language and adults learning their second or third.

Yet another point to remember is that audiolingualists divided the four language skills into two categories: active and passive. Speaking and writing were considered active skills, and reading and listening were considered passive skills. Today, such a suggestion "makes us smile" (Sandra Savignon, 1990, p. 207) because we now know that there is nothing passive about reading and listening. Readers and listeners have to actively engage their minds and actively process the information in order to make meaning. Eventually, the terms *active* and *passive* were replaced by *productive* (speaking and writing) and *receptive* (listening and reading). Although these new terms represent a sort of improvement over the earlier ones, they, too, are problematic because "it is now generally agreed that effective listening and reading require as much attention and mental activity as speaking and writing" (Paul Davies and Eric Pearse, 2000, p. 74). Thus, neither set of terms effectively captures the true nature of communication and "lost in this encode/decode, message-sending representation is the collaborative nature of meaning-making" (Savignon, 1990, p. 207).

Reflective task 10.2

There are textbooks that combine reading and writing as one unit, and listening and speaking as another. Recall any L2 class you recently taught or observed. What do learners actually do in class: don't they listen to the teacher attentively and take notes furiously, thereby combining listening and writing? If yes, how does this reality fit in with what popular textbooks profess?

Taking an empirical look at the separation of skills, and finding no substantial evidence to support any pedagogic decisions based on such a separation, Larry Selinker and Russ Tomlin (1986) call such decisions a "pedagogical artifact" (p. 230). In another study, Swaffar, Arens, and Morgan (1982) found the separation of skills to be inadequate for developing integrated functional skills. Its inadequacy arises because language skills are essentially interrelated and mutually reinforcing. Fragmenting them into manageable, atomistic items runs counter to the parallel and interactive nature of language and language use.

It is then fair to say that, in the absence of any empirical support, language skills are being taught in isolation more for logistical than for logical reasons; that is, it is done more out of administrative convenience and availability of time and resources than out of any sound theoretical or experiential knowledge. As was pointed out by Freeman and Freeman (1992, p. 138), a recognition of the tension between what should be rightfully done and what is actually done is clearly brought out by textbook writers who continue to write separate books or separate chapters for each of the skill areas, while at the same time find it necessary, in their editorial comments, to readily acknowledge the importance of the integration of language skills.

The Need for Integration

Theoretical as well as experiential knowledge overwhelmingly point to the importance of integrating language skills. It is likely that the learning and use of any one skill can trigger cognitive and communicative associations with the others. Several scholars have attested to this likelihood. Emphasizing the connection between reading and other skills, Krashen (1989, p. 90) argues that reading may very well be "the primary means of developing reading comprehension, writing style, and more sophisticated vocabulary and grammar." Similarly, listening activities have been found to help learners make the broader connection between the sociolinguistic concept of form and function and the psycholinguistic processes of interpretation and expression (Rost, 1990).

Linking speaking with other skills, Martin Bygate (1998, p. 34) found it "inevitable that the real time processing of listening activities, the exposure to language via reading and listening, and the attention to form-meaning relations in all skills can wash forward to help the development of speaking." Such a connection is true of writing as well, as observed by Wilga Rivers (1981, pp. 296–7): "Writing is not, then, a skill which can be learned in isolation. . . .

the most effective writing practice, and the most generally useful, will have a close connection with what is being practiced in relation to other skills."

In addition to these theoretical insights, there is yet another advantage for replicating the natural integration of skills in the classroom. As we saw in the chapter on learner autonomy, various learners bring various learning styles and strategies to class. Integration of language skills has the potential to offer "different opportunities for different types of learners, for example, the extroverts who like to speak a lot, the introverts who prefer to listen or read, and the analytically or visually oriented learners who like to see how words are written and sentences constructed" (Paul Davies and Eric Pearse, 2000, p. 75). While, as Selinker and Tomlin (1986) rightly urge, more classroom-oriented research is required to determine the full impact of integration and separation of skills, all available theoretical and experiential information stress the need to integrate language skills for effective language learning and teaching.

Reflective task 10.3

Pause here for a minute and think about all the ways in which you can integrate language skills in your class. If possible, brainstorm with another colleague and make a list.

Integrating Language Skills

In the last fifteen years or so, several types of classroom activities have entered the field of L2 learning and teaching. There are, as mentioned in the previous chapter, interactive scenarios (Di Pietro, 1987) and problem-solving tasks (Prabhu, 1987; Nunan, 1989; Willis, 1996). In addition, there are content-based activities (Crandall, 1987), project-based activities (Legutke and Thomas, 1991), whole-language activities (Goodman, 1986; Freeman and Freeman, 1992), and experiential activities (Kohonen, et al., 2001). All these classroom activities have one thing in common: they stress interactive language use that requires a synthesis of various language skills and various language components. Additionally, these integrated activities are all relevant for learners of different levels of proficiency, provided the degree of conceptual, communicative, and linguistic challenge is monitored and maintained.

Any of the above types of classroom activities, if properly designed and implemented, can easily lead to the integration of language skills. For instance, in performing a well-planned integrated activity, learners may

- try to understand the teacher's directions, seek clarifications, and take notes (listening, speaking, and writing);
- brainstorm, in pairs or in small groups, and decide to use library resources or the Internet to collect additional information (listening, speaking, reading, and writing);
- engage in a decision-making process about how to use the collected information and proceed with the activity (listening, speaking, and reading);
- carry out their plan of action (reading, writing, speaking, and listening);
- use the notes taken during their group discussion, and present to class what they have accomplished (reading, speaking, and listening); and
- finish the activity with a whole class discussion (listening and speaking).

The following illustrative microstrategies show how the language skills can be profitably integrated.

Microstrategies for Integrating Language Skills

As with most other microstrategies illustrated in this book, resources such as newspapers, news magazines, and the Internet (where available) provide excellent materials for designing microstrategies for integrating language skills. Additional resources can be found in TV shows—particularly excerpts from short documentaries—talk shows, and sitcom episodes as well as radio broadcasts. An easier alternative, of course, is textbook activities that can be suitably adapted to cover integrated skills. It should be remembered that a great way of motivating the learners is to involve them in the material selection process by asking them to suggest topics and themes that then can be discussed in class in order to arrive at a consensus list of topics they would like to address.

The following microstrategies, as well as exploratory projects, show how channels of communication such as newspapers, radio, TV, and the Internet can be effectively used for the purpose of integrating language skills.

Microstrategy 10.1: A Matter of Money and Motherhood

10.1.0 A regular column feature that appears in newspapers or news magazines in many parts of the world is the advice column. Readers who participate in these columns generally describe a personal experience or a social situation and seek advice from experts in the relevant field of activity. These columns can be a good source for generating meaningful discussion in class, since everybody will have an opinion on most of the personal and social issues raised by readers. Most of these are syndicated columns, that is, the same columns appear in several newspapers. It is fairly easy to use newspaper columns to design a classroom activity involving all four language skills and at different levels of linguistic and communicative challenge. Here's one way of doing it; you may wish to modify some parts of the microstrategy to suit your learning and teaching situation.

10.1.1 Select a short piece from an advice column that you believe will interest your learners. Make sure the issue raised lends itself to different interpretations and solutions based on different beliefs and expectations. The following sample text is taken from an advice column, titled "Miss Manners," that appeared in the *San Jose Mercury News*.

> Dear Miss Manners: While we were expecting our fourth son, my mother offered to come and assist with our family during his birth, using a plane ticket she already had. We were glad to have her here to help with transportation, meal preparation, etc. Because of unforeseen circumstances, she ended up staying for 13 days. During her stay, she made many trips to the grocery store: some I requested, some she did on her own. Whenever she purchased something for our family, I told her I would pay her back.
>
> Upon departure, she presented me with a total of over $400! I wrote her a check. Later, I looked at the receipts she had left. She charged us for all the food she ate, numerous magazines and cookbooks she purchased for herself, special soap she wanted instead of the brand we use, and gifts for the dog ($10 for the dog bones) and the children! In addition, she bought many expensive items (large bags of macadamia nuts and almonds, brand-name grocery items

when I usually purchase store brands) that I would never have purchased. She is not poor and neither are we, but my husband and I are at a loss as to why she would take advantage of us in this way. She didn't even leave the used magazines for us to see!

Should I confront her or just let sleeping dogs eat their $10 bones? (Source: *San Jose Mercury News*, 3/18/2001)

10.1.2 Make photocopies of the selected text, or copy it onto an OHP transparency. In class, before you distribute it to your learners, read the text aloud in normal speed, pausing at crucial places. For instance, read aloud the first two sentences. Pause. Ask the learners to guess what they would expect the writer to say about her mother. Read the next three sentences. Pause. Ask. Then, read the first sentence of the second paragraph, and so on. At an appropriate point in the reading (e.g., at the end of the first paragraph), ask them what the writer is seeking advice about.

10.1.3 Distribute copies of the text, or project it on the OHP. Ask your learners to read it carefully. Encourage them to seek clarification to help them understand the text.

10.1.4 Form small groups and have them discuss the immediate issues raised in the text, zeroing in on the mother's action and the daughter's reaction.

10.1.5 Ask each group to prepare a consensus report of what they would have done if they were in the position of the daughter.

10.1.6 Depending on the proficiency level, encourage them to discuss larger issues of cultural and social beliefs involving the concept of family, which individuals are considered to constitute a family, and a mother's relationship with her daughter's family and vice versa.

10.1.7 Have a representative from each group present the group's consensus report to the class, and lead a discussion on what emerges.

10.1.8 After giving adequate time for preparation, ask a couple of active, enterprising students to role-play a possible mother-daughter encounter assuming that the daughter has been advised, and has decided, to confront her mother.

10.1.9 Ask them to pretend that they are the experts the writer is turning to for advice. Have them write in class, individually, an appropriate response to the writer, specifically addressing the last question raised by her. If there are learners from different cultural or subcultural backgrounds, encourage them to write about how members of their cultural community would have reacted to the daughter's complaint about her mother.

10.1.10 Finally, alert your learners (if they do not already know) about advice columns in local newspapers, and ask them to read them regularly and bring a story or two to class if they find them interesting and would like to discuss them in class.

Microstrategy 10.2: A Matter of Reality and Falsehood

10.2.0 A recent source of entertainment is what is called reality TV. It has been a phenomenal success in North America and Europe, and is fast spreading to other parts of the world as well. Some successful reality shows include *Survivor, Big Brother, Temptation Island,* and *Loft Story*—the first three are North American and the last one French. Episodes of *Survivor* and *Loft Story,* for instance, have both been the most-watched TV shows in their respective countries.

In reality TV shows, participants are not professional actors and actresses but people selected from various walks of life. A small group of adventurous people is selected and taken to exotic places like Australian coasts or Kenyan villages and are given very few amenities. They have to survive and "outwit, outplay, outlast" each other in order to win a million dollars, as in the case of *Survivor*. Or, in the case of *Loft Story,* eleven young couples are housed in a small loft for seventy days, and one loft-dweller is kicked out after each episode. The couple remaining after everyone else is evicted wins a $400,000 house. In both shows, the cameras are turned on the participants almost twenty-four hours a day, and their every move is recorded and broadcast.

Reality TV with its exotic appeal can provide an extraordinary source of materials for L2 teachers if they wish to promote meaningful interaction in class and integrate language skills. Here's a suggestion; adapt as necessary:

10.2.1 To set the stage, write "Reality TV" on the board and ask your learners what it means and what they know about it. Ask them if they have seen or heard/read about any such shows. Let them share what they know with the class, including their opinions about why they appeal to people of different generations and interests.

10.2.2 Select an episode from any of these shows, videotape it, and play it in your class. You may also pause at crucial moments and ask the students to guess what they expect the participants to do next. If you teach in an area where these shows are not shown or are not available on video, you may give your learners a minilecture on the subject by collecting relevant information from newspapers and the Internet. If you are surfing the Internet, search for "reality TV" on any of the search engines (e.g., Yahoo.com or Google.com), and you will find hundreds of Web sites. Or, you may also go to specific shows; for instance, if you wish to know about *Survivor*, go to CBS.com. Print out information about the show you wish to focus on, and make enough photocopies for use in class.

10.2.3 Form small groups. If they viewed a video, have your students discuss what they saw. Guide them to discuss first the episode itself— what it is about and what the participants actually do, etc.—and then ask them what is real and unreal about this particular episode. If you used a newspaper cutting or a printout from the Internet (instead of showing a video), ask your learners to read it and discuss it in small groups.

10.2.4 Have the groups report back to the class about what they discussed followed by question-and-answer.

10.2.5 Have them go to the library, read back-volumes of newspapers or surf the Internet to collect information about the reality show they watched (or read about) in class. Or, if they wish, let them collect information about any reality TV show they like. Putting together what they discussed in class and what they collected in the library, ask them to write a brief reflective essay on what they think about the show, why it does or does not appeal to them.

10.2.6 In class, form pairs and ask them to read what the other partner has written and, if necessary, seek clarification.

10.2.7 Ask a select number of students to briefly tell the class about anything unusual or unexpected that they read in their partner's write-up.

10.2.8 Depending on the proficiency level of your students, take the discussion to a higher level of critical reflection. Focus on some of the criticisms about shows like *Survivor* or *Loft Story*. For instance, French critics call reality TV *télévision poubelle*—trash television. Commenting on *Loft Story*, one French television producer is reported to have said, "To me, *Loft Story* is non-television. It's just crap—no actors, no script, no production value. . . . As a television professional, there's nothing easier than picking 10 idiots off the street and asking them to be idiots in front of the camera" (From an article on "Culture Schlock in France: New Reality Television Show Draws a Crowd of Viewers and Critics," written by Keith Richburg, published in the on-line edition of the *Washington Post*, May 17, 2001, p. C01). Ask your students what they think about comments like this.

10.2.9 A different kind of observation, no less perceptive, came from a villager in Kenya. In the summer of 2001, CBS, the TV network that produces and broadcasts the most successful reality TV show, *Sur-*

vivor, took its crew and participants to a village in Kenya to film its new *Survivor: Africa* series. The story line is, of course, the same: the participants have to live under severe conditions and survive with meager food and other resources while outwitting, outplaying, and outlasting everybody else to win a million dollars. Project the following excerpt from a local newspaper on an OHP:

> "A million dollars? Just for surviving? . . . I could win that show. I live for several days without eating, just a little water."
>
> Mohammed Leeresh, a bemused Kenyan villager, commenting on "Survivor: Africa," the latest installment of the "reality TV" series that's taping in his neighborhood. Local people said they remained puzzled even after the show's concept was explained to them.
>
> (Source: *San Jose Mercury News*, August 19, 2001, p. C2)

Ask your learners to think about Mohammed Leeresh's comment. Have them discuss why they think Kenyan villagers are "bemused" and "puzzled." If your learners themselves are not doing it, lead them to consider the above piece of information from the perspective of those Kenyan villagers. Here they are, presumably living under severe conditions, facing starvation as part of their everyday existence. They cannot understand why anyone would create an artificial scarcity of food and other resources, and then pay a million dollars for somebody to survive such conditions, while, for those Kenyans, such conditions are part of their everyday reality. And, nobody pays them even a penny to applaud their survival. Alert your students to these perspectives and lead a critical discussion.

Exploratory Projects

The following exploratory projects are aimed at providing a general plan for designing microstrategies to integrate language skills. You need to decide what to do and how exactly you wish to do it.

Project 10.1: Comic Situations

10.1.0 Apart from the newly introduced reality shows, television everywhere has traditionally shown and continues to show sitcoms (situation comedies)—brief episodes that humorously bring out the strengths and weaknesses of human beings. These sitcoms are loaded with cultural and subcultural beliefs and value systems. Sitcoms produced in North America, for instance, depict, almost exclusively, the lives and loves of people of different ethnic communities. Any of the episodes of a sitcom can be used as a resource around which to design classroom activities, since each episode is short and self-contained with a beginning and an end.

10.1.1 Select any currently popular sitcom, one that you think is suitable for your class. Videotape an interesting episode. (If you do not have a videorecorder, your school may have one you can borrow. Some schools may do recordings for teachers, if requested.)

10.1.2 Watch the selected episode again, closely. Jot down questions that you might want to ask your learners before showing the video so that they will know what to anticipate.

10.1.3 Divide the episode into three or four segments and, focusing on each segment, think of listening comprehension questions that you can ask to help your students to understand the episode.

10.1.4 Focus on and prepare questions about conversational features that you want to highlight in class—such as the informal and colloquial nature of language used, how participants take turns, and how openings are provided for the listener to speak, etc.

10.1.5 Focus on features other than the lexical items that carry meaning so that you can direct your learners' attention to them. These may include: stress, intonation, rhythm, and body language. Think about what your learners already know and what needs to be highlighted.

10.1.6 Focus also on characterization to help learners identify any strong views or mannerisms or behavior patterns that are unique to a particular character in the episode.

10.1.7 In addition to the above, make sure you address the following questions as you design your microstrategy: Do the learners need any assistance with any of the jokes? What kind of linguistic and cultural prior knowledge is assumed here? Does the episode depict a particular set of attitudes and beliefs that you need to highlight?

10.1.8 Think about the kind of a class project that will help them do some reading and writing around this episode. Would it be possible to ask your students, in small groups, to make a transcript of the episode? To rewrite the script from the point of view of a different belief system? And, enact the revised version in class?

10.1.9 Finally, try to implement your microstrategy in class and monitor how it develops. Reflect, revise, and reuse.

Project 10.2: Radio Days

10.2.0 In learning/teaching environments where Internet surfing and videotaping are difficult, radio broadcasts can offer unlimited resources for language related activities. Local or international radio broadcasts in certain target languages, particularly English, are readily available in many countries. Generally, radio broadcasts offer a variety of programs including songs, music, news items, speeches, interviews, and sports commentaries. Depending on the interest and proficiency level of your learners, select any of these programs for designing a microstrategy to integrate language skills. Here's one possibility.

10.2.1 Select an evening news broadcast from a popular radio station. Audiotape it. Listen to it again, looking for possible segments for classroom use, and jot them down.

10.2.2 Normally, news broadcasts begin with headlines. Think about how you incorporate that aspect by the questions you can ask your learners. How would you help them anticipate the details of the news by merely listening to the headlines? And, how would you help them understand that headlines are to news broadcasts what titles and subtitles are to a text?

10.2.3 Focusing on each of the main news stories, think of listening comprehension questions that you can ask to help your students understand the day's news.

10.2.4 Think of any prior knowledge of political or social events that is needed for learners to fully understand the day's news.

10.2.5 Focus also on difficult lexical and grammatical structures so that you can direct your learners' attention to them.

10.2.6 Let's say you wish to zero in on one or two stories for detailed analysis and understanding. What preparation do you have to make? How would you encourage an extended discussion on the selected news items? A debate? A group work?

10.2.7 How would you relate the listening and speaking activity to reading and writing? Normally, newspapers have more in-depth coverage of a particular news story than radio news broadcasts; therefore, would it be advisable to ask the learners to bring a copy of the day's newspaper to class? How would you relate the radio story to what appears in the newspaper to create an opportunity for learners to read in class?

10.2.8 Think of a writing assignment that would be appropriate to help learners connect the radio news broadcast, the same story in the newspaper, and their discussion in class.

10.2.9 If you teach a class consisting of students from different countries, how would you make use of the rich array of political and cultural background knowledge that is available in the class?

10.2.10 Think of a project in which the learners consult the library or surf the Internet to gather more information about any news item discussed in class, write a brief report, and present it in class.

In Closing

What we learn from the general discussion, the microstrategies, and the project proposals is that integration of language skills is natural to language communication. By designing and using microstrategies that integrate language skills, we will be assisting learners to engage in classroom activities that involve a meaningful and simultaneous engagement with language in use. As Oxford (2000, p. 18) puts it eloquently, for the instructional loom to produce a large, strong, beautiful, colorful tapestry, the strands consisting of the four primary skills of listening, reading, speaking, and writing must be closely interwoven. I have tried to show in this chapter that the best way of interweaving the four strands is to go beyond the limitations of commercially available textbooks that are still based on the separation of language skills, and learn to exploit various resources and channels of communication such as newspapers, radio, TV, and the Internet.

The emphasis on the integration of language skills is a logical continuation of the emphasis on contextualizing input embedded in linguistic, extralinguistic, situational, and extrasituational contexts that we discussed in the previous chapter. This logical connection is extended in the next chapter, where we look at the relevance of the social context in which L2 learning and teaching takes place.

CHAPTER 11

Ensuring Social Relevance

> It is simply impossible to isolate classroom life from the
> school's institutional dynamics, the ever-present tensions
> within the community, and the larger social forces. . . . In
> order to act effectively we have to recognize the influence
> of the social context.
>
> —DANIEL LISTON AND KENNETH ZEICHNER,
>   1990, p. 612

No classroom is an island unto itself. Every classroom is influenced
by and is a reflection of the larger society of which it is a part. The
term *society* itself refers to a very large unit consisting of a community of communities. In the specific context of language education,
it stands for "all of those wider (and overlapping) contexts in which
are situated the institutions in which language teaching takes place.
These include—but are not limited to—the international, national,
community, ethnic, bureaucratic, professional, political, religious,
economic and family contexts in which schools and other educational institutions are located and with which they interact" (Hywel
Coleman, 1996, p. 1).

Within a society, one comes across many forms of accommoda-
tion and assistance as well as domination and resistance. These forms
are generally based on factors such as class, gender, race, ethnicity,
nationality, religion, language, and sexual orientation. The same factors play a role in shaping classroom discourse as well (see Kumaravadivelu, 1999b, for details). In order to make L2 learning and
teaching socially relevant one has to recognize that the broader social, political, historical, and economic conditions that affect the lives
of learners and teachers also affect classroom aims and activities.

What such a recognition entails is that all those who are concerned with language education have to consider several factors
before determining the content and character of language policy,

planning, learning, and teaching. Given the depth and breadth of the subject, I shall restrict my discussion in this chapter to the learning and teaching of English as a national and international language. Within such a setting, I shall briefly focus on issues related to (a) the status of English as a global language, (b) the role of the home language in the learning and teaching of English, and (c) the use of appropriate teaching materials. As we discuss these issues, it will become fairly apparent that language pedagogy is closely tied up with power politics.

The Status of English as a Global Language

"A language achieves a genuinely global status," observes David Crystal (1997), the author of *English as a Global Language*, "when it develops a special role that is recognized in every country." English has developed such a role. In the international arena, it has increasingly become the language of war and peace, science and technology, commerce and communication. The advent of the Internet has only accelerated its spread, with more than 80 percent of home pages on the World Wide Web using English. At present, up to 380 million people speak English as their native language, up to 300 million speak it as their second language, and up to 1 billion speak it as a foreign language (Crystal, 1997). Thus, in its spread and use the English language is unrivaled in human history.

It is inevitable that a language of such spread and use will develop a large number of local varieties. There are several varieties of English even among those who speak it as native language: American English, Australian English, British English, etc. And, within these, there are domestic variations. In the United States alone, for instance, there are regional variations found in areas such as Boston, New York, Texas, and the southern states, and ethnic variations such as African-American Vernacular English.

The non-native varieties of English include Indian English, Kenyan English, Nigerian English, Singaporean English, etc. All these varieties are rule-governed, that is, they are conditioned by phonological, syntactic, semantic, and rhetorical rules. They are used for intranational as well as international communication; more for the former than for the latter. Even when used outside their countries, they are used to communicate more with other non-native speakers than with native speakers. Besides, a number of non-native varieties have developed a rich body of literature and other creative writings that demonstrate the use of English to express local sociocultural nuances.

In fact, the number of varieties of English has multiplied to the point of pluralizing it as World Englishes. Given the linguistic spread and the cultural richness of World Englishes, a crucial question arises regarding which standard or variety one should adopt for the purpose of learning and teaching English in various educational settings.

Reflective task 11.1

What criteria, do you think, must a language variety meet before it can be considered a "standard" variety? Who or what agency has the authority to declare a variety, a "standard" variety? Do you speak the "standard" variety of your first language? How do you know?

The Politics of Standardization

The term *standard* refers to a prestige variety of a language. It is commonly and vaguely defined as "the variety of a language which has the highest status in a community or nation and which is usually based on the speech and writing of educated native speakers of the language" (*Longman Dictionary of Applied Linguistics*, 1985, p. 271). A definition like this begs a number of questions including: How does one determine "the highest status"? Who determines it? Who constitutes a community for this purpose? How educated is "educated"?

A variety does not become "standard" just because educated native speakers speak it. A case in point is the following episode reported in a major newspaper during the 1992 U.S. presidential campaign involving Bill Clinton, the then-governor of the southern state of Arkansas. Consider this:

> Gov. Clinton, you attended Oxford University in England and Yale Law School in the Ivy League, two of the finest institutions of learning in the world. So how come you still talk like a hillbilly?

> (Mike Royko, "Opinion," *Chicago Tribune*, October 11, 1992, cited in Lippi-Green 1997, p. 211).

Hillbilly is a reference to the fact that Clinton hails from the South and speaks "Southern," a variety of English that is not considered "standard" in the United States.

Realistically, then, a variety is considered "standard" only because it is spoken by those who control the social, political, and cultural power centers within a nation. Thus, the standard variety of French is based on educated Parisian French. The standard variety of British-spoken English refers to Received Pronunciation (RP), historically derived from the speech of the Royalty based in southern London. Similarly, standard American English refers to the variety spoken and written by persons

- with no regional accent;
- who reside in the Midwest, far west or perhaps some parts of the northeast (but never in the south);
- with more than average or superior education;
- who are themselves educators or broadcasters;
- who pay attention to speech, and are not sloppy in terms of pronunciation or grammar;
- who are easily understood by all;
- who enter into a consensus of other individuals like themselves about what is proper in language.

(Rosina Lippi-Green, 1997, p. 53)

A standard variety, thus, gets its prestige owing to social, political, and economic factors and not linguistic ones. Linguistically speaking, a standard variety is neither superior nor inferior to any other. Given these facts, it is easy to conclude that "the custodians of standard English are self-elected members of a rather exclusive club" (Widdowson, 1994, p. 377).

The issue of "standard" becomes even more complicated in the context of several varieties of World Englishes because of colonial history and national identity. Colonialism used language as an instrument of political, social, and cultural control. Postcolonial theorists tell us that language "is a fundamental site of struggle for postcolonial discourse because the colonial process itself begins in language. The control over language by the imperial centre—whether achieved by displacing native languages, by installing itself as a 'standard' against other variants which are constituted as 'impurities,' or by planting the language of empire in a new place—

remains the most potent instrument of cultural control" (Bill Ash-croft, Gareth Griffiths and Helen Tiffin, 1995, p. 283).

Connecting this line of thinking specifically to English language teaching (ELT), Alastair Pennycook (1998) offers an in-depth analysis of what he calls "the continuity of cultural constructs of colonialism" and demonstrates how ELT is deeply interwoven with the discourses of colonialism. ELT, he argues, "is a product of colonialism not just because it is colonialism that produced the initial conditions for the global spread of English but because it was colonialism that produced many of the ways of thinking and behaving that are still part of Western cultures. European/Western culture not only produced colonialism but was also produced by it; ELT not only rode on the back of colonialism to the distant corners of the Empire but was also in turn produced by that voyage" (p. 19). Based on his analysis, Pennycook calls for concerted efforts to decolonize English language education by finding alternative representations and alternative possibilities in English language classes.

Consolidating an alternative approach to the issue of standardization, Peter Lowenberg (2000, p. 69–70) observes that "the norms of Standard English in any variety—native-speaker or non-native—are not what any outsider—native speaker or non-native speaker—thinks they should be." Accordingly, he operationally defines the standard model of a variety of English—native or non-native—as "the linguistic forms of that variety that are normally used in formal speaking and writing by speakers who have received the highest level of education available in that variety." The assumption that native speakers should determine the norms for teaching and testing Standard English around the world, he rightly asserts, betrays a neocolonial attitude. Lowenberg's observations are consistent with the stand other scholars have taken in the field of World Englishes such as Kachru (1982), Krishnaswamy and Burde (1998), and Kandiah (1998). They hold the view that the pluralistic nature and the dynamic linguistic and creative processes of non-native varieties express the social identity and the cultural values of the speakers of those varieties, thus constituting standard varieties by themselves.

Reflective task 11.2

Focus on three different settings, i.e., (a) immigrants in an English-speaking country like the United States or United Kingdom, (b) learners of English as a second language in countries like India or Singapore, and (c) learners of English as a foreign language in countries like China or Japan. If you were part of the language policy planning team in these countries, what variety (or standard) would you recommend for purposes of learning and teaching in these settings? Why?

Raising and answering the question, Who owns English? Widdowson (1994, p. 384) argues that "the very fact that English is an international language means that no nation can have a custody over it. To grant such custody of the language is necessarily to arrest its development and so undermine its international status." He further reckons that native speakers of English cannot claim the language to be exclusively their own because it is "not a possession which they lease out to others, while still retaining the freehold. Other people actually own it."

If "other people" actually own a variety of the English language and use it effectively within their speech community, how does such ownership conflict with the politics of standardization? And, how does that conflict affect English language learning and teaching in various educational settings? Let us consider these and other related issues with reference to two different settings: (a) English in the L1 setting, (b) English in the L2 setting.

Standardization in the L1 Context

Aboriginal English spoken in Australia, Scottish and Irish spoken in the United Kingdom, and African-American Vernacular English spoken in the United States are all examples of English that are in contact with a dominant variety of English. All these varieties are rule-governed with phonological, morphological, syntactic, semantic, and rhetorical structures. Speakers of these varieties use them with members of their families or with members of their communities but may switch to a dominant variety for other purposes. While the history and status of these varieties are very different, they all share similar experiences of coming into conflict with the politics of standardization.

A case in point is the cultural politics of Ebonics that flared up recently in the United States. Ebonics, a blend of *ebony* and *phonics*, is the popular name given to African-American Vernacular English (AAVE). In 1996, authorities in Oakland, California, passed a resolution declaring Ebonics to be the primary language of the African-American students in Oakland's schools and recommended that students be taught in such a way that they maintain their home language Ebonics as well as learn Standard American English.

The move was strongly opposed by the American media and the American public, including some prominent African-American leaders. The *New York Times* wrote that it is a "blunder" to give "black slang" a place of honor in the classroom. It objected that "by labeling them as linguistic foreigners in their own country, the new policy will actually stigmatize African-American children—while validating habits of speech that bar them from the cultural mainstream and decent jobs" (*New York Times*, 1996, cited in Dennis Baron, 2000, p. 7). Faced with severe criticism, Oakland quickly retracted its resolution and replaced it with a milder one stating that the objective of the resolution was to teach teachers about the language their students brought to school, and to teach Standard American English to students who speak AAVE as home language (see, for instance, Baron, 2000, for more details).

The widespread debate that followed the Oakland decision seems to have reinforced the general consensus that knowledge of the "standard" variety is necessary for social and economic uplift. However, serious concerns were expressed about the need for maintaining the linguistic and cultural identity of the speakers of minority varieties, and also for linking the variety spoken at home with the variety taught at school. These concerns reflected an earlier assertion by Lisa Delpit (1990, p. 53) that it is the responsibility of teachers to "recognize that the linguistic form a student brings to school is intimately connected with loved ones, community, and personal identity. To suggest that this form is 'wrong' or, even worse, ignorant, is to suggest that something is wrong with the student and his or her family."

There is also evidence suggesting that an understanding of the

norms of interaction in home language and home culture can significantly help teachers create the conditions necessary for their
learners to master the "standard" variety taught at school. In her
well-known study on this subject, Shirley Brice Heath (1983)
demonstrated how the discontinuity in the patterns of language
learning and language use in schools and communities of children
from African-American families in the southeastern United States
adversely affected their language development. When teachers were
made aware of this discontinuity and changed their teaching strategies, students were found to be more active and more motivated to
participate in classroom events. Summarizing research studies in
this area, Geneva Smitherman (1998, p. 142) observes, "When students' primary/home language is factored into language planning
policy and the teaching-learning process, it is a win-win situation
for all."

Standardization in the L2 Context

The need to recognize the legitimacy of "nonstandard" varieties becomes even more acute in the context of the different varieties of
World Englishes that are learned and taught in various parts of the
world. In most cases, these varieties came about because of colonial
history and are retained because of postcolonial economy. As Thiru
Kandaiah (1998, p.104) succinctly puts it, the users of these varieties "take hold of an originally alien code which, moreover, was
imposed on them. But without disregarding entirely the nature of
the rule-governed system they received from its original users, they
still go on to reconstruct it to make it serve their semantic, actional
and interactional purposes. In doing so, they operate in immediate
interaction with the social, cultural, historical and other such particularities of their contexts."

At times, the particularities of these varieties conflict with the
process of standardization. Consider, for example, the English language policy of two nations with two different varieties—India and
Singapore. As former British colonies, they both share a common
colonial heritage. They both are multilingual and multicultural societies, though of very different magnitude in terms of economy,
size, and population. In both countries, English functions as a *lingua
franca*, a common language that links people of different languages

and cultures. They have, however, taken two different paths to the issue of standardization.

Considered to be "among the most distinctive varieties in the English-speaking world" (Crystal, 1997, p. 41), Indian English represents the extent to which a foreign language can be profitably reconstructed into a vehicle to express sociocultural norms and networks that are typically local. The process of Indianization of English has not left any of the linguistic systems—syntactic, lexical, semantic, or rhetorical—untouched (see Kachru, 1985, for details). Enjoying the constitutionally guaranteed status of an "associate" official language, English is used within the legal system, administration, secondary and higher education, the armed forces, the media, and industry. Although only a fraction of the population are fluent in English, it has penetrated most layers of the society through English words borrowed into Indian languages.

In spite of its deep penetration, the English language has not, argue Krishnaswamy and Burde (1998, p. 153), "made any serious inroads into the social customs, ceremonies connected with births, marriages and deaths, religious functions and rituals that go with festivals, worship in temples, intimate interactions in the family and in the peer group—even in urban areas." Because of this phenomenon, they suggest that English in India should be treated as a "modulect." It is the modular use of English, they assert, "that allows some Indians to use English according to their needs, and yet keep it separate from their local 'identity' which is deeply rooted in their ancient past and in the several layers of a pluralistic pattern."

It is certainly the emphasis on individual and collective identity that allows Indians to accept the variety spoken by educated Indians as norms for standardization rather than looking up to the norms associated with the British variety. For educational purposes, then, it is the Indian variety that is given prominence. While Indian writing in English—creative, professional, or journalistic—is expected to conform to international grammatical norms, all other forms of language use is shaped by the local variety. In fact, in schools and colleges, English is taught by Indian teachers using Indian textbooks written by Indian authors. Neither the policy makers nor the general public seek native speakers from English-speaking countries for purposes of English language education.

In Singapore, English is an official language along with three others: Malay, Mandarin, and Tamil. All Singaporeans are at least bilingual, the common language being English. One in five uses English in family settings. In fact, it is stated that "English can be used in all aspects of daily life. There are a few Singaporeans who seldom, if ever, need to use any other language; who perform all their work life, all their emotional life, and all their commercial transactions in English" (Anthea Gupta, 1998, p. 123).

The issue of standardization has been made simple and straightforward by declaring Standard Singapore English (SSE), which is closely modeled on Standard British English, as the norm to follow both for writing and for speech. For purposes of accelerating industrialization and modernization, for ensuring effective international communication, and for providing equal opportunities (as well as equal challenges), Singapore decided to opt for British Received Pronunciation (see Foley, et al., 1998, for more details) as a matter of government policy.

In order to implement its English-language policy, Singapore has been actively recruiting native speakers from Britain and other English-speaking countries to be teachers and teacher educators. In addition, most of the textbooks used in schools and colleges have been written and produced by native speakers of English. Singapore has also sought the expertise and the experience of The British Council, which, along with local institutions such as the Regional Language Centre (RELC), have been making a concerted effort to spread "proper" English.

Sustained institutional efforts seem to have yielded good results in that most educated Singaporeans are considered to speak standard English. However, also creeping in has been Colloquial Singapore English (CSE), or, more popularly, Singlish, which is a blend of simplified English with words and sentence patterns from local languages. When, during the early 1990s, there was a proliferation of TV shows that used Singlish, the government-run Singapore Broadcasting Corporation (SBC) decided not to allow Singlish on TV. It issued guidelines allowing the use of Standard English only. It defined Standard English as "grammatically correct and pronounced in the correct way," and local English as "grammatically correct but spoken in a recognizably Singaporean accent" (see Wendy Bokhorst-Heng, 1998, p. 305). Bokhorst-Heng goes on to remark that the assumption "was that what is 'correct' pronunciation is British Received Pronunciation." She also finds the SBC definitions "rather curious" because "Singlish is not spoken by only those with a 'poor command of English.'" It is spoken by highly educated Singaporeans as well.

Singlish "is part of the search for a Singaporean identity," said David Wong, Chair of the Speak Good English Movement (Associated Press, August 26, 2001). The Speak Good English Movement is a Singapore government initiative to encourage the use of proper English. The Associated Press also reported that Singapore's Prime Minister Goh Chok Tong warned that Singapore could lose out if vital foreign investors and multinational company executives face a variety of English that they don't understand. The persistent use of Singlish, even by highly educated Singaporeans, in spite of official discouragement, indicates the dynamic nature and the communicative potential of varieties of English that are not considered prestigious.

To sum up this section, standardization is essentially a political act over which teachers may not have any direct control. They may have to deal with students who come to class with a home language and home culture that are different from the ones they will encounter in the classroom. The least teachers can do is to recognize the rich linguistic and cultural heritage the learners bring with them and use them as resources to build bridges between what is known and what is new.

Reflective task 11.3

Pause here briefly to consider, either individually or with a peer partner, different ways in which L2 teachers can link learners' home language/culture with target language/culture. What opportunities and limitations do you anticipate here?

The Role of the First Language

First language is perhaps the most useful and the least-used resource students bring to the L2 classroom. This is partly due to two interrelated factors: the theory and practice of established methods (see Chapter 2 for details) discourage the use of L1 in the L2 classroom, and the political economy of English Language Teaching promotes the interests of native speakers of English who do not normally share the language of their learners. There are, however, sound arguments that support the use of L1 in the L2 classroom. I shall discuss these with reference to two different learning and teaching settings: (a) minority learners in Britain and (b) L2 learners in Sri Lanka.

Minority Learners in Britain

Since the mid-1980s British schools, particularly in multilingual urban areas, have been offering home language support for learners from minority ethnic communities. It has come to be known as bilingual support. The aim is to help learners access the curriculum until they develop sufficient English to move on to monolingual education through the medium of English. It is believed that such a practice would offer psychological and social support for minority children and provide a much-needed continuity between the home and school environment.

Marilyn Martin-Jones and Mukul Saxena (1996) have studied the effect of home language use in primary classrooms in England, where a majority of learners are speakers of Panjabi and Urdu. In these classes, typically, a bilingual assistant will provide a simple explanation in the learner's mother tongue. Here's a sample classroom interactional episode taken from their study, reproduced here as episode 12.1. I have retained the transcription convention given in the original text.

Transcription convention:

Italics	=	translation of Urdu/Panjabi into English
Normal	=	transcription for English utterances
Bold	=	transcription for U/P utterances
CT	=	Class Teacher
BA	=	Bilingual Assistant

L   =   one learner
LL   =   several learners
E   =   English
P   =   Punjabi

Episode 11.1

CT: . . . what did the thin snow man have?

L1:   I know, glasses

BA: no (P) **enoo** . . . **enoo** (points to book) e What's this called? This

CT: (E) (not glasses)

L: ([*Tailifoon*])

BA: **enoo aaxde ne** (E) pipe (P) **jeRe** (E) [*sigrat*](P) **hunde,** This is
         called a pipe. Do you know cigarettes? **Naa? Ik hundaa? . . . e
         jeRaa lakRii** There's a-this-that's made of wood. (BA mimes ac-
         tion of holding a pipe. Filling with tobacco, and smoking pipe)
         daa banyaa e. ede vic tabako paade naa? Fer onoo They put
         tobacco in this, then they light this. (E) light (P) **karde, naa? Taa
         fer enoo piinde naa?** (E) [*sigrat*] And then they smoke this like
         cigarettes (E) pipe (P) **aaxde. Kii e?** a pipe. What is it?

LL: (E) pipe, pipe, pipe

BA: [*sigrat*] (P) **piinde?** [They/he] smoke cigarettes?

L: (E) do you know my cousin

BA: he's got a pipe?

L: he not got a pipe he's got he . . . he (smokes cigarettes) everybody

BA: he smoke everyday?

CT: shall we give one to this snowman then? Like that, put it in his
         mouth? Oh he is that alright?

LL: yeh

CT: OK

                  (Data source: Martin-Jones and Saxena, 1996, p. 117–8)

The class teacher (CT) was discussing a story called *The Two Snowmen*. One was tall and thin and the other was short and fat. The
answer she expected to her question "What did the thin snowman
have?" was "a pipe." One learner volunteered "glasses" instead. At

this point, the bilingual assistant (BA) stepped in to explain in Panjabi the difference between a pipe and a cigarette. Explaining the episode and referring to the bilingual assistant, Martin-Jones and Saxena observe: "When discussing this event with us later, she said that she had realized that children were not familiar with the practice of putting pipes in the mouths of snowmen and were also unlikely to have seen anyone in their immediate family smoking a pipe" (p. 120).

More importantly, the researchers point out that when one learner introduced a point in English about a cousin of hers who smoked cigarettes, the bilingual assistant realized the significance of this point for the child because smoking was frowned upon in her local Muslim community. Not realizing the significance of the child's point, the class teacher terminated this exchange between the learner and the bilingual assistant, directing everyone's attention to the board, thus failing to utilize a learning opportunity created by a learner (see Chapter 3).

L2 learners in Sri Lanka

Consider the following three short interactional episodes from Sri Lankan classrooms consisting of Tamil learners of English. The data and explanation are taken from Canagarajah (1999, p. 132, 136).

Episode 11.2

S1:   (reading) Who owns the red car?
S2:   (reads) The red car belongs to // (to T) *itenna*, miss, eppiTi colluratu, (spells) e-n-o-s-h-a? What is this, MISS, how do I say this?
T: Enosha
S2:   (reads) The red car belongs to Enosha.

In this episode, where two learners role-play a dialogue, the task itself is performed in English while request for help is uttered in Tamil. Additionally, according to Canagarajah, making requests in L1 "has affective value and it conveys sincerity and an appeal for sympathy" (p. 132).

Episode 11.3

T: What is the past tense form of swim? // Come on. // *enna piL-LayaL,itu teriyaataa? Poona vakupilai connaiinkaL.* What, children, you don't know this? You told me in the last class.

S1: swimmed=

S2: =swam

In situations like this, where teachers need to encourage hesitant, frightened, or nervous students, they switch to the less formal and more personal Tamil. This results in "putting students at ease, conveying teacher's empathy and, in general, creating a less threatening atmosphere" (ibid., p. 132).

Episode 11.4

T: Trees and vegetation are also used as medicine. Can you mention some trees which are used like that? // Quinine is produced from citronella. What else?

S1: *tulasi?*

T: Yes.

S2: *tuutuvalai?*

S3: *canTi.*

As the above episode reveals, on occasions, it is easier to use L1 terms instead of attempting a confusing and misleading translation into the closest English equivalent. As observed by Canagarajah, by encouraging such answers in the L1, the teacher is able to ensure that the lesson relates well to the cultural background of the learners.

To sum up this section, the interactional episodes from the British and Sri Lankan classes reveal that there are several advantages to using the L1 as a resource in the L2 classroom. They include, but are not limited to,

- tapping the linguistic and cultural knowledge that the learners bring to class;

- managing linguistic and cultural identity in informal and friendly ways;

- giving clear directions in class thereby reducing the chances of mismatch between teacher intention and learner interpretation (cf. Chapter 4);

- providing simple explanations so that learners can easily grasp certain concepts that are being addressed; and

- personalizing routine classroom talk and topic management (cf. Chapter 5).

In short, the use of L1 helps learners make the connection between the home language and the target language, thereby ensuring social relevance to classroom aims and activities.

It is therefore pedagogically unsound not to use a rich resource like the home language of the learners whenever possible and appropriate. Elsa Auerbach (1993) cites evidence from both research and practice to show that the use of the L1 in early L2 classes is critical not only to later success but also to a smooth transition to the target language. What she points out about the American context is also true of other contexts, that is, the insistence of using English only in the classroom "rests on unexamined assumptions, originates in the political agenda of dominant groups, and serves to reinforce existing relations of power" (p.12).

In fact, sometimes learners themselves might resist any dogmatic insistence on the target language only policy in the classroom. Marilyn Martin-Jones and Monica Heller (1996, p. 7) report an incident from a French-language minority school in Canada. In one grade 8 classroom, a student approached the teacher and said, "Can I have the stapler, Monsieur?" In an attempt to uphold the official language policy of the school, the teacher replied, *"Parlez Français"* (Speak French). The student looked at the clock and said, "It's not nine o'clock yet, Monsieur!"—indicating that the class had not started yet. It appears that by making a structural distinction between class time and "other time," this learner is actually registering her resentment over the French-only policy of the school.

Thus, the case for using L1 in the L2 classroom is quite strong. What would, indeed, complement the appropriate use of L1 in the L2 classroom is the design and use of socially relevant teaching materials.

Reflective task 11.4

How would you define or describe "socially relevant teaching materials"? If you are given prescribed textbooks selected by your school authorities or by outside agencies, what are the ways in which you can adapt them to suit your social context?

The Use of Appropriate Teaching Materials

Textbooks are not a neutral medium. They represent cultural values, beliefs, and attitudes. They reflect "a social construction that may be imposed on teachers and students and that indirectly constructs their view of a culture. This aspect often passes unrecognized" (Martin Cortazzi and Lixian Jin, 1999, p. 200). Critical recognition of the hidden cultural values embedded in centrally produced textbooks is a prerequisite for ensuring social relevance in the L2 classroom.

Textbooks, to be relevant, must be sensitive to the aims and objectives, needs and wants of learners from a particular pedagogic setting. However, because of the global spread of English, ELT has become a global industry with high economic stakes, and textbook production has become one of the engines that drives the industry. It is hardly surprising that the world market is flooded with textbooks not grounded in local sociocultural milieu.

It is very common, as Sandra McKay (2000, p. 9) points out, to see teacher and students coming from the same linguistic and cultural background, but use textbooks that draw heavily on a foreign culture, as in the case of classrooms in Thailand or in Korea where local teachers use materials written in the United States or Great Britain. She cites two examples to bring out such a cultural anomaly. A Korean student experienced difficulty in using a U.S.-published textbook when he was teaching in Korea. One of the exercises instructed students to look at photographs of various events in American history and decide the decade in which the picture was taken! In another example, she talks about a lesson on garage sales in the United States. She rightly observes that those from cultures that have garage sales wouldn't think twice about it, while those from other cultures might be puzzled. She wonders whether students from another culture "would be surprised and perhaps offended by the idea of buying used mattresses, sheets, blankets and underwear" (p. 9).

Taking into consideration that English is a global language, Cortazzi and Jin (1999) suggest three types of cultural information that can be used in preparing teaching materials:

- target culture materials that use the culture of a country where English is spoken as a first language;
- source culture materials that draw on the learners' own culture as content; and
- international target culture materials that use a variety of cultures in English and non-English-speaking countries around the world.

This suggestion is based on the recognition that both local and global cultures, not just the culture of the target language community, should inform the preparation of materials for learning and teaching an L2. This is one sure way of ensuring social relevance in the L2 classroom.

Expanding Possibilities

Ensuring social relevance in the L2 classroom is closely linked to the pedagogy of possibility discussed in chapters 1 and 2. Recall that a pedagogy of possibility demands for us to take seriously the social and historical conditions that create the cultural forms and interested knowledge that give meaning to the lives of teachers and learners. As I have argued elsewhere (Kumaravadivelu, 2001), the experiences participants bring to the classroom are shaped not only by the learning and teaching episodes they have encountered in the past but also by a broader social, economic, and political environment in which they grew up. These experiences have the potential to affect classroom practices in ways unintended and unexpected by policy planners, curriculum designers, or textbook producers.

Two examples, one from Sri Lanka and another from South Africa, demonstrate how life in the street can easily influence lessons in the classroom. Canagarajah (1999) reports how Tamil students of English in the civil war–torn Sri Lanka offered resistance to Western representations of English language and culture. He shows how the students, through marginal comments and graphics, actually reframed, reinterpreted, and rewrote the content of their

ESL textbooks imported from the West. Similarly, analyzing L2 classroom data in terms of the ideology and structures of the apartheid South Africa, Keith Chick (1996) demonstrates how the classroom talk represented "styles consistent with norms of interaction which teachers and students constituted as a means of avoiding the oppressive and demeaning constraints of apartheid educational systems" (p. 37). While the Sri Lankan and South African cases may be considered by some to be extreme cases of classroom life imitating the sociopolitical turmoil outside the class, there are numerous instances where race, gender, class, and other variables directly or indirectly influence the content and character of classroom input and interaction.

In the process of sensitizing itself to the prevailing sociopolitical reality, a pedagogy of possibility is also concerned with individual as well as social identity. More than any other educational enterprise, L2 education that brings languages and cultures in contact provides its participants with challenges and opportunities for a continual quest for subjectivity and self-identity. In a sense, then, the classroom behavior of the Sri Lankan and South African students mentioned above is an unmistakable manifestation of their attempt to preserve and protect their individual and collective identity. At a different level, the same can be said about the persistence of Singlish in Singapore as well.

Reflective task 11.5

Considering the overall thrust of this chapter, what challenges do you think L2 teachers face in raising sociopolitical and sociocultural issues in class? And, how to overcome those challenges?

In answering this question, reflect on the following episode reported by Douglas Brown (1998, p. 256): "From China I received some very guarded personal comments from a native Chinese who asked not to be identified. I was told that, in fact, treatment of political issues must be covert, lest one lose more than one's job. He described two approaches that intrigued me. The first he called 'point at one but accuse another,' through which he has had students study oppression and suppression of free speech in the former Soviet Union, calling for critical analysis of the roots and remedies of such denial of freedom. In another approach, which he called 'murder someone with a borrowed knife,' he had students criticize Western news reports on Chinese politics. Without espousing any particular point of view himself, and under the guise of offering criticism of the Western bias, students were covertly led to comprehend alternative points of view."

What follows from the above discussion is that language teachers, if they are serious about ensuring social relevance in the classroom, can ill afford to ignore the sociopolitical and sociocultural reality that influences identity formation in the classroom nor can they afford to separate the linguistic needs of learners from their social needs. In other words, they can hardly satisfy their pedagogic obligations without at the same time satisfying their social obligations. In fulfilling these obligations, they will have to reconcile two apparently opposing tendencies: on the one hand, knowledge of a standard variety, however it is defined in a particular context, is essential for personal growth as well as professional opportunities; on the other hand, respect for and recognition of the home languages that learners bring to the class can only enhance their chances of developing linguistic and communicative competence in their L2. Keeping all this in mind, let us now turn to sample microstrategies that might help teachers ensure social relevance in their classroom. See also microstrategies in other chapters (e.g., chapters 7 and 10) that deal with sociopolitical relevance.

Microstrategies for Ensuring Social Relevance

As always, modify the following microstrategies to suit the proficiency level of your students. You might also wish to delete or add to the activities that constitute these microstrategies.

Microstrategy 11.1. *Una Coca Cola por favor*

11.1.0 As an L2 teacher, you might have noticed that learners, at least in private conversations, engage in what is called code mixing, that is, mixing features of L1 and L2, sometimes resulting in humorous situations. Try to pay attention and collect true stories that you can later use for a classroom activity. You can also collect such stories from students, newspapers, or Internet chat rooms. Here's one such example:

11.1.1 The following humorous story was contributed by Dominick Egan to *ESL Magazine*, January/February 1998, p. 26. Copy it onto a transparency and project it on an OHP screen. Ask your learners to read this silently.

Linguistic Laughs!
Every ESL teacher has his or her favorite class story; these stories usually concern comical linguistic/cultural misunderstandings. My own favorite story occurred many years ago in a small ESL school in Washington, DC. On the first day of school a young Hispanic student joined our beginners' English class; he had just arrived in the U.S.

During break he went to buy a Coke from the soda vending machine. This machine contained a little window with a digital display. The display indicated how much to insert for a soda, e.g., 60¢. The thirsty student inserted a quarter and the machine promptly displayed 35¢. After he inserted another quarter, the machine displayed the digital letters "d-i-m-e." To you and me this means ten cents. But he misread it as two separate words "di" "me" which means "tell me" in Spanish. He leaned closer to the vending machine and whispered: "una Coca Cola por favour." Needless to say, the other students died laughing and the story of the bilingual vending machine spread like wildfire!

11.1.2 First use this text as you normally would for teaching reading comprehension. Help your learners understand the text. In settings where vending machines are not a familiar concept, explain what they are and how they are used. If your class does not consist of Spanish-speaking students, ask them to guess the meaning of "una Coca Cola por favour" from the context. Focus also on phrases like "died laughing" and "spread like wildfire."

11.1.3 Form groups of three to five students. If yours is a multilingual class, put those who speak the same L1 in the same group(s). Ask each group to come up with at least one story or a joke based on linguistic or cultural misunderstanding. Let them know that the focus is on "linguistic jokes," not on "ethnic jokes," which could be embarrassing for some members of the class.

11.1.4 Select a few groups that have something to report and ask a representative from each group to share their story with the class. Let them, with your help, explain the linguistic nuances associated with the joke or story. Encourage others to ask questions and seek clarifications. Explain the punch line, if necessary.

11.1.5 Switch gears and turn to cognate words. Explain to your students that these are words from two different languages that are similar in form and meaning, because both languages may have the same origin. Give examples such as *brother* in English and *Bruder* in German. In small groups or as a whole class, depending on time, ask them to think of similar examples focusing on their L1 and L2. Discuss these examples. If they cannot come up with any examples in class, ask them to do the task as a take-home assignment, talking to people at home or consulting a dictionary, and bring examples to the next class session.

11.1.6 Then, focus on false cognates (also called false friends). Explain to them that these are words that have the same or very similar form in two languages, with a different meaning in each. Give an example such as the French word *expérience*, which means *experiment* and not *experience*. Then, follow the same procedure as in 11.1.5.

11.1.7 Turn now to borrowed words. Explain the concept with examples (e.g., *kampuni* in Swahili is a borrowing from English *company*). Then, follow the same procedure as in 11.1.5.

11.1.8 Devote a class session in which you allow students to present examples of cognates, false cognates, or borrowings in their home language and the target language. Encourage them to provide adequate explanations for the benefit of those who may come from a different L1 background.

11.1.9 Finally, pull all the class discussion together and explain how consciously looking for cognates, false cognates, and borrowings is a good learning strategy particularly for building vocabulary or for increasing one's reading comprehension.

Microstrategy 11.2: No Spanish, Please

11.2.0 As we discussed earlier in this chapter, language policy and planning have more to do with politics than with linguistics or even education. There are multilingual countries where the political establishment would like to encourage the use of a dominant language and discourage the use of minority ones, often resulting in personal or political tension. Issues arising out of such a tension can be raised in class not only for focusing on certain lexical or grammatical items but also for raising social consciousness among the learners. Newspapers are a good source of materials that can be used for this purpose. Here's an example. Adapt this microstrategy to suit your learning and teaching situation.

11.2.1   An interesting news item related to the use of first language and the target language at home appeared in *New York Times* September 30, 1995, page A10. It was titled "Mother Scolded by Judge for Speaking Spanish." I summarize it below. Copy this onto an OHP transparency for use in class, or make multiple copies to distribute to students.

In June 1995, in Amarillo, Texas, a district court judge named Samuel C. Kiser delivered a ruling in a child custody case involving a Spanish speaking couple. In his ruling, he accused the defendant, Martha Laureano, of child abuse for using Spanish at home to speak to her five-year-old daughter. He ordered the mother to speak only English to the girl, who was about to enter kindergarten that fall. He argued that English was necessary for her daughter to "do good in school." Otherwise, he warned, the girl would be condemned to a life as a maid.

When the news story was published, there was a public outcry against the court decision. Judge Kiser held a press conference and apologized to maids, insisting that he held them in high esteem. But he stuck to his English-only order.

Martha Laureano was bilingual in English and Spanish but, as a mother, she wanted to speak Spanish at home so that her child would not forget her native tongue as she learns in English at school.

11.2.2   As a prereading strategy, ask your learners general questions such as what role their native tongue plays in their life, what language they use with their mother, father, and other family members and why, etc.

11.2.3   Continue the prereading strategy with questions that are specific to the reading text, questions such as what constitutes child abuse, under what circumstances, if any, can a mother using her native tongue with her child be considered child abuse, etc.

11.2.4   Project the text onto the OHP screen and have your learners read it silently. Start with reading comprehension questions. Help your learners understand the text.

11.2.5   Depending on the proficiency level of your students, conduct a debate in class, with one group arguing for and another against the judge's decision. Divide the class into two groups, and ask each group to select a leader. Let them first discuss the pros and cons.

11.2.6   Moderate the debate. First, ask the group leaders to present their case. Then, have members of each group argue and try to convince the other. Sum up the debate at the end, remembering to commend your learners for their attempt.

11.2.7 Shifting attention of language use at home to the workplace, ask your learners to read the following "News Brief" (you can either write it on the board or project it onto the OHP screen). It is taken from the *Los Angeles Times*, September, 24, 2000. Here's the unedited version.

> Spanish-Speaking Workers Win English-Only Ruling
> Thirteen telephone operators who had been hired to field calls from Mexico won a record $709,284 judgment against a Texas company that fired them for refusing to abide by an English-only rule. The plaintiffs included a couple barred from speaking Spanish to each other in the lunchroom. A judge ruled against Premier Operator Services Inc., after a linguist testified that "code switching," an unconscious tendency to lapse into a native language, cannot easily be turned off.

11.2.8 First, help the learners comprehend the text. Have them talk about the rationale behind the Texas company's decision to fire some of the employees—including a married couple—because they were speaking in their native tongue during their lunch break.

11.2.9 If the linguistic and communicative levels of your learners permit, ask them to discuss the two court rulings in relation to the difficulties faced by minority communities in maintaining their linguistic and cultural identity. If not, then you should talk about them briefly.

11.2.10 Finally, give the students a take-home assignment in which they write an essay expressing their personal views on the issues raised in class.

Exploratory Projects

As indicated earlier in this chapter, one of the impediments teachers face in their attempt to ensure social relevance is that prescribed textbooks may not adequately deal with socially relevant issues. To overcome such an impediment, you may have to tap into (a) human resources, and (b) electronic resources. The following projects are designed to help you to explore both.

Project 11.1. Tapping Human Resources

11.1.0 We learned in this chapter that one way of easing the transition from home language to school language is for teachers to form bridges between the two. It is profitable to involve learners themselves in the task of bridge-building. One area of difficulty for L2 learners is the difference between management of talk at home and management of talk at school. It is often suggested that L2 learners from certain linguistic or cultural backgrounds hesitate to actively participate in class discussion. As Heath (1983) suggested, the reason may have to do with the disjunction between the nature of talk at home and the nature of talk at school. This exploratory project aims at connecting the two. It is based on ideas from Bean, Kumaravadivelu, and Lowenberg (1995).

11.1.1 First you need to find out about the interactive styles and preferences that learners bring with them to class. Even a roughly tuned survey questionnaire with open-ended questions will serve the purpose. It is true that open-ended questions yield less precise responses, but they are capable of bringing out more holistic insights into the students' take on interactional patterns. Think about possible areas of differences between home and classroom modes of interaction.

11.1.2 Make a list of probable questions that you might wish to ask your learners about interactive styles at home. Questions such as:

- Who initiates talk at home?
- Are turns allotted or taken?
- Are there any rules of conversation?
- Are there any restrictions about what to talk about and when?
- Are there any restrictions about what not to talk about and when?
- What variations do they notice in talking to parents, siblings, and friends?
- Any other?

11.1.3 Make a list of probable questions that you might wish to ask your learners about what they prefer in classroom interaction. Questions such as:

- What kind of interactional style makes them feel comfortable in class?
- Do they prefer teachers calling on students individually?
- Do they prefer questions addressed to the class as a whole?
- Do they prefer teachers correcting their errors?
- Do they like to help their friends with homework?
- Any other?

11.1.4 Add as many questions as you deem fit, and conduct the survey in class. Ask your students to do it anonymously. If necessary, allow them to complete the first part of the survey at home with the help of other members of the family. Collect and consolidate their responses.

11.1.5   Use the consolidated response as the basis of a discussion in class. Highlight the differences between management of talk at home and at school, and the need for transition.

11.1.6   Think about strategies and activities that will not only raise their consciousness about talk at home and talk at school, but also lessen their inhibitions to express their fears and discomforts, and to share their preferences and predilections.

11.1.7   Rather than forcing change, think about how you can be sensitive to the learners' interactive styles and expectations and move them gradually to do what is expected of them in the classroom context.

11.1.8   Reflect on other ways of involving your learners in the process of bridging the gap between home language/culture and school language/culture.

11.1.9   Take any one unit of lesson from the textbook prescribed for your class and see how you can modify some of the exercises or activities to make them more sensitive to learner preferences and expectations.

11.1.10   Finally, think about how you can tap the print media (such as newspapers) and the electronic media (such as the Internet) to collect materials that would help you ensure social relevance in class.

Project 11.2: Tapping Electronic Resources

11.2.0   As demonstrated in several chapters of this book, electronic media offer unlimited possibilities for teachers to transcend the limitations of predetermined curricula and prescribed textbooks. One such possibility is to subscribe (it's free and flexible!) to a so-called listserv. "Listservs are simply electronic discussion groups which allow ESL/EFL professionals all over the world to share ideas. When you subscribe to a listserv, you receive through your e-mail account, all of the messages posted by subscribers to that group. You will be able to post your own messages as well and participate in any ongoing discussions" (Christine Meloni, 1998, p.19). Here's how you can use this resource for designing your own microstrategies. I have drawn ideas from Meloni to inform the "technical" part of this exploratory project.

11.2.1   In order to find out what is available and to choose one that most suits your needs, try the Web site called "Liszt" (http://www.liszt

.com). If you are overwhelmed by the volume of electronic lists you see on your computer screen, try a narrower resource: http://www.tsol.net/ mailing.list.help.html.

11.2.2 According to Meloni (1998, p. 19), the two most popular discussion lists for ESL/EFL professionals are TESL-L and Neteach-L. The former is more suited for ESL teachers and the latter for both ESL and EFL teachers. To subscribe to TESL-L send an e-mail to: Listserv @cunyvm.cuny.edu. The text of the message should be: SUB TESL-L [your first name] [your last name]. Example: SUB TESOL-L Jane Doe.

11.2.3 To subscribe to Neteach-L send an electronic message to: listserv@thecity.sfsu.edu The text of the message should be: subscribe Neteach-L [your first name] [your last name]. Example: subscribe Neteach-L John Doe.

11.2.4 These listservs have branches that focus on several areas of interest. For the specific purpose of designing microstrategies for ensuring social relevance, choose special interest areas such as "Fluency First and Whole Language," "Literacy and Adult Education," or "Critical Language Education" (Caution: these sites might change from time to time, or new ones may come up).

11.2.5 If possible, form an informal Internet club consisting of a group of your workplace peers so that each member of the club can focus on special interest areas and gather ideas to be shared with other members of the club.

11.2.6 Within your area of interest, select some relevant messages posted by subscribers. You may wish to create an archive of messages and conversations on specific topics either by printing a hard copy or by saving them on a disk for later use.

11.2.7 When the occasion arises, design a suitable microstrategy on a specific topic using the information from your archive. Adapt the procedure I have outlined for the two microstrategies given above.

11.2.8 Implement the newly designed microstrategy in class and monitor its development.

11.2.9 Involve your students by inviting them to assess the relevance as well as the effectiveness of the microstrategy you have designed and implemented. Based on their feedback, revise it for further use.

11.2.10 Finally, reflect on the desirability and doability of this project. Think also about any additional resources you may need to carry out a project like this either individually or with colleagues.

In Closing

The general discussion, sample microstrategies, and exploratory projects in this chapter all highlight the view that language planning and pedagogy are closely linked to power and politics. Teachers and teacher educators, therefore, have to seriously consider several social, political, historical, and economic conditions that shape the lives of their learners and their linguistic and cultural identity. More specifically, any language learning and teaching enterprise, if it aims to be socially relevant, must critically consider, among other things, the process of standardization, the role of the home language, and the use of appropriate teaching materials.

The challenge facing the L2 teacher is how to help learners strike a balance between their desire to maintain their linguistic identity while at the same time prepare them to face the sociopolitical and economic imperatives that point to the need to master and use a dominant language. "I prefer to be honest with my students," asserts Lisa Delpit (1995, pp. 39–40), "I tell them that their language and cultural style is unique and wonderful but that there is a political power game that is also being played, and if they want to be in on that game there are certain games that they too must play."

As the Delpit quote and the general discussion in this chapter suggest, linguistic identity is closely linked to cultural identity. What are the challenges and opportunities that L2 learners face in preserving their own cultural identity while at the same time expanding their cultural horizon to survive in a culturally challenging world? We turn to that issue in the next chapter.

CHAPTER 12

Raising Cultural Consciousness

> . . . we want to urge teachers to make schooling equally
> strange for all students and thus to expand the ways of
> thinking, knowing and expressing knowledge of all stu-
> dents through incorporating many cultural tendencies.
>
> —SHIRLEY BRICE HEATH AND LESLIE MANGIOLA,
>   1991, p. 37

"Culture is one of the two or three most complicated words in the English language," says Raymond Williams (1976, p. 87), the author of *Keywords: A Vocabulary of Culture and Society*. Culture is such a complicated concept that it does not lend itself to a single definition or a simple description. It brings to mind different images to different people. In its broadest sense, it includes a wide variety of constructs such as the mental habits, personal prejudices, moral values, social customs, artistic achievements, and aesthetic preferences of particular societies. Recognizing the amorphous nature of the concept of culture, anthropologists thought it fit to distinguish between *Culture* with a capital C and *culture* with a small c. The former is a relatively societal construct referring to the general view of culture as creative endeavors such as theater, dance, music, literature, and art. The latter is a relatively personal construct referring to the patterns of behavior, values, and beliefs that guide the everyday life of an individual or a group of individuals within a cultural community.

Historically, the cultural orientation that informed L2 learning and teaching was confined mostly to Culture with a big C. It is only after World War II, when language communication became the primary goal of language learning and teaching, that learners and teachers alike started emphasizing the importance of everyday aspects of cultural practices, that is, culture with a small c. Whatever its orientation, culture teaching played a rather subterranean role in most L2 education. It became part of what Micheal Byram (1989) has called "the hidden curriculum," indirectly seeking to create in the learner an empathy toward and an appreciation for the culture of the target language community. This hidden agenda has been the order of things from time immemorial. In a comprehensive review of twenty-five centuries of language teaching, Louis Kelly (1966, p. 378) has pointed out that "the cultural orientation of language teaching has always been one of its *unstated* aims" (emphasis added).

According to a more recent review by H. H. Stern (1992), culture teaching has generally included a cognitive component, an affective component, and a behavioral component. The cognitive component relates to various forms of knowledge—geographical knowledge, knowledge about the contributions of the target culture to world civilization, and knowledge about differences in the way of life as well as an understanding of values and attitudes in the L2 community. The affective component relates to L2 learners' curiosity about and empathy for the target culture. The behavioral component relates to learners' ability to interpret culturally relevant behavior, and to conduct themselves in culturally appropriate ways.

A focal point of the cognitive, affective, and behavioral components of teaching culture has always been the native speaker of the target language. As Stern (1992) reiterates, "One of the most important aims of culture teaching is to help the learner gain an understanding of the native speaker's perspective" (p. 216). It is a matter of the L2 learner "becoming sensitive to the state of mind of individuals and groups within the target language community" (p. 217). The teacher's task, then, is to help the learner "create a network of mental associations similar to those which the items evoke in the native speaker" (p. 224). The overall objective of culture teaching, then, is to help L2 learners develop the ability to use the target language in culturally appropriate ways for the specific purpose of empathizing and interacting with native speakers of the target language.

Such an approach is based on a limited view of culture in at least two important ways. First, it narrowly associates cultural identity with national identity or linguistic identity. That is, it considers all the people belonging to a particular nation (e.g., the United States) speaking a particular language (e.g., English) as belonging to a particular culture. It ignores multicultural and subcultural variations within national or linguistic boundaries. We learn from the works of scholars such as Deborah Tannen (1992) in the United States, Ben Rampton (1995) in the United Kingdom, Robert Young (1996) in Australia, and Bonny Norton (2000) in Canada that cultural identity is likely to diverge based not only on learners' national and linguistic background but also on their ethnic heritage, religious beliefs, class, age, gender, and sexual orientation. Given such a perspective, raising cultural consciousness becomes an issue not only in ESL classes where students from different nationalities come together to learn a common second language, but also in EFL classes where students may share the same national and linguistic backgrounds.

Second, the traditional approach to the teaching of culture also ignores the rich diversity of world views that learners bring with them to the language classroom. That is, even if a group of learners, as in most educational contexts, appear to belong to a seemingly homogeneous national or linguistic entity, their life values, life choices, life-styles, and, therefore, their world view may significantly vary. In that sense, most classes are not monocultural cocoons but rather are multicultural mosaics. With its exclusive emphasis on a homogenized target language community and its cultural way of life, the traditional approach to teaching culture has failed to capitalize on the rich linguistic and cultural resources that characterize most L2 classes.

Reflective task 12.1

What are the implications—positive as well as negative—of culture teaching that is centered on the native speaker's perspective? To what extent do you think such an approach will help you to raise cultural consciousness in your L2 learners and to promote intercultural understanding?

Cultural Understanding

Recent explorations by L2 educationists such as Gail Robinson, Claire Kramsch, and Adrian Holliday seek to expand the horizon of culture learning and teaching in the L2 classroom by attempting to go beyond a preoccupation with native speaker perspectives. They emphasize how human beings interpret their cross-cultural experiences, and how they construct meaning in cross-cultural encounters. They point out that cultural understanding is more than a series of discrete objects to be gathered; rather, it is a serious effort to come to grips with how people live and express their lives.

Robinson was one of the first in the field of L2 education to argue that instead of treating culture as a collection of static products or facts that may be objectified and presented to learners in discrete items, it should be viewed as a process, that is, as a way of perceiving, interpreting, feeling, understanding. This perspective views culture as part of the process of living and being in the world, the part that is necessary for making and understanding meaning. Robinson (1985) talks about what she calls "cultural versatility," which implies "expanding one's repertoire of experiences and behaviors, not subtracting anything" (1985, p. 101). When people expand their cultural repertoire, they "would become a little bit of 'other,' and would have a degree of psychological match with more people" (p. 101).

In a subsequent work, Robinson (1991) develops a theory of second culture acquisition as the integration of home and target culture in a synthesis she refers to as the *Color Purple*. Her Color Purple is a productive, cognitive, perceptual, and affective space that results from meaningful cross-cultural contact. It is created when one becomes aware of one's own cultural lens (i.e., blue) and when one recognizes that a person from another culture has a different lens (i.e., red). Neither person can escape his or her own cultural lens, but each can choose to overlap lenses (i.e., purple) in order to understand better the other's perspectives and arrive at shared meaning.

The idea of culturally shared meaning has been further elaborated by Claire Kramsch (1993). She sees culture both as facts and as meanings, and she sees the L2 classroom as a site of struggle between the learners' meanings and those of native speakers. Through this struggle, L2 learners create their own personal meanings at the boundaries between the native speaker's meanings and their own everyday life. She asserts that "from the clash between the familiar meanings of the native culture and the unexpected meanings of the target culture, meanings that were taken for granted are suddenly questioned, challenged, problematized" (p. 238). She also believes that political awareness and social change can occur while leaving the cultural boundaries between people undisturbed and untouched.

Without seeking to blur the cultural boundaries between two

different cultural communities, Kramsch would like teachers and learners to create what she calls "a third culture" in the L2 classroom. She describes the third culture as a conceptual space that recognizes the L2 classroom as the site of intersection of multiple worlds of discourse. She advises teachers to encourage learners to create this third culture while, at the same time, not allowing either the home culture or the target culture to hold them hostage to its particular values and beliefs. She puts the onus of creating this third culture primarily on L2 learners. It is the responsibility of L2 learners "to define for themselves what this 'third place' that they have engaged in seeking will look like, whether they are conscious of it or not. Nobody, least of all the teacher, can tell them where that very personal place is; for each learner it will be differently located, and will make different sense at different times" (p. 257).

Reflective task 12.2

Which of the two cultural scenarios—Color Purple or third culture—appeals to you more, and why? What role do you think teachers and learners ought to play in jointly creating and understanding one or both of the scenarios in the L2 classroom?

Critical Cultural Consciousness

While there are merits in the notions of Color Purple and third culture, it seems to me that a true understanding of the cultural dynamics of the L2 classroom can emerge only through an understanding of the individual cultural identity that teachers and learners bring with them. Such an understanding is possible only if teachers and learners develop what I call *critical cultural consciousness*.

As I see it, the development of critical cultural consciousness requires the recognition of a simple truth: there is no one culture that embodies all and only the best of human experience; and, there is no one culture that embodies all and only the worst of human experience. Every cultural community has virtues to be proud of, and every cultural community has vices to be ashamed of. Developing critical cultural consciousness enables one to learn and grow, to change and evolve, so as to meet the challenges of today's emerging global reality.

What is the global reality today? It primarily manifests itself in the twin processes of economic globalization and cultural globalization. A 1999 United Nations Report on Human Development points out that globalization is changing the world landscape in three distinct ways:

- Shrinking space: People's lives—their jobs, incomes, and health—are affected by events on the other side of the globe, often by events that they do not even know about, much less control.
- Shrinking time: Markets and technologies now change with unprecedented speed, with action at a distance immediately affecting people's lives far away.
- Disappearing borders: National borders are breaking down, not only for trade, capital, and information but also for ideas, norms, cultures, and values.

In other words, the world has now truly become one big global village affecting economic growth as well cultural change.

One of the engines that drives both economic and cultural globalization is global electronic communication, the Internet. In fact, without global communication, economic growth and cultural change would not have taken place "with breakneck speed and with amazing reach" (UN Report, 1999, p. 30). The impact of this electronic communicational concept on cultural globalization is astounding. "Contacts between people and their cultures—their ideas, their values, their way of life—have been growing and deepening in unprecedented ways" (p. 33).

Thus, economic and cultural globalization along with electronic media have vastly increased the opportunities for the people of this planet to know more about each other, and also to shape and reshape each other's thoughts and actions. In other words, the informational resource necessary for an individual to construct a meaningful cultural identity is only a click away. What the individual needs more than anything else to make proper use of that resource is a critically reflective mind that can tell the difference between information and disinformation, between ideas and ideologies.

What guides an individual in such a critical self-reflection is his or her own value system sedimented from his or her own cultural heritage. One's learned knowledge and experience of other cultural contexts not only expands one's cultural horizon but also clarifies and solidifies one's own cultural heritage. This critical self-reflection helps one to identify and understand what is good and bad about one's own culture, and what is good and bad about other cultures. It eventually leads to a deeper cultural understanding, not just superficial cultural knowledge. In understanding other cultures, we understand our own better; in understanding our own, we understand other cultures better. Therein lies real and meaningful cultural growth.

Teachers and Learners as Cultural Informants

The above discussion points to one unmistakable conclusion about raising critical cultural consciousness in the L2 classroom: instead of privileging the teacher or the native speaker as the sole cultural informant, as the traditional approach to culture teaching would do, we need to treat the learner as a cultural informant as well. We can privilege our learners by identifying the cultural knowledge they bring to the classroom, and by using it to help them share their own individual perspectives with the teacher as well as other learners whose lives, and hence perspectives, differ from theirs. By treating learners as cultural informants, we can encourage them to engage in a process of participation that puts a premium on their own power/knowledge.

Raising critical cultural consciousness in its true sense then entails going beyond the textbook's frame of reference and attempting to bring the learner's home community into the classroom experience. As we saw in the previous chapter, using the learners' home language and culture to inform classroom activities enables students to become motivated and empowered. In addition, raising cultural consciousness in the L2 classroom will help learners to critically reflect on their own culture and (re)view it in relation to others, thereby gaining fresh perspectives about their culture and about themselves. Cultural consciousness thus becomes a tool for both self-reflection and self-renewal. Such a process of cultural self-reflection and self-renewal is not confined to learners alone. In responding to their learners' heightened cultural awareness, teachers are also challenged to reflect on their cultural selves as deeply as they expect their learners to do.

In a culturally conscious classroom, teachers are required to play the role not only of reflective practitioners but also of transformative intellectuals (cf. Chapter 1). Teachers have to allow themselves to bring the full range of appropriate sociocultural issues as topics for discussion in their classroom and use their learners' varied experiences as sources of data for furthering their instructional goals (cf. Chapter 11). More specifically, teachers need to consider the following criteria from a practical pedagogic point of view:

- how they can make their learners aware of the complex connection between language use and cultural identity;
- how they can sensitize themselves and their learners to the cultural richness that surrounds their classroom environment;
- how they can create conditions to enable and encourage their learners to participate in the negotiation and articulation of their cultural meanings and values;
- how they can treat learners as cultural informants, and recognize and reward their cultural knowledge and individual identities;
- how they can design tasks and assignments to dispel stereotypes that create and sustain cultural misunderstandings and miscommunications; and finally,
- how they can help learners to "read" cultural events and activities in ways that resonate with their experience.

The set of criteria listed above has the potential to inform teachers in their principled attempt to design location-specific, context-sensitive microstrategies aimed at implementing the essence of the macrostrategy of raising cultural consciousness.

Reflective task 12.3

Consider the problems and prospects of designing microstrategies that reflect the essence of critical cultural consciousness in the L2 classroom. In what ways can you actively involve your learners in selecting the cultural topics and activities to be included in the learning and teaching agenda?

Microstrategies for Raising Cultural Consciousness

Most human activities, ranging from individual beliefs to social customs to national celebrations, can potentially constitute the theme for exploring the nuances of cross-cultural practices. It is worth re-peating what I have said in other chapters: with some effort, teach-ers can individually or in small groups explore imaginative ways of designing their own microstrategies or try to creatively adapt com-mercially available textbooks to suit their specific needs, wants, and situations. A crucial point to remember in designing microstrate-gies for raising cultural consciousness is that teachers should make a serious attempt to access, respond, and build on learners' vast cultural knowledge in order to help them connect the norms of their own cultural practices with those of the target language com-munity, and of the wider world, and thereby gain a deeper under-standing of all. With that goal in mind, I present below three sample microstrategies with varying degrees of conceptual and linguistic challenge.

Microstrategy 12.1: Cultural Profile

12.1.0 Cultural Profile, as a microstrategic activity, is best done at the beginning of a new academic year, or a new semester, when you and your students come together as a class. You may lead them in any getting-to-know activity to familiarize themselves with one another, and then you may do Cultural Profile as a follow-up activity. Depending on your learners' proficiency level and participatory skills, you can skip parts, modify, or add to the activity.

12.1.1 Find out your learners' initial knowledge of the concept of culture. Ask simple questions and, as they respond, write down some of their key words on the board, preferably in two columns. The first column should contain items that may later be explained as Culture with a big C, and the second column items related to culture with a small c. Ask the students to guess the rationale behind the categoriza-tion. Then, briefly explain the two cultural constructs, emphasizing that the class will be focusing on culture with a small c.

12.1.2 Ask every learner to select one or two (or however many) fea-tures of home culture from the second column, or, if they wish, select features that are not listed on the board. Most probably, learners will volunteer practices related to their cultural customs: holidays, festi-vals, art, music, etc.

12.1.3 Give students time (a day or a week, depending on how much work is expected of them) to collect relevant information about the cul-tural elements they selected. List potential sources of information: the library, encyclopedias, the Internet, elders at home, or a combination of these.

12.1.4 Ask them to use the information they have gathered to draw a cultural profile that includes key words, symbols, or pictures to represent a part of their focus.

12.1.5 Arrange for them to display their cultural profiles. For instance, they may display their profiles on a poster board for everybody to see and read.

12.1.6 After giving them time to view the displays, have a few students (let them self-select) give a brief oral presentation explaining the cultural practice they selected. Depending on their proficiency level, ask them to explain the deeper, metaphorical meaning behind signs and symbols and their historical importance.

12.1.7 Have a discussion on the presentations, focusing on the content as well as the style. Encourage students to ask questions. Step in with your own questions if other students miss something or misunderstand what was presented.

12.1.8 After the presentations and discussion, ask students to tell the class what they think is the common thread in the different cultural practices presented by students from various cultural and linguistic backgrounds.

12.1.9 Take time to talk about the norms of similar cultural practices from the target language community. Help learners identify the conceptual pattern that connects the practices of the target language community and their own. If necessary, help them perceive the connection.

12.1.10 As a final step, have the students write a coherent narrative of not only the cultural practice(s) they chose to talk about but also the new knowledge they gained about the target culture and other cultures represented in class.

In this kind of activity, L2 learners get a chance to identify the important elements of their culture that have shaped their lives. In addition, through comparison and contrast, they can share their cultural knowledge in a way that enables them to see the differences and similarities between their own cultural practices and those of others. The strength of this kind of microstrategy is that it lets the students select and define the elements of their culture that are important to them, thereby encouraging them to be creative, original, and, above all, make their lived experiences part of their classroom activity. The same goals are shared by the next two microstrategies as well—at a different level of complexity.

Microstrategy 12.2: Thanksgiving

12.2.0 This microstrategy is best introduced during the month or semester when some form of thanksgiving or spring festival is celebrated. The United States celebrates its Thanksgiving in the month of November. Although the term *thanksgiving* or its translated equivalent may not be part of the event name itself, the idea of thanksgiving can be found in many cultures around the world. Thanksgiving is observed for different reasons and in different ways. Thanks may be given to God or Nature for such things as a good harvest, the triumph of Good over Evil, overcoming some collective hardship, etc. The celebration may involve religious rituals, social gatherings, feasts, games, or other forms of festivities. An occasion like Thanksgiving offers an excellent opportunity for an L2 teacher to promote cross-cultural understanding among students. There are, of course, several ways of implementing a microstrategy like this. I present below one version that I have found very useful in my class.

12.2.1 Ask your students to think about the meaning of Thanksgiving and the form it takes in their home culture. More often than not, as frequently happens in my class, the initial response from a group of international students would be something like: "Oh, we don't celebrate Thanksgiving; it's an American festival." Ask leading questions (Is there a spring festival in your home culture? Do people in your home culture thank God or Nature when there is a good harvest of crops? etc.) to create the grounds for the activity to be understood and pursued.

12.2.2 Explain the primary objective of the activity: to help learners get a cross-cultural perspective of Thanksgiving—its origins and what people actually do on the day of Thanksgiving. Have your students collect information about Thanksgiving (a) in the United States, (b) in their home culture, and (c) in a third culture or subculture of their choice, preferably one represented in class.

12.2.3 Give adequate time for your students to research the topic in the library. General and subject-specific encyclopedias are a good place to start. Parents and other elders at home are a friendly source of information about thanksgiving in their home culture.

12.2.4 Ask your students to use the information they have gathered to put together posters containing key words, pictures, and images that are associated with Thanksgiving in the two or three cultures of their focus.

12.2.5 Ask them to display their work on a poster board for everybody to see and read.

12.2.6 Select some students and ask them to give a brief oral presentation explaining the historical origin and practice of Thanksgiving in the cultures they selected. You may ask students at higher levels of proficiency to explain the historical and cultural rationale behind those practices.

12.2.7 Lead a discussion in class, giving time for students to answer questions from the class and the teacher.

12.2.8 After the presentations, ask students who volunteer to tell the class what they think are the common and different threads that run through different origins and practices of Thanksgiving.

12.2.9 Sum up the discussion, bringing out the similarities and dissimilarities in cultural practices, focusing mostly on what the learners may have missed.

12.2.10 Finally, ask the students to write a cross-cultural perspective of Thanksgiving in two or three different cultures, and include new cultural knowledge they may have gained by doing this project and from listening to other students in class.

Like Cultural Profile, Project Thanksgiving gives L2 learners an opportunity to compare and contrast popular festivities, thereby promoting the construction of cultural meanings. An important aspect of this project is that beneath the apparent differences in the cultural practice there is an underlying commonality in the cultural process that is more universal than one would presume. In fact, the next microstrategy demonstrates this point even more tellingly.

Microstrategy 12.3: Hero and Hero-Worship

12.3.0 I would like to begin with some detailed background information on this microstrategy because it was prompted by a teacher-student conflict I had to resolve (see also Kumaravadivelu, 1999b). A few years ago, I was teaching in the MATESOL program of a university in the southeastern United States. In addition to courses in TESOL, the program at that time offered classes for advanced international students aimed at improving their reading and writing skills. It was part of my administrative responsibility, as director of the program, to periodically review the teaching effectiveness of instructors teaching those classes.

One day, at about the midpoint in a semester, I observed a class taught by Debbie (pseudonym). The class consisted of students mostly from the Middle East and Southeast Asia. Debbie had put together a course pack of readings under the theme "American Heroes." It consisted of selected texts about outstanding American politicians, scientists, artists, and the like. The readings, I thought, were well chosen and well organized. On the day of my observation, Debbie chose to use a text on "Mission to the Moon." She started with pre-reading questions, which elicited no more than monosyllabic responses from her students. She explained the heroic contribution made by Apollo 11 astronauts to advance the frontiers of knowledge. She then asked several comprehension questions to which her students, again reluctantly, answered in monosyllables. She continued in the same vein, and ended the class after giving a writing assignment. As prearranged, she then left the classroom to enable me to talk to the students to get their perspective of classroom events.

As I was observing that class, it was fairly apparent that (a) this was a teacher-fronted class; (b) the students had not read the text; and (c) they were not able to participate in class discussions, in spite of their advanced level of proficiency in English. Given what I thought was a dismal lack of preparation and participation on the part of the students, I was wondering what Debbie could have done differently to make the class more productive. It was therefore with sympathy and support for her that I started talking to the students.

I had barely finished introducing myself when several of the students vociferously started complaining about Debbie. It was as if their silence in class was just a matter of the proverbial calm before the storm. They said that she was not at all helping them improve their reading/writing skills. "She is all the time talking about American culture and American heroes and nothing else," they complained bitterly. It soon became clear to me that the problem between the teacher and her students arose not because of the content of the text, but partly because of Debbie's method of teaching and partly because of the students' perception of her being ethnocentric. They felt that their identities were not being recognized and that their voices were not being respected. Their unwillingness to prepare for the class and to participate in class discussion appeared to me to be a form of passive resistance.

In my feedback to Debbie, I pointed out that the theme she selected for the course could be well suited for an instructional strategy that not only respected her students' sociocultural sensibilities and their sociopolitical awareness, but tapped their experiential knowledge as well. The instructional strategy I suggested to her is given below in the form of a microstrategy.

Because of the way this microstrategy originated, it appears, as presented here, to be more suitable for a multilingual and multicultural classroom consisting of international students. However, you can adapt this microstrategy by treating cultural variations, as we all should, not just in terms of national variations (as in Japanese culture, American culture, etc.) but in terms of subcultural variations within a nation, such as religion, language, gender, age, or even personal interests.

12.3.1 Ask some of your students to share with the class who their heroes are. Most probably, they will mention some people who are familiar and some who are not familiar to you and the other students. Ask them to explain briefly why they consider these individuals to be their heroes.

12.3.2 Divide the class into small groups. Have members of each group discuss their views about the concept of hero in their cultural or subcultural community, and come away with a consensus definition of hero, with examples.

12.3.3 Have a representative from each group report back to the class, summarizing the group discussion, followed by a brief question-answer session.

12.3.4 Ask them to read about the concept of hero and hero-worship presented in the textbook, or in any reading material you may have selected for them. Help them with their reading comprehension.

12.3.5 Ask the students to go back to their small groups again, this time to compare their cultural concept of hero and hero-worship with that of the one presented in the reading material.

12.3.6 Ask a representative from each group to report back to the class once again, this time to talk about perspectives on heroes and hero-worship across cultures or subcultures.

12.3.7 Depending on the proficiency level of the students, you may also direct the students' attention to, and have an informed dialogue on, the cult of hero-worshipping and its potential harmful effects.

12.3.8 Sum up and complete the discussion, drawing the class's attention to anything they may have missed about the cultural/subcultural concepts of hero and hero-worship, and also try to bring about a class consensus on the subject.

12.3.9 Give a writing task in which they write about which hero or heroes they would like to emulate and why.

12.3.10 Bring the project to a closure by asking a few student volunteers to share their thoughts on heroes they want to emulate.

Exploratory Projects

Here are two exploratory research projects intended to prompt you to design your own microstrategies to raise your students' critical cultural consciousness. Keep in mind that your primary objective is to help your students analyze and understand some aspects of their own culture, those of the target language community, and other cultures as much as possible. Try to help them accomplish this in a nonthreatening environment and without them or you making any value judgments of any of the cultures involved.

Project 12.1: Happy New Year

12.1.0 The following project focuses on New Year celebrations across cultures.

12.1.1 Study the chart in Figure 12.1 about how different cultural communities usher in their New Year.

12.1.2 Design a step-by-step microstrategy to help your learners understand New Year festivities in different cultural communities. Make a list of possible questions and activities.

12.1.3 Think about possible items or pictures or artifacts that you can ask your learners to bring to class to help other students understand some of the culture-specific New Year festivities. If necessary, suggest to your students possible sources of information such as the library, the Internet, and elders in the family.

12.1.4 Make a list of display and referential questions you may have to ask to help them understand the information in Figure 12.1.

12.1.5 Consider suitable individual or group activities to help your learners understand the similarities and differences between various cultural practices.

12.1.6 Think about specific questions that go beyond the superficial cultural information in the chart and reflect on reasons why cultural communities do what they do on New Year's Day.

12.1.7 Think up homework (reading/writing) assignments that would be appropriate to help your learners synthesize the information and ideas generated during class discussion.

12.1.8 What would be an appropriate sequence to introduce your questions and activities in order to make the entire classroom activity logical and coherent?

What?	When?	How?
American New Year	January 1	(a) Make New Year resolutions (b) In the morning, watch parade(s) on TV (c) In the afternoon, watch football game(s) (d) In the evening, family and friends meet for a meal, and/or go out to party
Chinese New Year	On the day of the first moon of the lunar calendar	(a) Family and friends gather (b) Pay respects to ancestors (c) Pay debts and resolve differences (d) Lion dance to ward off evil spirits (e) *Lei see* (red envelopes with money) given for luck
Japanese New Year	Both January 1 and Lunar New Year	(a) Ring bells at temples 108 times to exorcise 108 passions or evil spirits (b) Family and friends gather for breakfast and eat *mochi* (rice cakes) (c) Children are given *otoshi-dama* ("new year treasure") in the form of money
Korean New Year	Both January 1 and Lunar New Year	(a) *Jishin Balpgi* ritual accompanied by gongs and drums to ward off evil spirits (b) Pay respects to elders by kneeling and bowing (c) Children are given lucky money (d) Family and friends gather for breakfast with rice-cake soup
Vietnamese New Year	Lunar New Year	(a) *Le true,* a ceremony with firecrackers (b) Pay debts and resolve differences (c) Families plant a tree, called *cay neu,* wrapped in red paper for good luck (d) Fortunes are exchanged
Any other?	(add as appropriate)	(add as appropriate)

Figure 12.1

12.1.9 Monitor how the activity develops in the classroom. Try to get informal feedback from your learners about the effectiveness of this microstrategy. Consider what you need to do to improve it in order to make it work better the next time.

12.1.10 Finally, reflect on the usefulness and the limitations of doing an exploratory project like this, given your specific learning and teaching environment. If there are limitations, how can you overcome them?

Project 12.2: Culture and Airplane Crashes

12.2.0 As has been repeatedly stated in this book (with irritating persistence?), newspapers and other communication media offer timely and topical themes that can be exploited for classroom activities. Here's one that can be used for dispelling cultural stereotypes.

12.2.1 A lead front-page story in the *Seattle Times* (March 19, 1998, page A1), the largest newspaper in the state of Washington, featured a news analysis about Korean Air Flight 801, which crashed on August 6, 1997, killing 228 passengers. A part of the analysis is reproduced below:

> Do culture factors cause air crashes?
> Flight safety may be hurt
>   by deference to authority
> By Don Phillips
> The Washington Post
> The crew of Korean Air Flight 801 grew nervous as the Boeing 747 approached Agana, Guam, on a rainy night in August. Something didn't feel right.
> The plane, being flown by auto pilot, was descending steeply. The crew talked about the altitude, and someone said several times that the airport "is not in sight." But investigative sources said neither the co-pilot nor the flight engineer spoke out boldly, as trained, to alert the captain or even to urge breaking off the landing.
> Alarms suddenly sounded in the cockpit. After an excruciating pause of several seconds, the captain finally cut off the auto pilot and prepared to pull up. At almost that moment, the crew of another plane perhaps 50 miles away saw the clouds ahead glow bright red.
> The red glow was the Korean Air jet slamming into the top of Nimitz Hill, killing 228 of the 254 people on board. The moments of hesitation may have made the difference, because the jumbo jet would have cleared the hill if it had been just a few feet higher.
> The question haunting investigators is why the co-pilot and flight engineer failed to challenge the captain. Specifically, some investigators are wondering whether cultural factors—in this case, a traditional Korean deference to command authority—may have played a role in the crash.
> Other experts counter that cultural factors play only a minor role in air safety, and some fear that even raising the issue may smack

of racism. The question of why nobody in the cockpit spoke up force-fully is crucial because this kind of crash—in which a perfectly good plane flies into the ground—happens with alarming frequency worldwide. Such disasters account for as many as eight out of every 10 crashes and more than 9,000 deaths on commercial flights in the jet age.

12.2.2 Consider all the possibilities, if you wish to design a step-by-step microstrategy using this or any other local newspaper story that has a cultural component built into it.

12.2.3 Make a list of pre-reading and post-reading comprehension questions that would help your learners understand the text.

12.2.4 Focus then on the cross-cultural aspect of the story. Defer-ence to authority? Respect for elders? Cultural stereotypes? What else?

12.2.5 Consider possible activities to help your learners research the Korean perspective of this accident. Library search? Internet archives? Korean embassy in your country?

12.2.6 What activities can you design to help your learners respond to this story creatively? For instance, assuming that the cultural aspect of the story is true as reported, would your learners be able to put themselves in the shoes of the co-pilot and then imaginatively write about how they would have reacted when they realized that their cap-tain was making a terrible mistake that could cost the lives of all 254 passengers and crew?

12.2.7 Is it a good idea to raise the issue of cultural stereotypes? What specific activities would you design to bring out the cultural stereotype embedded in this text?

12.2.8 What are other ways in which you can make use of this news-paper story to raise critical cultural consciousness in your learners?

12.2.9 As always, reflect on the possibilities and limitations of doing an exploratory project like this, given your specific learning and teach-ing environment.

In Closing

I started this chapter with a general discussion on the concept of culture. I pointed out that the traditional pedagogic aim has been primarily to create in the L2 learner an empathy toward and an ap-preciation for the culture of the target language community. Such a view offers only a narrow view of culture because it ignores the rich diversity of world views L2 learners bring with them to the class. One possible alternative is to create critical cultural consciousness among our learners.

Creating critical cultural consciousness in the L2 classroom offers immense possibilities for teachers as well as learners to explore the nuances of cultural and subcultural practices in a meaningful way. It involves constant and continual self-reflection guided by one's own value system sedimented from one's own cultural heritage. This critical self-reflection eventually leads to meaningful cultural growth, which has to be constructed consciously and systematically through a meaningful negotiation of differences between the culture individuals inherited by birth and the culture they learned through experience. The inherited culture should be allowed to interact freely with the learned culture so that there is mutual enrichment. The key to this enrichment is the lived experiences of individuals, along with their capacity to develop critical cultural consciousness.

In the fast-emerging world of economic, cultural, and communicational globalization, creating critical cultural consciousness in the L2 classroom is not an option but an obligation.

CHAPTER 13

Monitoring Teaching Acts

What is *most seen* does not define what is *most lacking*.
—MICHEL DE CERTEAU, 1997, p. 19

In the previous chapters, I presented a pedagogic framework consisting of ten macrostrategies or guiding principles that teachers can use to make informed decisions about classroom processes and practices. Recall one of the basic premises of this framework: L2 learning and teaching needs, wants, and situations are unpredictably numerous; therefore, it is a futile exercise to try to prepare teachers in advance to tackle so many unpredictable needs, wants, and situations. What teacher educators can and must do is to help prospective and practicing teachers develop a capacity to generate their own context-specific theories of practice based on their professional, personal, and experiential knowledge and skill.

One of the most important aspects of learning to theorize from practice is knowing how to monitor one's own teaching acts. Monitoring, in this context, entails a close observation of classroom events and activities, a careful analysis of classroom input and interaction, and a critical evaluation of instructional objectives and outcomes. In this chapter, I shall highlight the importance of monitoring teaching acts and show how teachers can use the pedagogic framework presented in this book to self-observe, self-analyze, and self-evaluate their teaching acts.

Classroom Observation

In a formal educational context, the classroom is the crucible where the practice of everyday learning and teaching is concocted. It is there the prime elements of learning and teaching—ideas and ideologies, policies and plans, methods and materials, learners and teachers— all mix together. It is there the effectiveness of innovative thoughts on teaching is tried and tested. What actually happens there largely determines the extent to which learning potential is realized, and desired outcomes are achieved. The task of systematically observing classroom events, therefore, becomes central to the goal of monitoring teaching acts.

Several models of classroom observation are available in the professional literature on L2 teaching. It is not the purpose of this chapter to discuss them in detail (see Allwright, 1988, for a detailed discussion, and Kumaravadivelu, 1999b, for a recent critique). But, a brief background information is in order. For the purpose of this chapter, it is useful to classify classroom observation models into two types: product-oriented and process-oriented.

Product-Oriented Models

Product-oriented models of classroom observation (e.g., Jarvis, 1968; Moskowitz, 1971) are based on the assumption that a description of teacher behavior is necessary in order to build a classroom behavior profile of the teacher. These models use a finite set of preselected and predetermined categories for describing certain verbal behaviors of teachers and learners as they interact in the classroom. The categories mainly include teacher behavior (such as, "Teacher asks questions," "Teacher gives directions") and learner behavior (such as, "Learner responds," "Learner initiates"). They are intended to help observe, describe, classify, and, through quantitative or statistical method of analysis, assign certain numerical values (such as the number of times students respond) to verbal behaviors.

These models are useful for a partial understanding of classroom activities, particularly in terms of teacher talk and student talk. Nevertheless, they all share four crucial limitations:

- they focus exclusively on the product of verbal behaviors of teachers and learners and give little or no consideration to classroom learning and teaching processes that prompt those verbal behaviors;
- they depend on quantitative measurements, thereby losing the essence of communicative intent that cannot be reduced to numerical codification;

- they are unidirectional, that is, the information flow is generally from the observer to the teacher, the observer being a supervisor in the case of practicing teachers, or a teacher educator in the case of student-teachers; and
- they are unidimensional, that is, the basis of observation is largely confined to one single perspective, that of the observer.

These models then emphasize observer perceptions of observable teacher behavior for the limited purpose of building a teacher profile. By their very nature and scope, they can offer only a narrow view of classroom processes and practices.

Process-Oriented Models

Process-oriented models of classroom observation (e.g., Allwright, 1980; van Lier, 1988) are based on the assumption that an interpretation of classroom activities is necessary in order to understand classroom processes and practices. With that objective, they focus on classroom input as well as interaction, and also on managerial as well as cognitive aspects of classroom activities. They attempt to describe and account for individual behavior, and thus treat classroom participants as individuals rather than as a collective mass. Furthermore, they use qualitative methods of analysis, along with quantitative methods, to interpret classroom data.

Like the product-oriented models, most of the process-oriented ones are also intended to observe, describe, classify, and assign certain numerical values to verbal behaviors using a preselected and predetermined set of categorical items. However, they are different from and an improvement over product-oriented models in at least two important ways. First, through a qualitative or ethnographic method of analysis (such as interviews), they seek to *interpret* classroom events, not just *describe* them. Second, in order to achieve the goal of interpretation, some of them attempt to go beyond the observer perspective of classroom events and attempt to elicit other related perspectives as well.

Process-oriented observation models have undoubtedly strengthened our capacity to understand classroom events. However, they, too, have certain shortcomings:

- although they are meant to help teachers, they are designed primarily to be used by researchers, supervisors, and teacher educators.

- although they emphasize qualitative or ethnographic techniques, they are dependent to a large extent on quantification of classroom events.

- although they emphasize explanation and interpretation, they offer very little guidance about how to explain or interpret the observed phenomena.

Most of the classroom observation models, whether they are product- or process-oriented, use coding procedures that are seldom user-friendly. Anybody who has used them knows that they are cumbersome, time-consuming, and labor-intensive. Besides, any useful or usable information that can be derived from these observational tools is highly disproportionate to the time and effort that go into applying them. If the ultimate goal of classroom observation is to enable teachers to think systematically and critically about their classroom practices so that what they do in class may turn out to be a principled activity, then these classroom observation models can hardly accomplish that goal. That is perhaps one reason why Allwright (1988, p. 196) rhetorically asked: "Who needs category systems?"

Teachers Need a User-Friendly System

I believe that, to be relevant for teachers, any classroom observational tool must minimally offer them open-ended possibilities and user-friendly procedures for self-observing, self-analyzing, and self-evaluating their teaching acts. It should help them understand the opportunities and challenges facing them as teachers. It should direct them away from knowledge transmission and toward knowledge generation; away from pedagogic dependence and toward pedagogic independence. It should also enable them, where possible, to reflect on educational, institutional, and sociocultural forces that directly or indirectly shape the character and content of classroom discourse.

Only such a tool can help teachers transform their tacit understanding of classroom events into explicit knowledge that can feed directly into the construction of their own theory of practice. More specifically, and in the context of a postmethod pedagogy, an observational tool must help teachers analyze and understand (a) possible multiple perspectives to classroom events, (b) potential mismatches between teacher intention and learner interpretation, and

(c) pertinent macrostrategies that help the achievement of specific learning and teaching objectives. Such an analysis and understanding will help them begin to theorize from practice.

Multiple Perspectives to Classroom Events

The traditional practice of classroom observation, which emphasizes observer perception of observable teacher behavior, is a necessary but not a sufficient condition for a meaningful understanding of classroom events. This tradition has made us focus more on the observation of surface-level teacher performance than on a deeper understanding of teaching processes. Furthermore, it has also driven us to neglect the equally important task of understanding the learner perception of classroom events. In the context of meaningful classroom observation what we need, then, is a broader definition of teaching, learning, and observing.

As discussed in Chapter 3, the teaching act can be defined as an interactive activity by which learning opportunities are created by the teacher, the learner, or both. By logical extension, the learning act can be defined as a cognitive activity by which learning opportunities are utilized by the learner. Observation, then, becomes an interpretive activity by which the successful, partially successful, or unsuccessful creation and utilization of learning opportunities are observed and analyzed. In such a view, monitoring classroom events entails an understanding of not merely how learning opportunities are created and utilized, but also how they are perceived by the learner, the teacher, and the observer. Only such a multifaceted, stereoscopic view will help teachers get a full picture of the intended and unintended outcomes of classroom events.

For a meaningful analysis of teaching acts, teachers, observers, and learners have to function as collaborative partners in the joint exploration of classroom discourse. These partners, by virtue of their prior experience and exposure, bring with them their own perceptions and prescriptions about what constitutes teaching, what constitutes learning, and what constitutes learning outcomes. Therefore, one and the same classroom event can be, and in fact is often, interpreted differently by different participants.

A balanced understanding of different, even conflicting, teacher, learner, and observer perspectives of classroom events is not only feasible but also desirable. The emphasis on teacher perspective ensures self-monitoring and self-evaluation on the part of teachers. They are better placed than anybody to provide descriptions of their work, their thinking behind it, and their interpretations of it.

The emphasis on learner perspective envisages an important role for learners in the process of evaluating teaching acts. As interested participants, they are best suited to comment critically on various aspects of classroom discourse. By virtue of the fact that they are the stake-holders of the classroom enterprise, they can bring a unique interpretation of the usefulness of teaching.

The emphasis on observer perspective enables collaboration among colleagues. That is, working together, colleagues can create a conducive atmosphere where teamwork is encouraged, and where they help each other improve both the work environment and their own teaching performance. A purposeful and periodical dialogue with an observing—and observant—colleague gives an opportunity for teachers to examine their philosophical orientation and analyze their instructional performance. Such a collegial, collaborative process can produce valuable and valued insights into pedagogic processes, greatly facilitating teachers' attempts to construct their own theory of practice.

Reflective task 13.1

Do you agree that several individuals can observe the same classroom event and come out with different perceptions of what happened? Can you think of any specific classroom episode, either while you were teaching or while you were attending a class, that led to multiple, conflicting perspectives?

In the context of classroom learning and teaching, the three perspectives—those of the teacher, the learner, and the observer—are easily identifiable and analyzable. An understanding of all three perspectives is indispensable if we are serious about a meaningful assessment of teaching effectiveness in the classroom, for, as in the case of the proverbial six blind men and the elephant, each of the participants may touch upon one aspect of the classroom event that forms part of a whole. To be aware of multiple perspectives also means to be aware of potential mismatches between intentions and interpretations among classroom participants (see Chapter 4). There-fore, combining the ten macrostrategies and the ten sources of mis-match discussed in this book, I present what I call a macrostrategies/mismatch observational scheme (M & M observational scheme, for short) that can be used for monitoring teaching acts.

M & Ms for the Observing Teacher

The M & M observational scheme can be used as a frame of refer-ence and a point of departure for providing an initial set of explana-tory and interpretive strategies for teachers to observe, analyze, and evaluate their teaching acts. Using the framework, teachers can ask questions such as, "Did I utilize the learning opportunity created by the learner?" or "Did I promote learner autonomy?" or questions such as, "I sense an element of misunderstanding here. Could this be due to an instructional mismatch or a conceptual mismatch?" etc.

Observational Procedures

The M & M observational scheme consists of a three-stage activity: (a) preobservation, in which the observer and the teacher consult with each other regarding the aims, objectives, and activities of the class(es) to be monitored; (b) observation itself; and (c) post-observation, in which the observer and the teacher select a few episodes for detailed treatment, analyze classroom input and inter-action, interpret their analysis, derive pedagogic implications, and put all this experiential knowledge together to develop a personal theory of practice.

These three stages involve ten steps:

- Step 1: The interested teacher chooses one of her colleagues and apprises her of her intention to conduct a classroom observa-tional study, and invites her to observe and analyze one class or one unit of her class. A unit may mean two or three consecutive sessions during which the teacher focuses on a closely related se-quence of instructional activities that are designed to achieve a specific teaching objective.

- Step 2: The observer elicits from the teacher information about (a) the specific objectives of the class(es) to be observed, (b) how the teacher proposes to achieve those objectives, (c) the students' general level of preparedness, motivation, and participation, etc.

- Step 3: After going over the supplied information and other instructional material(s) to be used in the class(es) to be observed, the observer may seek necessary clarification from the teacher.

- Step 4: The observer attends the teaching of one class or one unit of lessons over several class sessions and videotapes the class(es). The observer also takes notes on certain interactional episodes that, from her personal point of view, sound interesting or intriguing, something that needs to be jointly explored with the teacher. Even short episodes are sufficient. The purpose is intensive, not extensive, analysis.

- Step 5: As soon as possible—so as not to lose memory of classroom experience—the teacher watches the video and, like the observer, also takes notes on certain interactional episodes that, from her personal point of view, sound interesting or intriguing, something that needs to be jointly explored with the observer. At this crucial stage, the teacher might ask questions such as: Did I initiate all the topics or did my students initiate some? Are most of the questions display questions or referential questions? What is the nature of teacher/student talk—initiating, responding, explaining, modeling, negotiating? Are there learner-learner exchange of ideas? What part of my instruction has been successful or unsuccessful? What might be the reason(s) for the success or failure? What macrostrategy could have been used in this or that episode? What mismatch could have been anticipated and avoided? What changes might I like to effect? etc.

- Step 6: Based on their notes, the observer and the teacher exchange their initial views and jointly decide to select a few interactional episodes for further exploration and, if necessary, transcribe the data pertaining to those segments of classroom interaction where the episodes occur.

- Step 7: The observer and the teacher meet with group(s) of learners who figured in the episodes selected for analysis, and talk about learner-learner, learner-teacher input and interaction in those episodes. This provides the much-needed learner perspective to classroom events.

- Step 8: The observer and the teacher meet again for a post-observation analysis to discuss the already analyzed interactional episodes and to exchange their perspectives on what did or did not occur in the class(es) observed.

- Step 9: The observer and the teacher pull together all three perspectives (teacher, learner, observer) and, using the macrostrategies and the mismatches as a general guide, interpret the class-room events.

- Step 10: Finally, the teacher makes use of all the interpretive data in order to self-evaluate her teaching acts. Such an evaluation can help her refine her teaching beliefs and classroom practices and eventually lead her to construct her own personal theory of practice.

Reflective task 13.2

Before reading further, consider the feasibility of the ten-step procedure. What difficulties do you anticipate in following this procedure? What modifications would you suggest and why?

Using the M & M Scheme

By way of illustration, I present one aspect of a project I conducted to assess the extent to which the M & M scheme can help teachers reflect on their practice and begin to theorize from their practice (see Kumaravadivelu, 1999a, for details). Two female ESL teachers based in a California community college participated in this part of the project—one as teacher (T) and the other as observer (O). They both have a master's degree in TESOL. The observer has been teaching for nearly eight years. The teacher has been teaching for two and a half years. There were thirty students in the class that was observed, and approximately one-half spoke Spanish as their first language. Others spoke Vietnamese, Korean, or Chinese. Most were recently arrived immigrants. On the day of observation, the teacher was focusing on reading comprehension.

Before the actual observation, the observer gathered the following background information about the teacher and the class: the teacher was going to use a lesson titled "Looking for an apartment" for teaching reading comprehension; she did not subscribe to any particular method, "not even the communicative method." She believed in doing "whatever works." She also said, "I don't teach them grammar; I teach them what they need to know." She felt that even though hers was a low intermediate class, at least half the students were very active in class participation, and that most of the students

were highly motivated to learn. A transcript of the classroom interaction is given below.

Classroom Interactional Data

Read the following classroom transcript, given here as Episode 13.1.
The transcription convention is the same as the one I have used in
this book.

Episode 13.1

1.	T:	How many of you live in an apartment? How many of you live in an apartment?
2.	S1:	(Raises hand)
3.	T:	OK, only one? How many of you live in a house?
4.	Ss:	(Raise hands)
5.	T:	OK, any other place?
6.	S2:	Condo.
7.	T:	A condo? (Laughs). We have an apartment, a house . . .
8.	S3:	Condo?
9.	T:	A condo. It's like a house. Any other place?
10.	S4:	Mobile home.
11.	T:	Mobile home, OK.
12.	S5:	Under the bridge. (Ss laugh)
13.	T:	Oh, under the bridge! We've got some under the bridge. We've got four locations. Under the bridge, the mobile home, the apartment, and the house.
14.	S2:	Condo.
15.	T:	Oh, yah, condo, that makes it five.
16.	S6:	What's a condo?
17.	T:	Apartment complex. Like an apartment house.
18.	S6:	Apartment house?
19.	S7:	In the car (laughs).
20.	T:	I feel like I live there too sometimes. Carrying everything around, um . . . in this class, one of the things we'll be talking about is neighborhoods, and what to look for when

you're looking for a home. And also . . . last week, we spent time reading ads from the newspaper. So . . . sometimes you may have to go to the newspaper to locate a place to live. So . . . that's why we spent last week reading ads from the newspaper. And . . . you noticed that the ads in the newspaper were written in abbreviated form, for bedroom, you might find in the newspaper, what?

21. Ss: xxx

22. T: BD? OK . . .

23. S3:   DW.

24. S6:   What's DW?

25. T: Well, there were abbreviations for different things. So . . . they don't write out the words. It's important that you familiarize yourself with abbreviations. This article on houses . . . OK . . . on houses. I'm going to have someone read it. Read out loud please, S2.

26. S2:   (reads introductory questions at the beginning of lesson)

27. T: OK, three questions. Why did you choose, choose your present apartment and neighborhood? What do you like about it, what don't you like about it, and how are the schools in your neighborhood? OK, we got through writing yesterday, and I told you about indenting for a paragraph. Do you notice any paragraphs on this page? Anybody notice any paragraphs on this page?

28. S8:   What is paragraph?

29. T: What is a paragraph? Good question. A paragraph is . . . (addressing students who are writing) no writing, no writing. Yesterday, we focused on writing; now it's reading . . . OK? . . . A paragraph is the part that is indented. (Addressing another student) Writing again! You just love to write, don't you? (Turning to class) She's just writing away . . . So . . . if you find the words that are indented, that means that they start kind of in a little bit? Which words do you see?

30. S3:   There.

31. T: There is one of them. OK, the second word is . . .

32. S9:   After.

33. T: After. And the third word is look. Can everyone find those words? There, after, and look. Is there anyone who doesn't

see those three words? Let us know if you don't see them . . . So . . . on this page, this story has how many paragraphs?

34. Ss: Three.

35. T: Three paragraphs. So . . . when I told you yesterday to write a paragraph, that's what I wanted you to do. I wanted you to indent the first line, and continue writing until you got to the end. Do you understand? OK? So . . . that shows you have three paragraphs. Let's start with the first paragraph. Um . . . S10, read the first paragraph.

36. S10: (Reads the paragraph)

37. T: Can you read the same paragraph, S11?

38. S11: (Reads the paragraph)

39. T: OK, in your . . . in your particular situation, what is most important to you? Of the things listed, which would be the most important? The size of the apartment, the quality of the school system, or, if you were close to work? . . . Those three things . . . S12?

40. S12: Close to work.

41. T: OK, would you be concerned with the school system?

42. S12: (shrugs)

43. T: Would you be concerned with the school system, S12?

44. S12: I don't understand.

45. T: You picked, you picked the close to work, right? Why didn't you pick the school system?

46. S12: You mean why I didn't think of it?

47. T: Well, I guess a really simple question I'm going to ask you, do you have any children?

48. S12: I'm not even married. (Ss laugh)

49. T: So . . . maybe you're not concerned about the school system, right?

50. S12: xxx (Looks puzzled)

51. T: Because maybe if you had children that might be your first consideration. But since you don't have any children, you're more concerned with whether or not you are close to work . . . for transportation . . . OK, so . . . S13, what is most important to you? Size of the house? The quality of the school system?

52. S13:   The quality of the school system.

53. S14:   Why school system?

54. T: Yah, why did you choose that?

55. S13:   My children at home . . .

56. S14:   I don't understand school system.

57. T: OK, he has children that live with him at home. So . . .
            that's the most important to him. OK . . . ?

58. S14:   I am confused.

59. T: All right, all right. You're confused. Let's get unconfused.
            His children go to school, so he wants to live near a
            school . . . OK? . . . Now, you tell me . . . what's the most
            important to you?

60. S14:   (Still looking puzzled) . . . Um . . . close to work.

61. S15:   (Turning to S14) You got no work. (Ss laugh)

62. T: That's funny . . . what about you, S16?

63. S16:   Close to school.

64. T: Close to school. So, everybody's situation is different. What
            I'm looking for and what you're looking for, and what they
            are looking is completely different. But, it is important that
            you identify what is important. Because you don't want to,
            say, live in San Jose and work in San Francisco if you don't
            have any transportation. That just might be an impossible
            situation . . . OK . . . Now . . . (lesson continues).

                                              (Data source: Kumaravadivelu, 1999a)

Reflective task 13.3

Study the nature of input and interaction in the above classroom episode. If
you were teaching this class, what teaching strategies would you retain and
what would you change, and why? In what way, do you think, can the M & M
scheme help you analyze, interpret, and understand the data?

Analysis and Interpretation of the Data

"A good class"—that was the initial impression of the teacher as
well as the observer about this class. They felt that, overall, the par-

ticipants maintained a friendly and positive atmosphere conducive to learning. The class was highly interactive without the teacher dominating the conversational turns. They noticed that, out of the sixty-four conversational turns, there were thirty teacher turns and thirty-four student turns, however brief the student turns may have been. They also noted that a substantial number of questions asked by the teacher were referential in nature, that is, they were meant to elicit new information from the learners (e.g., turn 27: "Why did you choose . . . choose your present apartment and neighborhood?"), not just to display teacher knowledge (e.g., turn 29: "What is a paragraph?"). The teacher gave ample opportunities for the learners to participate meaningfully in classroom interaction, thus helping them stretch their still-developing linguistic repertoire.

At a more detailed level of analysis, the teacher and the observer tried to engage in a critical interpretation of the episode aimed at a comprehensive understanding of classroom events. I present below a synopsis of the teacher, observer, and learner perspectives in relation to the M & M scheme.

Consider the first eighteen turns. Several things are happening here. First of all, by asking two different questions, "How many of you live in an apartment? (turn 1), and later, "How many of you live in a house?" (turn 3), the teacher has already created a distinction between an apartment and a house. S2 suggests yet another housing possibility, a condo (turn 6). S3 wants to know what a condo is. The teacher says, "It's like a house" (turn 9). Another student, S6, is still unclear about the meaning of condo, even after the teacher's explanation: "What's a condo?" (turn 16). The teacher replies, "Apartment complex. Like an apartment house." Now, a condo, an apartment, and a house have all been synonymously used by the teacher, although she started with a distinction between an apartment and a house. Confusion was confounded.

What did the teacher and the observer learn from the analysis? When they talked to the two students (S3 and S6) involved in this exchange, they found out that the students were still not clear about condo, and about the difference between an apartment, a house, and a condo. Reflecting on this episode, the teacher said she wasn't conscious of the contradictory signals she was sending. "I just didn't notice," she said. The observer said she knew something was amiss but could not figure it out until they examined the transcript. They termed this a cognitive mismatch and said teachers should monitor

themselves and be on the lookout for possible conceptual misunderstanding they may create in the learner.

Go back to the same segment, turns 1–18. In turn 10, S4 suggests
"mobile home." The teacher merely acknowledges it and moves on.
Prompted by the observer, the teacher later felt that most students,
being recent immigrants to the United States, might not have
known what a mobile home is. The teacher could have used this opportunity to explain or at least encourage the student who gave that
answer to describe his mobile home or the neighborhood. Again, in
turn 12, S5 says, "Under the bridge." The teacher accepted that as a
matter of fact—as if to say, "you know, you live in an apartment,
you live in a house, you live in a condo, and you live under the
bridge!" As she discovered later, the student was clearly making a
reference to the problem of homelessness among the poor in the
San Francisco Bay area. The teacher was aware of that, as she told
the observer later, but she didn't pursue the student's reference to
the social problem of homelessness because she thought that it was
not relevant to the topic at hand.

After further discussion, the teacher and the observer said that
the two examples had something in common: in both cases, they
hypothesized, the teacher could have utilized the learning opportunity created by learners. And, in the case of the bridge example, they
both agreed that language teachers should not hesitate to talk about
socially relevant issues, particularly as glaring an issue as homelessness, especially when a student himself brought it up. There are
other examples where the teacher overlooked the learning opportunities created by learners. For instance, in turn 24, S6 wanted to
know the meaning of the abbreviation DW. The teacher ignored the
request although she went on to say, "It's important that you familiarize yourself with abbreviations."

Now, consider turns 28 and 29. Only the day before this particular class, the teacher had explained the concept of a paragraph and
used the word *paragraph* several times during that class. Yet, when
S8 asked, "What is paragraph?" she took the question in stride, and
correctly used the opportunity to explain how to recognize a paragraph. The observer asked her why she picked up on this learning
opportunity and ignored several others created by the learners. The
teacher replied that this student-initiated learning opportunity was
in line with her own agenda. The student offered her an opportunity
to clarify and reinforce her earlier lesson, so she recognized it and
responded to it.

Analyses of extended data (not included here) showed that the teacher consistently followed a pattern: she recognized those learner-initiated opportunities that were in support of her lesson plan, and ignored those that were not part of her planned agenda. When the observer, being a more experienced teacher, argued that teachers in an L2 class should make use of all the learning opportunities created by learners even if they go against their planned agenda, the novice teacher seemed skeptical. They agreed, however, that the teacher should have facilitated more meaningful interaction in class. Considering that only the previous day she had spent a lot of time explaining what a paragraph is, she could have asked other students to explain instead of providing a readymade answer. This would have given other students an opportunity to interact.

The same segment provides an example of a series of disruptive mismatches. Twice the teacher interrupts her own explanation of what a paragraph is in order to admonish students who were trying to take notes. She thought that students shouldn't write anything during a part of the lesson that she considered "reading comprehension time." Later on, during her conversation with students, she found out from the offending students that they were trying to write down the definition of paragraph and were perplexed why the teacher was preventing them from taking notes. The teacher had wrongly thought that the students were actually writing a paragraph about renting an apartment, which was the next exercise in the textbook, and therefore wanted them to stop writing and concentrate on reading.

The teacher and the observer discussed this misunderstanding at length and thought that this illustrates a combination of mismatches: instructional, procedural, and attitudinal—instructional mismatch because the teacher's directions were not clear to the students; procedural mismatch because the teacher was not aware of the path chosen by the learner to achieve an immediate goal; and attitudinal mismatch because of the teacher's attitude toward the nature of L2 learning and teaching, i.e., a strong belief on the separation of skills and a strict adherence to a predetermined lesson plan. They hypothesized that teachers who firmly keep students focused on the lesson can easily lead them to overlook many learning opportunities created by students, and also make them fail to promote negotiated interaction.

There is yet another segment (turns 52–62) that is as interesting as it is intriguing. In turn 52, S13 expresses the opinion that the quality of the school system would be his first consideration for deciding on an apartment. S14 asks, without any emphasis on any of the words, "Why school system?" The teacher thought that S14 was actually addressing S13, asking him in effect why the school system was his first consideration. That's why she reinforced the question to S13: "Yah, why did you choose that?" And S13 replies suitably. He has schoolchildren (turn 55). Now S14 says: "I don't understand school system." The teacher tries to explain: "He has children that live with him at home. So, that's the most important to him." But, S14 is not giving up. "I am confused," he says. The teacher, clearly irritated, says sternly, "All right, all right. You're confused. Let's get unconfused. His children go to school, so he wants to live near a school . . . OK?" By that time, S14 lost all interest and that's why, when the teacher asked him for his most important consideration for renting an apartment, he nonchalantly responds, "Close to work," even though he doesn't have any part-time work, something that his friend S15 (turn 61) gleefully points out.

In class, the observer did not have a clue what was happening. But she teased it out after talking to the teacher and S14, who incidentally is one of the brighter students in class. Here's the deconstructed version: Go back to turn 53. S14 asks: "Why school system?" That was not a question addressed to S13, as the teacher concluded. Rather, that was a question addressed to the teacher herself. S14 wanted to know why the word *system* is used in relation to *school*. He wanted to know why it is called a school *system*, even though he did not use this emphasis. Now, the teacher, knowing fully well that S14 is a bright student, thought that he was just being mischievous as usual. She didn't think that he really was confused. That's why she got irritated and said, "Get unconfused."

Later, when the student told her that he didn't really understand the phrase "school *system*," she was very apologetic. She explained that the word *system* is used to refer to a cluster of schools managed and run by a central authority within a county, all having a common curriculum. The teacher and the observer thought that this segment was a very good example of a combination of mismatches: cognitive mismatch because the student didn't know the concept of a school system, linguistic mismatch because he didn't understand the particular use of the word *system* in this context, instructional mismatch because the teacher failed to diagnose the problem and provide proper guidance. This segment also illustrates missed chances to promote interaction, and to utilize learning opportunities created by learners.

It is clear from the above analysis and interpretation that the M & M scheme with its emphasis on macrostrategies and mismatches, along with its emphasis on multiple perspectives, helped the teacher and the observer understand the complexity of this particular classroom event. Through critical monitoring of their teaching acts, they were able to sensitize themselves to various perspectives of classroom aims and events. Such a systematic monitoring of teaching acts, leading to a sustained process of self-reflection and self-renewal, has the potential to open up new vistas for teachers to construct their own theory of practice.

Theory construction, then, "does not move away from the concrete, only to be returned to it in the form of some sort of practical application. Instead, theory is continually moving toward the complexity of the concrete and, in the measure that it is correct in indicating the underlying concrete and contradictory tensions in reality, it is capable of guiding the transformation of reality" (Lamb, 1982, pp. 49–50). A crucial aspect of this reality is the creation of opportunities for the construction of meaning that has the potential to shape and reshape the thought processes of participating teachers, resulting in mutual enrichment.

Reflective task 13.4

Consider the desirability and the doability of a classroom observation project like the one described above. Is this something that you as a prospective or practicing teacher can do? What are the institutional resources and constraints that you think can help or hinder your desire to conduct a similar self-observational study?

While the of use the M & M scheme as a classroom observational tool may not be painless, hands-on experience with the scheme will show that it is less painful and more productive than the process of using traditional observational tools. Some of the built-in advantages of the M & M scheme are:

- it is designed to be used by those who matter most: teachers, not just professional researchers, teacher educators, or academic supervisors;
- it engages prospective and practicing teachers in a continual and dynamic process of reflection, reevaluation, and renewal;
- it puts a premium on teachers and their self-observation, self-analysis, and self-evaluation of their own teaching acts;
- it is multidimensional and multidirectional, ensuring a three-way information flow between teachers, learners, and observers, and a purposeful interaction among them;
- it is relatively user-friendly, not requiring any cumbersome process of quantification of classroom events using predetermined coding procedures;
- it provides simple, nontechnical language necessary for talking about the analysis and interpretation of classroom interactional data; and
- it is cost-effective in the sense that, for the time and effort it takes to do an observational study, it has the potential to provide rich insights into classroom events that can be used by teachers for constructing their own theory of practice.

A Note of Caution

It is important that teachers who would like to be observed take care to choose a concerned and cooperative colleague as an observing partner—someone who has the desired knowledge, skill, and attitude to observe and analyze classroom events, someone who is able and willing to give fair, frank, and friendly comments on the teacher's classroom performance. The primary role of the observer is to analyze and interpret teaching acts, not to judge and evaluate the teacher. In other words, the observing partner should take on the role of a counselor, not that of a supervisor. The actual evaluation should be done by teachers themselves, using the partner's comments as one source of input for evaluation. If it becomes difficult for teachers to find observing partners as often as they want, they may opt to videotape their own class(es) periodically. They then can watch the video as participant-observers, and do the analysis, interpretation, and evaluation by themselves.

It should also be remembered that systematic classroom observation is not a one-time activity. It can be repeated as often as teachers wish. The procedural steps illustrated above require a considerable amount of time and effort on the part of teachers at the outset, but, as they get used to it, they may be able to monitor their teaching acts with relative ease and comfort. It is useful for teachers to videotape their classes periodically, each time focusing on different aspects of teaching, thus collecting a rich source of information about their teaching. In fact, re-viewing their videos collected over a period of time is sure to give them an idea of the changing profile of themselves as teachers. Keep in mind that, after all, "as in all things, change in teaching behaviours is neither painless nor linear" (Thornbury, 1996, p. 287).

Exploratory Research Projects

Here are three possible projects in classroom observation for prospective and practicing teachers. Project 13.1 relates to information-gathering about your classroom performance. Project 13.2 is about the analysis and interpretation of classroom data already provided for you. Project 13.3 is rather challenging and relates to classroom observation including observation, data collection, analysis, and interpretation.

Project 13.1: Logging to Learn

13.1.0 This project is specifically designed for those who may be unable to videotape their classes and also for those who may be looking for ways to monitor their teaching acts between videotaping sessions. The primary purpose of the project is to help you gather information about your teaching, so that you can keep track of what you do in your class. It involves keeping a log of how you perform as a teacher, hour by hour, for one full week.

13.1.1 Decide whether you want your log to take the form of a paper-and-pencil note-taking exercise, or an electronic journal in which you make your daily entry on your computer.

13.1.2 Select any one week during which you wish to monitor your teaching in order to keep a log. A possible choice is sometime in the middle of your semester, when beginning- and end-of-semester hassles are not present. Moreover, by the middle of the semester, you would have familiarized yourself with your students.

13.1.3 Select any one of the classes you teach. This is the class you are going to focus on for the purpose of monitoring your teaching.

13.1.4 Select a particular time of day when you can spend ten or fifteen minutes writing your log. A good time to do that is at the end of the selected class, or at the end of the day. Whatever time you choose, make sure you do it at the same time each day to make it a habit, and do it before you forget what actually happened in the class. You may find it useful to take notes in class that you may use later to write your log.

13.1.5 The next step is to write. To make daily entries in your log, create a questionnaire template with the items shown in Figure 13.1 (and any other item you may wish to add) and complete the questionnaire every day that week. Be as specific as possible in your response.

On a general level, you may focus on any pedagogic issue(s) you were forced to confront in the classroom, or anything (or anybody) that forced you, directly or indirectly, to change your way of teaching or your attitude toward teaching. On a more specific level, you may use the M & M scheme to focus on aspects of your teaching that you think needed some attention. For instance, you might ask questions such as: Did I initiate all the topics or did my students initiate some? Are most of the questions display questions or referential questions? Are there learner-learner exchange of ideas? What macrostrategy could have been

---

Class: Date: Time:

1. One good thing about my teaching that I noticed today.

2. One big weakness about my teaching that I noticed today.

3. One thing I really wanted to do in class today but couldn't do.

4. One reason why I couldn't do what I wanted to do in class today.

5. One lesson I learned from keeping this log today.

Figure 13.1

used in this or that episode? What mismatch could have been anticipated and avoided?

13.1.6 After your week-long period of monitoring and logging, take a close and critical look at all your entries. Without being oversensitive or hypercritical, try to get a clear and coherent picture of your teaching acts during the week of your observation. Consider questions such as: What aspect of my teaching would I keep or change and why? What have I learned from this process of keeping a log? Etc.

13.1.7 Repeat the logging exercise at least once a semester for as many semesters as you like, varying the class you wish to observe. Over a period of time, you will have collected a rich body of information about your own growth and development as a teacher. This body of information may be used to begin to construct your own theory of practice.

Project 13.2: Analyzing Input and Interaction

13.2.0 Below are transcripts of two episodes of classroom interaction. Both episodes occurred in the same intermediate level class (i.e., same group of learners featured in both episodes) in an English Language Institute. Episode 1 is from a speaking class taught by Teacher 1 (T1); episode 2 is from a grammar class taught by Teacher 2 (T2). Both T1 and T2 have an M.A. degree in TESOL. T1, a male, has been teaching for 3.2 years, and T2, a female, has been teaching for 4.1 years. On the day of data collection, fifteen international students were present in class. Since the data were in the midst of an eight-week term, the learners were familiar with their teachers and their teaching style, and also with each other.

T1 was fully briefed on the theoretical and pedagogic aspects of macrostrategies and was asked to design classroom microstrategies using as many macrostrategies as possible. T2 was not aware of the macrostrategic framework and was told to use whatever techniques she would have normally used. The classroom activities were videotaped and transcribed.

Episode 1 starts with a simulated conversation (not included in the transcript) between a man and a woman. The woman was not interested in the man; she just listens to him without any interest, not even looking in his direction. After the simulated conversation, T1 seeks the students' response to the conversation.

You may do this project individually or in small groups. If you are part of a teacher education program, form small groups of three classmates. If you are a practicing teacher, try to do the project with one or two other colleagues. Here's what you have to do to complete the project:

13.2.1   Read the transcripts carefully. Transcription conventions are the same as those used in this chapter.

13.2.2   Analyze and interpret the data in terms of the M & M scheme. Focus on, among other things, input and interaction. Specifically, for input analysis, focus on teacher talk (i.e., length, comprehensibility, the type of questions [display/referential], etc.), and learner talk (i.e., length, communicative appropriateness, grammatical accuracy, etc.). For interaction analysis, focus on turn taking and turn giving techniques, (i.e., do learners initiate interaction, do they merely respond to teacher questions, do they ask questions, etc.), learners' enthusiasm for participating in interaction, the degree of success achieved by the teachers (i.e., the teachers' ability to create learning opportunities and to utilize those created by learners, etc.). Focus also on any other aspect of classroom processes and practices that interests you.

13.2.3   Compare and contrast your (individual/group) analysis and interpretation with those of another individual/group.

13.2.4   Apart from the background details given above, what additional information do you think would have helped you do the project in a more satisfying manner, and why?

Interactional data:

Episode 13.2: (Intermediate — Speaking)

[The class begins with a role play by T1 and his colleague—not included in the transcript.]

1	T	Now, the purpose of that was to see what you think about conversations. What do you think about the conversations we've just had? Were they good conversations?
2	Ss	No . . . (laugh)
3	J	No, not the acting . . . not the acting . . . we know that. [J is the colleague who participated in the role play.]
4	T	Yah, we know we are good actors. (Ss laugh) But what about the situations? Did you notice anything about it?
5	S5	You speak with her but she is not giving you any . . . you know . . . xxx she goes yah . . . I like this you know . . . she must say alright good, I think . . . the University of Georgia is best . . . or something like this . . .

6	T	Why does she need to do that? Does anyone have an idea? Why didn't she do that?
7	S7	She is not interesting about . . . your conversation.
8	T	How do you know that she is not interested?
9	S1	She doesn't like you. (Ss laugh)
10	T	Maybe she doesn't like me. But what makes you say that? What makes you say she doesn't like . . .
11	S1	Her face . . . the emotions . . . it seems she is not xx.
12	T	Ah . . . ok. So, she doesn't talk to me. That's one thing that maybe we could improve. What's another thing in . . . the other situations that you noticed?
13	S3	mmm . . . she might be Japanese . . . (Ss laugh)
14	T	She might be Japanese. What makes you say that?
15	S3	She doesn't understand . . .
16	T	She doesn't understand. (Ss laugh) Alright. Why do you say she doesn't understand? . . . Any idea?
17	S3	Maybe she is shy . . . she is afraid to talk to you because her English is no good.
18	T	Ok, what about the first situation . . . you remember what I was talking to her . . .
19	S8	You don't understand what to talk about . . .
20	T	Maybe I did understand . . .
21	S8	You don't care . . . you said . . . you said that's good. I don't want to . . . I want to . . .
22	T	Was there something wrong with what I said to her?
23	Ss	Yah . . .
24	T	Why?
25	S8	Oh . . . that's great. Her car is broken and you said, "Oh that's great" . . .
26	T	So that's not a good conversation?
27	Ss	No . . .
28	T	What about the . . . mmm
29	S2	She misunderstood what you said.
30	T	She misunderstood what I said?
31	S6	You misunderstood what she said.
32	T	Ok. Right. Maybe there's a misunderstanding. Good. What

about . . . when I was going to be the editor of the school newspaper . . .

33	S7	She didn't interest you . . . xxx
34	T	She is not interested . . . What makes you say that she wasn't interested?
35	S7	Because she's not paying attention to you . . . she's facing the wrong . . .
36	T	Not paying attention . . . what do we know about paying attention . . . when you are paying attention to someone . . .
37	S9	Eye . . . straight . . . xxx
38	T	Eye contact . . . very good. So when we had these conversations, have you ever felt like in one of these situations?
39	Ss	Yah . . . (Ss laugh)
40	T	Ok, that's what we are hoping to do in this class is to give you some opportunity to interact with each other and . . . ah . . . respond in an appropriate way. You know sometimes there may be situations like Julia's car is broken and she is worried about this. She needs to, she needs some help from a friend. Can you think of some other situations that might make a person to be worried? What situations can you think about . . . that might make a person to be worried?
41	S	Fire in the apartment . . .
42	T	Fire in the apartment . . . (writes on BB) good . . .
43	S11	Car accident.
44	T	Car accident . . . right . . .
45	S2	Sick . . .
46	T	Sick . . . in what way would you be sick . . . can you . . .
47	S	xx
48	T	You are sick . . . and . . .
49	S	xx (Ss laugh)
50	S2	Sick . . . xx . . . mind . . .
51	T	(laughs) Maybe a mental sickness . . . but . . . maybe you're sick and . . . need a doctor fast . . . ok. What else?
52	S12	Your wife . . . baby . . . xx (gestures)
53	T	Your wife is having a baby.
54	S	She's having a baby xx (Ss laugh)
55	T	Oh . . . yes . . . there's a movie called *She's Having a Baby*. So

what else might . . . ah, these are situations that might mean an emergency. What if you are just worried about something?

56 S   xx future.

57 T   Your future, ok.

58 Ss   xxx (laugh)

59 T   Future plans.

60 S10 Homework . . .

61 T   Worried about your homework . . . Alright . . .

62 S   xx (Ss laugh)

63 T   You are worried about me?

64 S2   Grade . . . grade . . .

65 T   Oh worried about grade . . . ok. That's good. Now . . .

Episode 13.3: (Intermediate — Grammar)

1 T   There are different ways of comparing things, you know. We can compare things . . . and one is just as the other. You know what a scale is? A scale: When you weigh things on it. You know I weigh myself . . . (pretends to weigh herself on a scale) I am . . . woo A hundred and fifty pounds. I weigh a hundred and fifty pounds. You know what a scale is? . . . Sometimes it is easier for you to understand what it is if it's written, is that correct? (Writes "scale" on BB). Do you know what a scale is?

2 Ss   Yah.

3 T   Alright you weigh things . . . ok? You weigh things on a scale. Ok. and . . . s . . . when we have a scale . . . and we put two things on a scale they are the same. It will not go up or down, right? It will be like this, alright? When one is heavier than the other, what happens? (gestures) boop . . . goes down, alright? Or, the other one goes down, right? And in between the two extremes, there is a variety, right? We can express that in language, right? We can express the idea in language, right? We can say you are as tall as I am, right? You are . . . eh . . . taller than I am. What happens here? We are the same, right? Everybody . . . he is as tall as I am. He is taller than I

am, right? You are . . . nothing personal, I am just playing right now . . . you are smaller than I am, right? And, Mr. X [refer-ring to the colleague operating the camera] is the tallest . . . of, all right? eh . . . but then we can also say (writes on BB), ok . . . Mr. X is the tallest . . . of what . . . the tallest. Some-times you don't have to use all of it because we know what we are talking about, right. In a conversation if we don't know sometimes we may just have to say yes or no you know and sometimes we have to make give more information, ok? (writes on BB) is the tallest of the class, right? Alright? eh . . . x let's see . . . Let's make a sentence with eh the same, ok? I am . . .

4	S5	. . . as tall as you.
5	T	You don't understand what I am what I want.
6	S5	The same?
7	T	The same, yah . . . give me a sentence with the same.
8	S3	I am as tall as you are.
9	T	Ok, (writes on BB: "I am as tall as you are") Ok. eh . . . most of the time . . . most of the time . . . or, let me put it this way . . . there are probably more things that are different right than the same. Would you agree with me? Yah?

[Break in interactional sequence]

10	T	Let's see if we can talk about the worst . . . the coldest . . . you know the most the most negative . . . Ok. All right, the most negative . . . ok. Alright, the most negative. What's the worst for you? The worst experience . . . or something, something that you really . . . now we've talked about tornado and earth-quakes, right?
11	S9	We xx Tuscaloosa is the worst thing xxx tornado . . .
12	T	Tornado?
13	S9	Yes.
14	T	The worst thing that they have in . . . ok. What about your country? What is the worst thing in your country? We've talked about some good things . . . Let's see the . . . we have also to talk about bad . . . right? What's the worst you can think about your country? If you have to say one thing really bad, what would you say? . . . (Long pause) . . . you have to think . . . alright? That's good. You know . . . think . . . xx one thing about country xx . . . I can tell you one bad thing about

the Midwest . . . Midwest has very bad weather . . . It has perhaps the worst weather of all . . . states that I have lived in. It's not true . . . but it seems . . . It's very cold. It's much colder than here . . . much, much colder than here . . . and the sun does not shine very often . . . Ok, the sun doesn't shine enough. You understand what I mean . . . doesn't shine enough, alright. Now, what about your country?

15	S7	Japan has a lot of xxx.
16	T	A lot of . . .
17	S7	Earthquakes.
18	T	Earthquakes . . . earthquakes.
19	S7	Earthquakes.
20	T	mmm yah, that sounds . . . eh . . . that sounds scary . . . does it does it interfere with your daily life?
21	Ss	mm.
22	T	Yes. Everywhere in Japan? Are there earthquake dangers everywhere in Japan?
23	S7	Almost everywhere.
24	T	Almost everywhere. hm . . . alright. Ok. What about your country?
25	S1	We have a lot of typhoons.
26	T	What is a typhoon? Does everybody know what a typhoon is? Right, if we all know we don't have to waste our time, right? That's good. Do you agree? I mean. Yah?
27	S1	I agree.
28	T	hmm I would think that . . . what about language? Some of you . . . not Japan . . . but . . . Taiwan . . . is a problem of language, right because there are so many different dialects . . . right . . . of China . . . Chinese? Isn't there a problem? When there are . . . communication problems, right?
29	S9	xxx xxx we have the same . . . so many xxx that's no problem.
30	T	But, Chinese language . . . has many different dialects right?
31	S9	Yes.
32	T	And that's a, that is a most serious problem if you want to . . . be able to communicate . . . There is another country that has the same problem. Which is that? Which country?
33	S5	India? Problems of xxx.

34   T   India . . . too many languages . . . the most languages of all
           countries . . . I don't know what the number of languages . . .
           ok . . . Alright.

                                   (Data source: Kumaravadivelu, 1993b)

Project 13.3: Conducting an Observational Study

13.3.0 You may do this project individually or with a partner. If
you are part of a teacher education program, select another classmate to work with. If you are a practicing teacher, try to do the
project with a colleague. Your primary objective is to understand
classroom events, and how different participants (the teacher, the
learner, and the observer) see and interpret the same event in different ways, all of which could be equally valid. Your objective is to
learn from your observation and not to pass any value judgment
about the class(es) or the teacher(s). Here's what you have to do to
complete the project:

13.3.1 Select an L2 class/teacher you wish to observe. Explain your
objective to the teacher and seek his/her permission to observe a unit
of his/her class. A unit is defined as a series of (two or more) related lessons with specific learning and teaching objectives. You may record
classroom instruction on an audio- or videotape if the teacher and the
students give you permission to do so. If permission is not granted, you
may have to take extensive notes. It is better to find a teacher who permits video-recording because, obviously, videotaped classes are a rich
source of information for analysis and interpretation.

13.3.2 For your observation, focus on three perspectives of classroom
events: the teacher perspective, the observer perspective (i.e., your perspective), and the learner perspective. For the teacher perspective, talk
to the teacher you have chosen to observe before and after your observation; ask about what he/she planned to do (specific objectives, classroom techniques, etc.) and what he/she actually did in the classroom (as
perceived by him or her). For the observer perspective, take detailed
notes on your class observation and your opinions about learning and
teaching in the classes you observed. For the learner perspective, talk to
three or four students (the more the better) in the class, ask them what
they thought the specific objectives of the classes were and what they
actually learned in those classes. You may also direct your question(s)
toward the learners' participation in class interaction. It is, of course,
useful to select those students who have actively participated in the class.

13.3.3 Analyze and interpret classroom events in terms of the M & M scheme. Pull together all three perspectives, consider their similarities and dissimilarities, and identify probable reasons for the differences you might have observed.

13.3.4 You may also reflect on what you have learned (and on the difficulties you have faced) in the process of carrying out this project.

13.3.5 If possible, compare and contrast your learning experience with that of another individual/group. That others may have observed different classes/teachers does not really matter. What matters is the sharing of the observational experience and the lessons learned.

In Closing

The M & M scheme for classroom observation presented in this chapter offers new possibilities of, and procedures for, self-observing, self-analyzing, and self-evaluating teaching acts. It is only by systematically analyzing classroom input and interaction, interpreting their analysis, evaluating their teaching effectiveness, and putting all this developing experiential knowledge together that teachers can make sense of what happens in their classroom.

The M & M scheme provides the necessary knowledge and skill for teachers to explore their classroom processes and practices. When they engage in such an exploration, and perceive it as a valuable professional activity, they will eventually become teacher-scholars capable of generating their own personal pedagogic knowledge. The challenge facing them is how to integrate such a professional activity with their activity of everyday teaching. The observational scheme, with macrostrategies and mismatches as points of departure, provide a productive way of integrating the twin pedagogic activities so that they can develop the capacity to theorize from practice, and practice what they theorize.

Afterword

The purpose of this Afterword is to have a personal word with prospective and practicing teachers.

My primary goal in this book has been to provide a postmethod pedagogic framework to enable you to develop the knowledge, skill, attitude, and autonomy necessary to devise for yourself a systematic, coherent, and relevant personal theory of practice.

The postmethod pedagogic framework is founded on the parameters of particularity, practicality, and possibility. Consistent with that conceptual foundation, I have suggested ten macrostrategies derived from theoretical, empirical, and experiential knowledge. One way you can actualize this framework is by using the suggested macrostrategies to design your own situated microstrategies. Such a strategic activity, if carried out seriously and systematically, has the potential to transform you into strategic thinkers, strategic teachers, and strategic explorers.

An Alphabet of Pedagogic Thought

What I have attempted to present in this book is no more than an alphabet of pedagogic thought. Just as the alphabet of a language allows various permutations and combinations of letters, words, and sentences, making it possible for you to construct your own text with your own ideas, the alphabet of pedagogic thought, I hope, will enable you to construct your own personal pedagogic knowledge to suit your local learning/teaching needs, wants, and situations. Just as the creative aspect of language use enables us to produce sentences never spoken before and to understand sentences never heard before, the creative use of the alphabet of pedagogic thought, I hope, will make it possible for you to design micro-strategies that you have never designed before.

The possibilities this book opens up are unlimited; they present you with challenges as well as opportunities. Just reading this book, even if you have done some of the reflective tasks and carried out some of the exploratory projects, may not be sufficient to make you a strategic thinker and a strategic teacher. What will make you a strategic thinker and teacher is a conscious, continual, and constructive engagement that prompts you to reflect, review, and reinvent what you do in the classroom. The macrostrategic framework, then, is not a body of knowledge to be learned to satisfy your intellectual curiosity; rather, it is a set of tools to be used to develop your own theory of practice.

Developing your own theory of practice requires patience and perseverance. It does not develop instantly before your eyes, as film develops in a Polaroid camera. It evolves over time, through determined effort. It involves the development of a level of knowledge, skill, attitude, and autonomy that is necessary to give you the confidence and the competence to embrace a self-directed pedagogy. Above all, it involves the ability to critically engage your own beliefs and values, understandings and assumptions, and change them if necessary.

Paving the Path as You Walk It

This book does not represent a final product; rather, it represents a starting point, both for me and for you. For me, it represents my initial attempt to come to grips with the limitations of a method-based pedagogy and with the challenges of a postmethod pedagogy. Much work remains to be done. This book does not give answers to many of the doubts and uncertainties that we all face in the practice of our everyday teaching. However, I would be happy and satisfied if your response to this book goes something like this: "Before I read this book, I had a lot of doubts and uncertainties about language learning and teaching. After reading this book, I still have those doubts and uncertainties, but on a much higher level of cognition!"

For you as well, this book is a starting point in the sense that all you have here are raw materials necessary to lay a solid foundation on which you can begin to construct a postmethod pedagogy. But, the edifice of a postmethod pedagogy has to be constructed by you. You can hope to do that only by anchoring yourself in the social, political, economic, and educational particularities that surround you and your learners, and by integrating, in an informed way, what you have read in this book with your ever-evolving and ever-widening professional and personal knowledge base. In other words, the suggested macrostrategies and the sample microstrategies are not meant to be transplanted; rather, they are meant to be transformed.

As you begin your long journey to transform your postmethod pedagogic thoughts, it is worthwhile to remember Antonio Machado's poem:

Caminante, no hay camino, se hace el camino al andar

(Traveler, there are no roads. The road is created as we walk it.)

What this book asks you to do is to pave your own pedagogic path as you walk it.

References

Alexander, R. J. (1986). "Innovation and continuity in the initial teacher education curriculum," in R. J. Alexander, M. Craft, and J. Lynch (eds.). *Change in Teacher Education: Context and Provision Since Robbins*. London: Holt, Rinehart and Winston, pp. 103–60.

Allwright, R. L. (1980). "Turns, Topics, and Tasks: Patterns of Participation in Language Learning and Teaching," in D. Larsen-Freeman (ed.). *Discourse Analysis in Second Language Research*. Rowley: Newbury House Publishers, Inc.

Allwright, R. L. (1981). What do we want teaching materials for? *ELT Journal* 36:1:5–19.

Allwright, R. L. (1984). The importance of interaction in classroom language learning. *Applied Linguistics* 5, 156–71.

Allwright, R. L. (1986). Making sense of instruction: What's the problem? *Papers in Applied Linguistics-Michigan* 1:2:1–10.

Allwright, R. L. (1987). "Classroom Observation: Problems and Possibilities," in B. K. Das (ed.). *Patterns of Classroom Interaction in Southeast Asia*. Singapore: SEAMEO Regional Language Center, pp. 88–102.

Allwright, R. L. (1988). *Observation in the Language Classroom*. London: Longman.

Allwright, R. L. (1993). "Integrating 'research' and 'pedagogy': appropriate criteria and practical problems," in J. Edge and K. Richards (eds.). *Teachers Develop Teachers Research*. London: Heinemann, pp. 125–35 (1993).

Allwright, R. L., and K. M. Bailey (1991). *Focus on the Language Classroom*. Cambridge: Cambridge University Press.

Ashcroft, B., G. Griffiths, and H. Tiffin (eds.) (1995). *The Post-Colonial Studies Reader*. London: Routledge.

Auerbach, E. R. (1993). Reexamining English-only in the ESL classroom. *TESOL Quarterly* 27:1:9–32.

Auerbach, E. R. (1995). The politics of the ESL classroom: Issues of power in pedagogical choices. In J. W. Tellefson (ed.). *Power and Inequality in Language Education*. Cambridge: Cambridge University Press, pp. 9–33 (1995).

Barkhuizen, G. P. (1998). Discovering learners' perceptions of ESL classroom teaching/learning activities in a South African context. *TESOL Quarterly* 32:1:85–108.

Baron, D. (2000). Ebonics and the politics of English. *World Englishes* 19:1:5–19.

Bates, E., and B. MacWhinney (1982). "Functionalist Approaches to Grammar," in L. Gleitman, and E. Wanner (eds.). *Language Acquisition: The State of the Art* New York: Cambridge University Press, pp. 173–128.

Bean, M., B. Kumaravadivelu, and P. Lowenberg (1995). Students as experts: Tapping the cultural and linguistic diversity of the classroom. *Journal of Excellence in College Teaching* 6:2:99–112.

Benesch, S. (2001). *Critical English for Academic Purposes: Theory, Politics, and Practice*. Mahwah, New Jersey: Lawrence Erlbaum Associates, Inc.

Benson, P. (1997). "The philosophy and politics of learner autonomy," in P. Benson and P. Voller (eds.). *Autonomy and Independence in Language Learning*. London: Longman (pp. 18–34).

Benson, P. (2001). *Teaching and Researching Autonomy in Language Learning*. London: Longman.

Benson, P. and P. Voller (eds.) (1997). *Autonomy & Independence in Language Learning*. London: Longman.

Berns, M. (1990). *Contexts of Competence: Social and Cultural Considerations in Communicative Language Teaching*. New York: Plenum Press.

Block, D. (1994). A Day in the life of class: Teachers/Learner perceptions of task purpose in conflict. *System* 22:4:473–86.

Block, D. (1996). "A window on the classroom: classroom events viewed from different angles," in K. M. Bailey and D. Nunan (eds.). *Voices from the Classroom: Qualitative Research in Language Classrooms*. Cambridge: Cambridge University Press, pp. 168–93.

Blyth, S. C. (1998). *Untangling the Web: St. Martin Guide to Language and Culture on the Internet*. New York: St. Martin's Press.

Breen, M. P. (1985). The social context for language teaching: A neglected situation? *Studies in Second Language Acquisition* 7:2:135–58.

Broady, E., and M. M. Kenning (1996). *Promoting Learner Autonomy in University Language Teaching*. London: CILT.

Brock, C. (1986). The effects of referential questions on ESL classroom discourse. *TESOL Quarterly* 20:1:47–59.

Brown, D. H. (1998). "The place of moral and political issues in language pedagogy," in W. A. Renandya and G. M. Jacobs (eds.). *Learners and Language Learning*. Singapore: SEAMEO Regional Language Centre.

Brown, K. (1999). *Developing Critical Literacy*. Sydney: Macquarie University Press.

Byram, M. (1989). *Cultural Studies in Foreign Language Education*. Clevedon, United Kingdom: Multilingual Matters.

Cameron, D., E. Frazer, P. Harvey, M. B. H. Rampton, and K. Richardson (1992). *Researching Language: Issues of Power and Method*. London: Routledge.

Canagarajah, A. S. (1997). Safe houses in the contact zone: Coping strategies of African-American students in the academy. *College Composition and Communication* 48:2:173–96.

Canagarajah, A. S. (1999). *Resisting Linguistic Imperialism in English Teaching*. Oxford: Oxford University Press.

Candlin, C. N. (1997). "Preface," in P. Benson, P. and P. Voller. *Autonomy & Independence in Language Learning*. London: Longman, pp. x–xiii.

Celce-Murcia, M. and D. Larsen-Freeman (1983). *The Grammar Book*. Boston: Heinle & Heinle Publishers.

Celce-Murcia, M., and E. Olshtain (2000). *Discourse and Context in Language Teaching: A Guide for Language Teachers*. Cambridge: Cambridge University Press.

Chamot, A. U., S. Barnhardt, P. B. El-Dinary, and J. Robbins (1999). *The Learning Strategies Handbook*. London: Longman.

Chick, K. J. (1996). "Safe-talk: Collusion in apartheid education," in H. Coleman (ed.). *Society and the Language Classroom*. Cambridge: Cambridge University Press, pp. 21–39.

Chomsky, N. (1965). *Aspects of the Theory of Syntax*. Cambridge: MIT Press.

Chomsky, N. (1970). "BBC interviews with Stuart Hampshire. rpt. Noam Chomsky's view of language," in M. Lester (ed.). *Readings in Applied Transformational Grammar*. New York: Holt, Rinehart, pp. 96–113.

Clarke, M. A. (1983). "The scope of approach, the importance of method, and the nature of technique," in J. E. Alatis, H. Stern, and P. Strevens (eds.). *Georgetown University Round Table on Languages and Linguistics 1983: Applied Linguistics and the Preparation of Second Language Teachers*. Washington, D.C.: Georgetown University, pp. 106–15.

Coleman, H. (1996). "Autonomy and ideology in the English language classroom," in H. Coleman (ed.). *Society and the Language Classroom* Cambridge: Cambridge University Press, pp. 1–15.

Corder, S. P. (1967). The significance of learners' errors. *International Review of Applied Linguistics* 5, 161–70.

Cortazzi, M. (1991). Primary Teaching How It Is: A Narrative Account. London: David Foulton. *Critical Inquiry* 17 (Winter), 336–57.

Cortazzi, M. and L. Jin (1999). "Cultural mirrors: Materials and methods in the EFL classroom," in E. Hinkel (ed.). *Culture in Second Language Teaching*. Cambridge: Cambridge University Press, pp. 196–219.

Crandall, J. (ed.) (1987). *ESL Through Content-Area Instruction; Mathematics, Science, Social Studies*. Englewood Cliffs, New Jersey: Regents/Prentice Hall.

Crookall, D. and R. Oxford (eds.). (1990). *Language Learning Through Simulation/Gaming*. Rowley: Newbury House.

Crookes, G., and S. Gass (eds.) (1993). *Tasks and Language Learning: Integrating Theory and Practice*. Clevedon, Avon: Multilingual Matters.

Crystal, D. (1997). *English as a Global Language*. Cambridge: Cambridge University Press.

Cuban, L. (1989). The at-risk label and the problems in urban school reform. A study of two learners. *System* 17, 249–62.

Davies, P. and E. Pearse (2000). *Success in English Teaching*. Oxford: Oxford University Press.

de-Certeau, M. (1974). *Culture in the Plural*. Minneapolis: University of Minnesota Press.

Delpit, L. (1995). *Other People's Children: Cultural Conflict in the Classroom*. New York: Norton.

Dewey, J. (1933). *How We Think*. Chicago: Henry Regnery.

Di Pietro, R. (1987). *Strategic Interaction: Learning Languages Through Scenarios*. Cambridge: Cambridge University Press.

Dickinson, L. (1987). *Self-Instruction in Language Learning*. Cambridge: Cambridge University Press.

Dirven, R. (1990). Pedagogical grammar. *Language Teaching* 23, 1–18.

Doughty, C. and J. Williams (eds.) (1998). *Focus on Form in Classroom Second Language Acquisition*. Cambridge: Cambridge University Press.

Elliott, J. (1991). *Action Research for Educational Change*. Buckingham: Open University Press.

Ellis, G. and B. Sinclair (1989). *Learning to Learn English: A Course in Learner Training*. Teacher Handbook. Cambridge: Cambridge University Press.

Ellis, R. (1992). "The classroom context: An acquisition-rich or an acquisition-poor environment?" in C. Kramsch and S. McConnell-Ginet (eds.). *Text and Context: Cross-Disciplinary Perspectives on Language Study*. Toronto: D.C. Heath and Co., pp. 171–86.

Ellis, R. (1995). Uptake as language awareness. *Language Awareness* 4:3:147–60.

Ellis, R. (1997). *SLA Research and Language Teaching*. Oxford: Oxford University Press.

Ellis, R. (1999). *Learning a Second Language Through Interaction*. Philadelphia: John Benjamins.

Fairclough, N. (1995). *Critical Discourse Analysis: The Critical Study of Language*. London: Longman.

Fairclough, N. (ed.) (1992). *Critical Language Awareness*. London: Longman.

Foley, J. A., T. Kandiah, B. Zhiming, A. F. Gupta, L. Alsagoff, H. C. Lick, L. Wee, I. S. Talib, and W. Bokhorst-Heng (1998). *English in New Cultural Contexts: Reflections from Singapore*. Singapore: Singapore Institute of Management and Oxford University Press.

Freeman, D. (1991). "Mistaken constructs: Re-examining the nature and assumptions of language teacher education," in J. Alatis (ed.). *George-*

town University Round Table on Languages and Linguistics 1991: Linguistics and Language Pedagogy: The State of the Art. Washington, D.C.: Georgetown University Press, pp. 25–39.

Freeman, D. (1998). *Doing Teacher Research.* Boston: Heinle & Heinle Publishers.

Freeman, Y. S. and D. E. Freeman (1992). *Whole Language for Second Language Learners.* Portsmouth, New Hampshire: Heinemann.

Freire, P. (1972). *Pedagogy of the Oppressed.* Harmondsworth, United Kingdom: Penguin Books.

Freire, P. (1998). *Pedagogy of the Heart.* New York: Continuum.

Gass, S. M. (1986). An interactionist approach to L2 sentence interpretation. *Studies in Second Language Acquisition* 8:19–37.

Gass, S. M. (1997). *Input, Interaction, and the Second Language Learner.* Mahwah, New Jersey: Lawrence Erlbaum Associates, Inc.

Giddens, A. (1999). *Runaway World.* New York: Routledge.

Giroux, H. A. (1988). *Teachers as Intellectuals: Toward a Critical Pedagogy of Learning.* South Hadley, Massachusetts: Bergin & Garvey.

Goodman, K. (1986). *What's Whole in Whole Language?* Portsmouth, New Hampshire: Heinemann.

Grosse, C. U. (1991). The TESOL methods course. *TESOL Quarterly* 25:1:29–50.

Gumperz, J. J. (1982). *Discourse Strategies.* Cambridge: Cambridge University Press.

Halliday, M. A. K., and R. Hasan (1976). *Cohesion in English.* London: Longman.

Hansen, D. T. (1995). *The Call to Teach.* New York: Teachers College Press.

Harmer, J. (1991). *The Practice of English Language Teaching.* London: Longman.

Hatch, E. (1978). "Discourse analysis and second language acquisition," in E. Hatch (ed.). *Second Language Acquisition,* Rowley, Mass.: Newbury House, pp. 401–35.

Hatch, E. (1992). *Discourse and Language Education.* Cambridge: Cambridge University Press.

Hawkins, E. (1984). *Awareness of language: An Introduction.* Cambridge: Cambridge University Press.

Heath, S. B. (1983). *Ways with Words: Language, Life, and Work in Communities and Classrooms.* Cambridge: Cambridge University Press.

Heath, S. B. (1993). Inner city life through drama: Imagining the language classroom. *TESOL Quarterly* 27:2:177–92.

Heath, S. B. and L. Mangiola (1991). *Children of Promise: Literate Activity in Linguistically and Culturally Diverse Classrooms.* Washington, D.C.: National Education Association Publications.

Horwitz, E. K., M. B. Horwitz, and J. Cope (1986). Foreign language classroom anxiety. *Modern Language Journal* 70:125–32.

Hymes, D. (1970). "On communicative competence," in J. J. Gumperz and D. Hymes. *Directions in Sociolinguistics*. Austin, Texas: Holt, Rinehart, and Winston.

Illich, I. (1970). *Deschooling Society*. Harmondsworth, United Kingdom: Penguin Books.

International Dictionary of English. (1995). Cambridge: Cambridge University Press.

Jarvis, G. A. (1968). Behavioral observation system for classroom foreign language skill acquisition activities. *Modern Language Journal* 52:335–41.

Jarvis, G. A. (1991). "Research on teaching methodology: Its evolution and prospects," in Barbara Freed (ed.). *Foreign Language Acquisition Research and the Classroom*. Lexington, Massachusetts: D.C. Heath and Company, pp. 295–306.

Jesperson, J. O. (1904). *How to Teach a Foreign Language*. London: George Allen and Unwin.

Johnson, K. E. (1999). *Understanding Language Teaching*. Boston: Heinle & Heinle Publishers.

Kachru, B. B. (1982). *The Other Tongue: English Across Cultures*. Chicago: University of Illinois Press.

Kachru, B. B. (1985). *The Alchemy of English: The Spread, Functions and Models of Non-Native Englishes*. Oxford: Pergamon.

Kachru, B. B. (1990). World Englishes and applied linguistics. *World Englishes* 9, 3–20.

Kandiah, T. (1998). "The emergence of new Englishes," in J. A. Foley et al. (eds.). *English in New Cultural Contexts*. Singapore: Singapore Institute of Management and Oxford University Press, pp. 73–105.

Kelly, L. G. (1969). *25 Centuries of Language Teaching*. Rowley, Massachusetts: Newbury House Publishers.

Kincheloe, J. L. (1993). *Toward a Critical Politics of Teacher Thinking*. Westport: Bergin & Garvey.

Kohonen, V., R. Jaatinen, P. Kaikkonen, and J. Lehtovaara (2001). *Experiential Learning in Foreign Language Education*. London: Longman.

Kramsch, C. (1993). *Context and Culture in Language Teaching*. Oxford: Oxford University Press.

Krashen, S. (1985). *The Input Hypothesis: Issues and Implications*. London: Longman.

Krashen, S. (1989). *Language Acquisition and Language Education*. London: Prentice Hall.

Krashen, S. (1998). Comprehensible output? *System* 26, 175–82.

Krashen, S. D. and T. D. Terrell (1983). *The Natural Approach: Language Acquisition in the Classroom*. Hayward, California: The Alemany Press.

Krishnaswamy, N. and A. S. Burde (1998). *The Politics of Indians' English: Linguistic Colonialism and the Expanding English Empire*. Delhi: Oxford University Press.

Kumaravadivelu, B. (March 1989). Task-based learning: Teacher intention and learner interpretation. Paper presented at 23rd Annual National TESOL Convention, San Antonio, March 7–11, 1989.

Kumaravadivelu, B. (1991). Language learning tasks: Teacher intention and learner interpretation. *ELT Journal* 45:2:98–107.

Kumaravadivelu, B. (1992). Macrostrategies for the second/foreign language teacher. *Modern Language Journal* 76:1:41–49.

Kumaravadivelu, B. (1993a). "The name of the task and the task of naming: Methodological aspects of task-based pedagogy," in G. Crookes and S. Gass (eds.). *Tasks in a Pedagogical Context*. Clevedon: Multilingual Matters, pp. 69–96.

Kumaravadivelu, B. (1993b). Maximizing learning potential in the communicative classroom. *ELT Journal* 47:1:12–21. Reprinted in T. Hedge and N. Whitney (eds.). *Power, Pedagogy & Practice*. Oxford: Oxford University Press, pp. 241–353 (1996).

Kumaravadivelu, B. (1994a). The postmethod condition: (E)merging strategies for second/foreign language teaching. *TESOL Quarterly*, 28:1:27–48.

Kumaravadivelu, B. (1994b). Intake factors and intake processes in adult language learning. *Applied Language Learning* 5:1:33–71.

Kumaravadivelu, B. (1995). A multidimensional model for peer evaluation of teaching effectiveness. *Journal of Excellence in College Teaching* 6:3: 95–114.

Kumaravadivelu, B. (1999a). "Theorizing practice, practicing theory: Critical classroom observation," in H. Trappes-Lomax and I. McGrath (eds.). *Theory in Language Teacher Education*. London: Prentice-Hall, pp. 33–45.

Kumaravadivelu, B. (1999b). Critical classroom discourse analysis. *TESOL Quarterly* 33:3:453–85.

Kumaravadivelu, B. (2001). Toward a postmethod pedagogy. *TESOL Quarterly* 35:4:537–60.

Lamb, M. (1982). *Solidarity with Victims*. New York: Crossroad.

Larsen-Freeman, D. (1986). *Techniques and Principles in Language Teaching*. Oxford: Oxford University Press.

Larsen-Freeman, D. (1990). "On the need for a theory of language teaching," in J. E. Alatis (ed.). *Georgetown University Round Table on Languages and Linguistics, 1990*. Washington, D.C.: Georgetown University Press, pp. 261–70.

Larsen-Freeman, D. (2000). Grammar: Rules and reasons working together. *ESL Magazine* 3:1:10–12.

Leech, G. and J. Svartvik (1975). *A Communicative Grammar of English*. London: Longman.

Legutke, M. and H. Thomas (1991). *Process and Experience in the Language Classroom*. London: Longman.

Lippi-Green, R. (1997). *English with an accent: Language, ideology, and discrimination in the United States*. London: Routledge.

Little, L. (2000). Leading four generations. *Academic Leader*, March 2000: 4–5.

Long, M. (1981). "Input, interaction and second language acquisition," in H. Winitz (ed.). *Native Language and Foreign Language Acquisition* (pp. 259–78). New York, Annals of the New York Academy of Sciences, Series No. 379.

Long, M. and P. Robinson (1998). "Focus on form: Theory, research, and practice," in C. Doughty and J. Williams (eds.). *Focus on Form in Classroom Second Language Acquisition*. Cambridge: Cambridge University Press, pp. 15–41.

Long, M. and C. Sato (1983). "Classroom foreigner talk discourse: Forms and functions of teachers' questions," in H. Seliger and M. Long (eds.). *Classroom-oriented Research in Second Language Acquisition*. Rowley, Mass.: Newbury House, pp. 268–285.

Lowenberg, P. H. (2000). "Non-native varieties and the sociopolitics of English proficiency assessment," in J. K. Hall and W. G. Eggington (eds.). *The Sociopolitics of English Language Teaching*. Clevedon: Multilingual Matters Ltd., pp. 67–85.

Lutz, W. (1989). *Doublespeak: From "Revenue Enhancement" to "Terminal Living": How Government, Business, Advertisers, and Others Use Language to Deceive You*. New York: Harper & Row.

Macedo, D. (1994). "Preface," in P. McLaren and C. Lankshear (eds.). *Conscientization and Resistance*. New York: Routledge, pp. 1–8.

Mackey, W. F. (1965). *Language Teaching Analysis*. Bloomington: Indiana University Press.

Malinowski, B. (1923). "The problem of meaning in primitive languages," in C. K. Ogden and I. A. Richards (eds.). *The Meaning of Meaning*. New York: Harcourt, Brace and World, Inc., pp. 296–336.

Martin-Jones, M., and M. Saxena (1996). Turn-taking, power asymmetries, and the positioning of bilingual participants in classroom discourse. *Linguistics and Education* 8:105–23.

Martin-Jones, M., and M. Heller (1996). Introduction to the special issues on education in multilingual settings: discourse, identities, and power. Part I: Constructing legitimacy. *Linguistics and Education* 8:3–16.

McCaleb, S. P. (1994). *Building Communities of Learning: A Collaboration Among Teachers, Students, Families, and Community*. Mahwah, New Jersey: Lawrence Erlbaum Associates.

McKay S. L. (2000). Teaching English as an international language: Implications for cultural materials in the classroom. *TESOL Journal*, Winter 2000: 7–11.

McKay, S. L. and S. C. Wong (1996). Multiple discourses, multiple identities: Investment and agency in second language learning among Chinese adolescent immigrant students. *Harvard Educational Review* 3:577–608.

McLaren. P. (1995). *Critical Pedagogy and Predatory Culture*. London: Routledge.

Mehan, H. (1979). *Learning Lessons: Social Organization in the Classroom*. Cambridge: Cambridge University Press.

Meloni, C. (1998). The Internet in the Classroom. *ESL Magazine*, 1:1: 10–16.

Morgan, B. (1998). *The ESL Classroom: Teaching, Critical Practice, and Community Development*. Toronto: University of Toronto Press Inc.

Moskowitz, G. (1971). Interaction analysis—A new modern language for supervisors. *Foreign Language Annals* 5:211–21.

Norton, B. (2000). *Identity and Language Learning*. London: Longman.

Nunan, D. (1987). Communicative language teaching: Making it work. *ELT Journal* 41/2:136–45.

Nunan, D. (1989). *Designing Tasks for the Communicative Classroom*. Cambridge: Cambridge University Press.

Nunan, D. (1996). "Towards autonomous learning: Some theoretical, empirical and practical issues," in R. Pemberton, E. Li, W. Or, and H. Pierson (eds.). *Taking Control: Autonomy in Language Learning*. Hong Kong: Hong Kong University Press.

O'Hanlon, C. (1993). "The importance of an articulated personal theory of professional development," in J. Elliott (ed.). *Reconstructing Teacher Education: Teacher Development*. London: The Falmer Press, pp. 243–55 (1993).

Odlin, T. (1994). *Perspectives on Pedagogical Grammar*. Cambridge: Cambridge University Press.

Oller J. W., Jr. (1979). *Language Tests at School*. London: Longman.

Omaggio, A. C. (1986). *Teaching Language in Context*. Boston: Heinle & Heinle Publishers.

O'Malley, J. M., and A. U. Chamot (1990). *Learning Strategies in Second Language Acquisition*. Cambridge: Cambridge University Press.

Oxford, R. (1990). *Language Learning Strategies: What Every Teacher Should Know*. New York: Newbury House/Harper and Row.

Oxford, R. (2001). Integrated skills in the ESL/EFL classroom. *ESL Magazine*, January/February: 18–19.

Page, B. (1992). *Letting Go—Taking Hold: A Guide to Independent Language Learning by Teachers for Teachers*. London: CILT.

Peirce, B. N. (1995). Social identity, investment, and language learning. *TESOL Quarterly* 29:9–31.

Pennycook, A. (1989). The concept of method, interested knowledge, and the politics of language teaching. *TESOL Quarterly* 23:4:589–618.

Pennycook, A. (1997). "Cultural alternatives and autonomy," in P. Benson and P. Voller (eds.). *Autonomy and Independence in Language Learning*. London: Longman, pp. 35–53.

Pennycook, A. (1998). *English and the Discourses of Colonialism*. London: Routledge.

Pica, T., L. Holliday, N. Lewis, and L. Morgenthaler (1989). Comprehensible output as an outcome of linguistic demands on the learner. *Studies in Second Language Acquisition*, 11:63–10.

Pica, T., R. Young, and C. Doughty (1987). The impact of interaction on comprehension. *TESOL Quarterly* 21:737–58.

Pinker, S. (1994). *The Language Instinct: How the Mind Creates Language*. New York: HarperPerennial.

Prabhu, N. S. (1987). *Second Language Pedagogy*. Oxford: Oxford University Press.

Prabhu, N. S. (1990). There is no best method—why? *TESOL Quarterly* 24:2:161–76.

Richards, J. C. and C. Lockhart (1994). *Reflective Teaching in Second Language Classrooms*. Cambridge: Cambridge University Press.

Richards, J. C. and T. Rodgers (1986). *Approaches and Methods in Language Teaching*. Cambridge: Cambridge University Press.

Riggenbach, H. (1999). *Discourse Analysis in the Language Classroom: Volume 1. The Spoken Language*. Ann Arbor: The University of Michigan Press.

Rivers, W. M. (1964). *The Psychologist and the Foreign Language Teacher*. Chicago: University of Chicago Press.

Rivers, W. M. (1991). "Psychological validation of methodological approaches and foreign language classroom practices," in Barbara Freed (ed.). *Foreign Language Acquisition Research and the Classroom*. Lexington, Massachusetts: D.C. Heath & Co., pp. 283–94.

Rivers, W. M. (1992). "Ten principles of interactive language learning and teaching," in W. M. Rivers (ed.). *Teaching Languages in College: Curriculum and Content*. Lincolnwood: NTC, pp. 373–92.

Robinson, G. L. (1985). *Crosscultural Understanding: Processes and Approaches for Foreign Language, English as a Foreign Language and Bilingual Educators*. New York and Oxford: Pergamon.

Robinson, G. L. (1991). "Second culture acquisition," in J. E. Alatis (ed.). *Georgetown University Round Table on Languages and Linguistics, 1991*. Washington, D.C.: Georgetown University Press, pp. 114–22.

Rost, M. (1990). *Listening in Language Learning*. London: Longman.

Savignon, S. (1990). "Communicative language teaching: definitions and directions," in J. E. Alatis (ed.). *Georgetown University Round Table on Languages and Linguistics, 1990*. Washington, D.C.: Georgetown University Press.

Scharle, A. and A. Szabo (2000). *Learner Autonomy: A Guide to Developing Learner Responsibility*. Cambridge: Cambridge University Press.

Schmidt, R., and S. Frota (1986). "Developing basic conversational ability in a second language: A case study of an adult learner of Portuguese," in R. Day (ed.). *Talking to Learn: Conversation in Second Language Acquisition.* Rowley, Massachusetts: Newbury House, pp. 237–326.

Selinker, L. and R. S. Tomlin (1986). An empirical look at the integration and separation of skills in ELT. *ELT Journal* 40:3:227–35.

Sharwood Smith, M. (1991). Speaking to many minds: On the relevance of different types of language information for the L2 learner. *Second Language Research* 7:118–32.

Simon, R. I. (1987). Empowerment as a pedagogy of possibility. *Language Arts* 64:4:379–88.

Singleton, D. (1989). *Language Acquisition: The Age Factor.* Clevedon: Multilingual Matters.

Slimani, A. (1989). The role of topicalization in classroom language learning. *System* 17:2:223–34.

Slimani, A. (1992). "Evaluation of classroom interaction," in J. C. Alderson and A. Beretta (eds.). *Evaluating Second Language Education.* Cambridge: Cambridge University Press, pp. 197–221.

Smitherman, G. (1998). "Dat teacher be at us"—What is Ebonics? *TESOL Quarterly* 32:1:139–43.

Snow. C. E. and C. A. Ferguson (1977). *Talking to Children: Language Input and Acquisition.* Cambridge: Cambridge University Press.

Stern, H. H. (1992). *Issues and Options in Language Teaching.* Oxford: Oxford University Press.

Stevick, E. W. (1982). *Teaching and Learning Languages.* Cambridge: Cambridge University Press.

Swaffar, J., K. Arens, and M. Morgan (1982). Teacher classroom practices: Redefining method as task hierarchy. *Modern Language Journal* 66:24–33.

Swain, M. (1985). "Communicative competence: Some roles of comprehensible input and comprehensible output in its development," in S. Gass and C. Madden (eds.). *Input in Second Language Acquisition.* Rowley, Massachusetts: Newbury House, pp. 235–53.

Swain, M. (1995). "Three functions of output in second language learning," in G. Cook and B. Seidlhofer (eds.). *Principle and Practice in Applied Linguistics.* Oxford: Oxford University Press, pp. 125–44.

Swain, M. & S. Lapkin (1998). Interaction and second language learning. Two adolescent French immersion students working together. *Modern Language Journal* 83:320–37.

Sweet, H. (1899/1964). *The Practical Study of Languages,* 1899; rpt. 1964. Oxford: Oxford University Press.

Tannen, D. (1992). "Rethinking power and solidarity in gender and dominance," in C. Kramsch and S. McConnell-Ginet (eds.). *Text and Context: Cross-Disciplinary Perspectives on Language Study.* Lexington, Massachusetts: D.C. Heath and Company, pp. 135–47.

Thornbury, S. (1996). Teachers research teacher talk. *ELT Journal,* 50: 279–88.

Thornbury, S. (1997). *About Language: Tasks for Teachers of English.* Cambridge: Cambridge University Press.

van Lier, L. (1988). *The Classroom and the Language Learner.* London: Longman.

van Lier, L. (1996). *Introducing Language Awareness.* London: Penguin.

van Manen, M. (1977). Linking ways of knowing with ways of being practical. *Curriculum Inquiry* 6:3:205–228.

Wallace, C. (1992). "Critical literacy awareness in the EFL classroom," in N. Fairclough (ed.). *Critical Language Awareness.* London: Longman.

Wallace, M. (1991). *Training Foreign Language Teachers.* Cambridge: Cambridge University Press.

Walz, J. (1989). Context and contextualized language practice in foreign language teaching. *Modern Language Journal* 73:160–68.

Weedon, C. (1987). *Feminist Practice and Poststructuralist Theory.* London: Blackwell.

Wenden, A. (1991). *Learner Strategies for Learner Autonomy: Planning and Implementing Learner Training for Language Learners.* New York: Prentice Hall.

Widdowson, H. G. (1978). *Teaching Language as Communication.* Oxford: Oxford University Press.

Widdowson, H. G. (1990). *Aspects of Language Teaching.* Oxford: Oxford University Press.

Widdowson, H. G. (1994). The ownership of English. *TESOL Quarterly* 28:2:377–89.

Widdowson, H. G. (1998). Skills, abilities, and contexts of reality. *Annual Review of Applied Linguistics* 18:3223–333.

Williams, R. (1976). *Keywords: A Vocabulary of Culture and Society.* New York: Oxford University Press.

Wills, J. (1996). *A Framework for Task-Based Learning.* London: Longman.

Young, R. (1992). *Critical Theory and Classroom Talk.* Clevedon: Multilingual Matters.

Zeichner, K. M. and D. P. Liston (1996). *Reflective Teaching: An Introduction.* Mahwah, New Jersey: Lawrence Erlbaum.

Index